CHRIST

the CORNERSTONE

CHRIST
the CORNERSTONE

—

Collected Essays

of

JOHN
STOTT

LEXHAM PRESS

Christ the Cornerstone: Collected Essays of John Stott
Best of *Christianity Today*

Copyright 2019 Christianity Today International

Lexham Press, 1313 Commercial St., Bellingham, WA 98225
LexhamPress.com

Print ISBN 9781683593409
Digital ISBN Digital ISBN

Lexham Editorial: Elliot Ritzema, Danielle Thevenaz
Cover Design: Lydia Dahl
Typesetting: ProjectLuz.com

CONTENTS

INTRODUCTION

*C*hrist the Cornerstone aptly names this collection of essays by John Stott. It partially fits because these articles are drawn primarily from Stott's monthly "Cornerstone" column in *Christianity Today* written between 1977 and 1981. But far more importantly, especially to Stott, the column title itself reflects one of the ways the New Testament designates Jesus and his unique role in the building that is the church, God's people (Eph. 2:20–22; Acts 4:10–12; 1 Pet. 2:4–8). While the essays in this volume range from 1959 to 1992 and deal with a variety of topics, I'd like to draw attention to four themes that unite them and make them relevant for today.

First, *Stott writes for the honor and glory of Jesus Christ.* In all he did, Stott sought to articulate and demonstrate the comprehensive glory, power, truth, mercy, and justice of Jesus Christ, our Cornerstone. These essays cover a wide spectrum of theological, ethical, cultural, and global issues. In some ways, reading them feels like stepping back in time because of the varying shifts that have occurred since these pieces were first written. Looked at in this way, it is striking at several points to see how advanced Stott's evangelical voice was as he addressed the issues of his time. But in another way, it is remarkable how current his words can still seem, and how internally consistent they are over time. That is because these essays hold on display some of the most distinguishing features of Stott's life and ministry, above all his plain, relentless zeal to lift up Jesus as Lord and to allow his life, death, and resurrection to be the benchmark, the plumb line, the motivation, the inspiration for everything he addresses. Whatever or wherever the issue Stott is writing about, his standard is clear, and this explains the evergreen quality of his writing.

Second, *Stott writes with fairness and clarity.* These essays offer us a chance to learn from someone who tackles complex, and often contested, issues in ways that reflect his humble willingness to listen and learn (even from opponents), to receive and honor distinct points of view, and to be judicious and clear in offering his own point of view. I was struck by these same qualities when I first heard Stott as a preacher and teacher at the Urbana missions conference sponsored by InterVarsity Christian Fellowship. During the afternoon seminars, he was asked to hold a question-and-answer session in which, for two hours, he fielded a very wide set of questions. He was strong-minded, disciplined, biblically fluent, but relentlessly fair and clear. He treated people and ideas with respect. These same qualities are ones you will find throughout this collection of essays, making them a rich point of reflection especially in these current days of contentious, inhospitable, uncivil division.

Third, *Stott grounds his writing in a humble and confident reliance on the Bible.* These essays treat a myriad of global, ecclesiastical, and cultural issues, but the reference point for his most salient comments or responses start and finish with the teaching of the Bible. His use of Scripture avoids proof-texting; it is less about any one text and more about a text in its context, or a text in combination with the weight of a line of biblical teaching. This is undoubtedly part of the enduring force of his writing (and of his preaching), and why the re-publishing of these essays is welcome.

He is endlessly trying to raise the bar of biblical literacy and fluency, and wants to be held accountable more to the force of a biblical argument than to agreement or disagreement with his interlocutors. While working on the questions at hand, Stott is also working to form a "Christian mind" that is rich and nimble, humble and wise, assured but not over-reaching. The value of these essays may lie less in the contemporary relevance of their particular topics and more in the opportunity to watch a careful master student of the Scriptures simply do his work.

Finally, *Stott writes about the world with neighbor-love.* The commanding range of Stott's study and travel allowed him to make the distant appear near, but what he does in his writing is more profound and personal than that. Few Western Christian leaders have spent time in the global South as extensively as Stott did, and even fewer have done so as listeningly as Stott did. He put virtually all of his honoraria and royalties to work paying for his travels to remote places, speaking often to small gatherings and struggling institutions. In all his travels he was eager to listen, to care, and to learn from those he came to know. I can't adequately count the numbers of times Majority World leaders have told me that "Uncle John" listened and cared like few other Western leaders they have ever known. And having listened, he followed up with prayer and with practical and strategic actions of support and encouragement. He saw and touched the world in ways that are human, approaching others with compassion and empathy, not with abstraction and objectification. His traveling journals were filled with names and stories. In this way he not only made the distant *near*, but made it *close*, because that's what genuine love of neighbor means and does.

Having known John Stott first as a preacher and writer, then as a boss and colleague, and surely as a friend and brother, I eagerly commend this volume of essays. I believe you will be blessed by watching the way he addressed some of the many and varied people and concerns that occupied his attention. But read and listen more carefully, and John Stott will richly demonstrate and embody qualities of being a disciple that could not be more urgently needed in and among us today. May Christ the Cornerstone explain our lives as truly as it did his.

MARK LABBERTON

President, Fuller Theological Seminary

Part I

—

SCRIPTURE AND THEOLOGY

Chapter 1

———

CHRIST AND THE SCRIPTURES

You search the scriptures, because you think that in them you have eternal life; and it is they that bear witness to me; yet you refuse to come to me that you may have life. (John 5:39, 40 RSV)

T he two most important questions which must be asked and answered about the Bible concern its *origin* and its *purpose*. Where has it come from, and what is it meant for? Until we know whether its origin is ultimately human or divine, we cannot determine what degree of confidence may be placed in it. Until we have clarified the purpose for which its divine Author or human authors brought it into being, we cannot put it to right and proper use.

Both questions gain an answer from the words of Jesus to certain Jews, recorded in chapter 5 of John's Gospel, verses 39 and 40: "You search the scriptures, because you think that in them you have eternal life; and it is they that bear witness to me; yet you refuse to come to me that you may have life" (RSV). He was, of course, referring primarily to the Old Testament Scriptures. But if we concede that there is an organic unity in the Bible, and

3

that God intended his saving acts to be recorded and interpreted under the New Covenant as much as under the Old, then these words may be applied to the New Testament also.

The Scriptures Have a Divine Origin

The divine origin of the Scriptures is clearly implied in our Lord's statement: "It is they that bear witness to me." The scriptural witness to him is a divine witness. Jesus has been advancing some stupendous claims about his relation to the Father. The Father has committed to him the two tasks of judging and quickening (vv. 21, 22, 27, 28). But how are Christ's claims to be confirmed? They are confirmed, he says, by testimony, and the testimony he requires adequately to authenticate his claims is divine, not human. Self-testimony is not enough. "If I bear witness to myself, my testimony is not true" (v. 31 RSV). John the Baptist's testimony is not enough. "You sent to John, and he has borne witness to the truth" (v. 33). No. He adds: "Not that the testimony which I receive is from man" (v. 34). "There is another who bears witness to me, and I know that the testimony which he bears to me is true" (v. 32). He is referring, of course, to the Father. But how does the Father bear witness to the Son? In two ways; first, in the works of Jesus, and second, in the words of Scripture. "The testimony which I have is greater than that of John; for the works which the Father has granted me to accomplish, these very works which I am doing, bear me witness that the Father has sent me" (v. 36). This is familiar ground to readers of the Fourth Gospel. "If I am not doing the works of my Father, then do not believe me; but if I do them, even though you do not believe me, believe the works, that you may know and understand that the Father is in me and I am in the Father" (10:27, 38). "Believe me that I am in the Father and the Father in me; or else believe me for the sake of the works themselves" (14:11).

Our Lord asserts, however, that he has from the Father an even more direct testimony than his mighty works. "And the Father who sent me has himself borne witness to me" (5:37). But these Jews were rejecting this testimony. "You do not have his word abiding in you, for you do not believe him whom he has sent" (v. 38). What is this witness? Where is this word? Jesus immediately continues, "You search the scriptures ... and it is they that bear witness to me" (v. 39), and concludes this discourse with a specific example of what he means: "Do not think that I shall accuse you to the Father; it is Moses who accuses you, on whom you set your hope. If you believed Moses, you would believe me, for he wrote of me. But if you do not believe his writings, how will you believe my words?" (vv. 45–47).

The Scriptures are, then, in the thought and teaching of Jesus, the supreme testimony of the Father to the Son. They are the word and witness of God. True, they had human authors. It was Moses who wrote, and the writings of Moses are the Word of God (vv. 46, 47, 38). Jesus undoubtedly believed the Bible to be no ordinary book, nor even a whole library of ordinary books, because behind the human writers stood the one divine Author, the Holy Spirit of God, who, as the Nicene Creed affirms, "spake by the prophets." Because men spoke from God, or God spoke through men (for the process of inspiration is described in both ways in Scripture), the Bible is to be viewed not as a mere symposium of human words but as the very Word of God.

There are many grounds for this Christian belief. There is the Scriptures' own unaffected claim. There is their astonishing unity of theme, despite the extremely varied circumstances of composition. There is their power to convict and convert, to comfort and uplift, to inspire and to save. But the greatest and firmest ground for faith in the divine origin of Scripture will always remain that Jesus himself taught it. The living Word of God bore witness to the written Word of God. His opinion of, and attitude to, the Scriptures is not difficult to determine. Three striking indications are:

He Believed Them. Let one example suffice. On the way to the Mount of Olives he turned to the disciples and said: "You will all fall away." This categorical statement must have amazed and perplexed them. Had they not sworn allegiance to him and promised to be true to him? Had they not followed him these three years without thought of home and comfort and security? How could he assert with such definiteness and dogmatism that every one of them would desert him? The answer is simple. He continues: "You will all fall away; for it is written, 'I will strike the shepherd, and the sheep will be scattered'" (Mark 14:27). It is because the Scriptures had said so that he knew beyond peradventure or doubt that it would come to pass.

It is for this reason that the progress of events at the end of his career did not take him by surprise. He knew that what had been written about him would have its fulfillment. The word *gegraptai,* "it stands written," was enough to remove every doubt and silence every objection. So, with an assurance and clarity that over-awed the Twelve, he repeatedly predicted both his death and his resurrection, because the Old Testament had depicted the sufferings and the glory of the Christ. So plain was it to him that he soundly rebuked the Emmaus disciples after the resurrection, saying: "O foolish men, and slow of heart to believe all that the prophets have spoken! Was it not necessary that the Christ should suffer these things and enter into his glory? And beginning with Moses and all the prophets, he interpreted to them in all the scriptures the things concerning himself" (Luke 24:25–27).

No wonder he could say in his Sermon on the Mount, "Truly, I say to you, till heaven and earth pass away, not an iota, not a dot, will pass from the law until all is accomplished" (Matt. 5:18) and, again, later: "Scripture cannot be broken" (John 10:35). To him the Scriptures were unbreakable because they are eternal. It was impossible that one Scripture should fail or pass until it had been fulfilled.

He *Obeyed Them*. Even more impressive than the fact that Jesus believed the Scriptures is that he obeyed them in his own life. He practiced what he preached. He not only said he believed in their divine origin; he acted on his belief by submitting to their authority as to the authority of God. He gladly and voluntarily accepted a position of humble subordination to them. He followed their teaching in his own life.

The most striking example of this occurs during the period of temptation in the wilderness. The synoptic evangelists record the three principal temptations with which he must later have told them he had been assaulted. Each time he countered the devil's proposal with an apt quotation from chapters 6 or 8 of the Book of Deuteronomy, on which he appears to have been meditating at the time. It is incorrect to say that he quoted Scripture *at the devil*. What he was actually doing was quoting Scripture *at himself in the hearing of the devil*. For instance, when he said, "It is written, 'Thou shalt worship the Lord thy God, and him only shalt thou serve,'" or "It is written, 'Thou shalt not tempt the Lord thy God,'" he was not telling Satan what to do and what not to do. He was not commanding Satan to worship God and forbidding Satan to tempt God. No. He was stating what he himself would and would not do. It was his firm resolve to worship exclusively, he said, and not to tempt God in unbelief. Why? Because this was what was written in the Scriptures. Once again, the simple word *gegraptai*, "it stands written," settled the issue for him. What was written was as much the standard of his behavior as the criterion of his belief.

Moreover, Jesus obeyed the Scriptures in his ministry as well as in his private conduct. The Old Testament set forth the nature and character of the mission he had come to fulfill. He knew that he was the anointed King, the Son of man, the suffering servant, the smitten shepherd of Old Testament prophecy, and he resolved to fulfill to the letter what was written of him. Thus, "the Son of man goes as it is written of him" (Mark 14:21), and again, "Behold, we are going up to Jerusalem, and everything that is written of the Son of man by the prophets will be accomplished" (Luke 18:31). Indeed, Jesus felt a certain compulsion, to which he often referred, to conform his ministry to the prophetic pattern. Even as a boy of 12, this sense of necessity had begun to grip him: "Did you not know that I must be in my Father's house?" What is the meaning of this "must"? We hear it again and again. It was the compulsion of Scripture, the inner constraint to fulfill the messianic role which he found portrayed in the Old Testament and which he had voluntarily assumed. So, "He began to teach them that the Son of man *must* suffer many things" (Mark 8:31). "I *must* work the works of him that sent me while it is day" (John 9:4). When Peter attempted to defend him in the garden and prevent his arrest, he forbade him, saying: "How then should the scriptures be fulfilled, that it *must* be so?" (Matt. 26:54). Again, "Was it not *necessary* that the Christ should suffer these things?" (Luke 24:26).

He Quoted Them. Not only did Jesus believe the statements and obey the commands of Scripture in his own life, but he made the Scriptures the standard of reference when engaged in debate with his critics. To him the Scriptures were the arbiter in every dispute, the canon (literally, a carpenter's rule) to measure and judge what was under discussion, the criterion by which to test every idea. He made the Scriptures the final court of appeal.

This can be seen from his attitude to the religious parties of his day, the Sadducees and the Pharisees.

When the Sadducees (who denied the immortality of the soul, the resurrection of the body, and the existence of spirits and angels) came to him with their trick question about the condition in the next world of a woman married and widowed seven times, he replied: "You do greatly err" or (RSV) "Is not this why you are wrong, that you know neither the scriptures nor the power of God?" (Mark 12:24). He went on to refute them, not only in the silly problem they had propounded to him, but in their whole theological position, by quoting Exodus 3:6 and expounding its implications.

As for the Scribes and Pharisees, Jesus rejected their innumerable man-made rules and traditions and referred them back to the simple, unadulterated Word of God. Whether the question was sabbath observance, ceremonial laws, or marriage and divorce, it was to the original divine Word that he made his appeal. You make the word of God void by your tradition, he said, and "You have a fine way of rejecting the commandment of God, in order to keep your tradition!" (Mark 7:13, 9). And during the Sermon on the Mount, in the six paragraphs introduced by the formula "You have heard that it hath been said ... but I say to you ..." Jesus is contradicting not the law of Moses but the unwarranted scribal interpretations of Moses' law. This is clear from the fact that he has just said "Think not that I have come to abolish the law and the prophets; I have come not to abolish them but to fulfill them" (Matt. 5:17). Besides, where does the law say, "You shall love your neighbor and hate your enemy" (v. 43)? The law says "Thou shalt love thy neighbor." It was the Scribes who attempted to restrict the reference of this command to friends and kinsmen, and Jesus rejected their interpretation.

All of this is of the greatest importance. Jesus of Nazareth, the Son of God, with all his supernatural knowledge and wisdom, accepted and endorsed the divine origin and authority of the Old Testament Scriptures. He believed them. He obeyed them in his own life and ministry. He quoted them in debate and controversy.

The question is, Are we to regard lightly the Scriptures to which he gave his reverent assent? Can we repudiate what he embraced? Are we really prepared to part company with him on this issue and assert that he was mistaken? No. He who said "I *am* the truth" undoubtedly *spoke* the truth. If he taught that the Scriptures were a divine word and witness, the Christian is committed to believe this. Never mind, in the last resort, what the rationalists and the critics say, or even what the theologians and the churches say. What matters to us supremely is: What did Jesus Christ say?

The Scriptures Have a Practical Purpose

We have considered the origin of the Scriptures; we must now consider their purpose. We have seen from whom they have come to us; we must now ask for what they have been given. It is important to grasp that their purpose is not academic but practical. No doubt the Scriptures contain both science and history, but their purpose is neither scientific nor historical. The Bible also includes great literature and profound philosophy, but its purpose is neither literary nor philosophical. The so-called "Bible Designed to be Read as Literature" is a most misleading volume, for the Bible never was designed to be read as literature. The Bible is not an academic textbook for any branch of knowledge, so much as a practical handbook of religion. It is a lamp to our feet and a light to our path.

This Jesus made plain in the verses we are studying. "You search the scriptures, because you think that in them you have eternal life; and it is they that bear witness to me; yet you refuse to come to me that you may have life." The Jews were in the habit of "searching the scriptures." The verb used here, comments Bishop B. F. Westcott, indicates "that minute, intense investigation of Scripture which issued in the allegorical and mystical interpretations of the Midrash." They thus studied and sought to expound the Scriptures, while fondly imagining that salvation and eternal life were to be found in accurate knowledge!

But the purpose of the Scriptures is not merely to impart knowledge, but to bestow life. Knowledge is important, but as a means to an end, not as an end in itself. The holy, God-breathed Scriptures, wrote Paul to Timothy, "are able to make thee wise unto salvation through faith which is in Christ Jesus" (2 Tim. 3:15, 16 KJV). Their purpose is not just to "make wise" but to "make wise unto salvation" and that "through faith in Christ Jesus." Their ultimate purpose is to lead to salvation; their immediate purpose is to arouse personal faith in Christ in whom salvation is to be found. This, albeit in different terms, is exactly what Jesus in John 5:39, 40 is recorded as saying. Three stages are discernible in the purpose of Holy Scripture.

The Scriptures Point to Christ. "It is they which bear witness to me," he said. The Old Testament points forward, and the New Testament looks back, to Jesus Christ. English theologians of a former generation were fond of saying that as in England every track and lane and road, linking on to other thoroughfares, would ultimately lead the traveler to London, so every verse in Scripture, leading to other verses, would ultimately bring the reader to Christ. Or we might say that as seven or eight different streets converge on Piccadilly Circus in the heart of London, so all the prophetic and apostolic strands of biblical witness converge on Jesus Christ. He is the grand theme of Holy Scripture. Reading the Bible is like an exciting treasure hunt. As each clue leads to another clue until the treasure is discovered, so every verse leads to other verses until the glory of Christ is unveiled. The eye of faith, wherever it looks in Scripture, sees him, as he expounds to us "in all the scriptures the things concerning himself" (Luke 24:27; cf. v. 44). We see him foreshadowed in the Mosaic sacrifices and in the Davidic Kingdom. The law is our schoolmaster to bring us to Christ, and the prophets write of his sufferings and glory. The evangelists describe his birth, life, death, and resurrection, his gracious words and mighty works; the Acts reveals him continuing through his Spirit what he had begun to do and to teach in the days of his flesh; the apostles unfold the hidden glory of his person and work; while in the Revelation we see him worshiped by the hosts of heaven and finally overthrowing the powers of evil. No man can read the Scriptures without being brought face to face with Jesus, the Son of God and Savior of men. This is why we love the Bible. We love it because it speaks to us of him.

The Scriptures Affirm That Life Is to Be Found in Christ. The purpose of the Scriptures is not just to reveal Christ, but to reveal him as the only Savior competent to bring forgiveness to sinners, secure their reconciliation to God and make them holy. That is why they concentrate on his "suffering and glory." The Gospel they enshrine is that "Christ died for our sins in accordance with the scriptures, that he was buried, that he was raised on the third day in accordance with the scriptures, and that he appeared ..." (1 Cor. 15:3–5). As Dr. Marcus Dods writes in the *Expositor's Greek Testament*, the Scriptures "do not give life; they lead to the Lifegiver." This is what our Lord meant in saying that the Jews thought they could find life in the Scriptures and would not come to him that they might receive life. Of every Scripture, and not just of the Fourth Gospel, it may be said: "These are written that you may believe that Jesus is the Christ, the Son of God, and that believing you may have life in his name" (John 20:31).

The Scriptures Invite Us to Come to Christ to Receive Life. The Scriptures do not just point; they urge us to go to the One to whom they point. They do not only make an offer of life; they issue a challenge to action. What the star did for the Magi, the Scriptures do for us. The star beckoned and guided them to Jesus;

the Scriptures will lighten our path to him. That is why Jesus blamed his contemporaries for not coming to him. Their study of the Scriptures was purely academic. They were not doers of the Word, but hearers only and thus self-deceived. They *searched* the Scriptures, but did not *obey* them. Indeed, they *would* not come to Christ to receive life. Their minds may have been busily investigating, but their wills were stubborn and inflexible.

We must come to the Bible as sick sinners. It is no use just memorizing its prescription for salvation. We must go to Christ and take him as the medicine our sick souls need.

These verses from John 5 show our Lord's view of the divine origin and practical purpose of the Scriptures. We learn their divine origin from his testimony to them. We learn their practical purpose from their testimony to him. There is therefore between Christ (the living Word of God) and the Scriptures (the written Word of God) this reciprocal testimony. Each bears witness to the other. It is because he bore witness to them that we accept their divine origin. It is because they bear witness to him that we fulfill their practical purpose, come to him in personal faith, and receive life. May God grant in his infinite mercy that Jesus may never have to say to us what he said to his contemporaries: "You search the scriptures, because you think that in them you have eternal life; and it is they that bear witness to me; yet you refuse to come to me that you may have life."

John R. W. Stott, "Christ and the Scriptures," *Christianity Today* 4, no. 4 (November 23, 1959): 6–10.

Chapter 2

IS THE INCARNATION
A MYTH?

I was in Latin America when *The Myth of God Incarnate* (edited by John Hick) was published in faraway London. But within a day or two the ripples (even shock waves?) had reached Argentina, and people were asking me if English churchmen were still Christians.

The book is unworthy of its highly competent contributors. Of course, every symposium is uneven, but this one contains several inner contradictions. My problem with the book concerns the questions of language, authority, and heresy.

Language

First, the debate is confused by a failure to agree on the meaning of the word "myth" and to distinguish between substance and form, or doctrine and language. Sometimes "mythical" is used quite harmlessly to mean no more than "poetic" or "symbolic." Frances Young contrasts "myth" with "science" in the sense that religious reality is inaccessible to scientific investigation, indefinable in human language, and inconceivable to the finite mind.

Her use of the word "myth" may be injudicious, but we have no quarrel with her and others' desire to preserve the element of mystery in Christian faith and experience. Maurice Wiles makes a conscious attempt to define the term, though he admits it is "loose and elusive." He takes four biblical doctrines (creation, fall, incarnation-atonement, and resurrection-judgment) and argues that to call any of these a "myth" implies that there is "some onto-logical truth" which corresponds to the central characteristic of the myth and some "appropriateness" about it. The weakness of his argument may be judged when he goes on to write of the "Incarnation myth." Despite the variant uses of the word "myth" all the contributors deny that Jesus either claimed to be or was the God-man of historic Christianity. The book airily dismisses the claims of Jesus on the ground that they are Johannine not synoptic. No serious attempt is made to face the claims—often indirect rather than direct—that the Synoptic Gospels do record or explain how *ho kurios,* the Septuagint title for Yahweh, could be applied to Jesus *so early and without controversy,* as in the Pauline epistles, which indicated that the divine lordship of Jesus, demanding worship and obedience, was already the universal faith of the church.

Authority

The contributors don't recognize the authority of the New Testament. They have no objective standard or criterion by which to test their views. The book is divided into two halves, "testing the sources" and "testing the development," but the sources are not the New Testament documents against which the later develop-ment of doctrines is assessed. New Testament writers and patristic writers are quoted without any distinction drawn between them.

What, then, are the sources of incarnational belief? Michael Goulder constructs an ingenious but largely unsupported theory that it arose from "the Galilean eschatological myth" and "the Samaritan gnostical myth" (the latter emanating from Simon Magus) in dialectic with one another. Instead of these "two roots" Frances Young prefers "a tangled mass" of divine births, claims, titles, appearances, and expectations—pagan and Jewish—all creating a "cultural atmosphere" conducive to the deification of Jesus.

Granted such an atmosphere, what sparked off belief in the Incarnation of God in Jesus? The authors reply that it was an experience of salvation through Jesus. There was no "revelation," only an inference from their experience. The same is true today, they say. They retain some kind of commitment to Jesus because he means something special to them.

Now we evangelicals have ourselves often stressed that creed without experience is valueless. Nevertheless, to base creed upon experience is a very different and a very precarious practice.

Heresy

What should the contemporary church do with heretics? Is that a harsh word? I think not. A humble and reverent probing into the mystery of the Incarnation is the essence of true Christological scholarship. But attempted reconstructions that effectively destroy that which is supposed to be being reconstructed is Christological heresy.

Let me defend my question further. It is based on three convictions: there is such a thing as heresy, that is, a deviation from fundamental, revealed truth; heresy "troubles" the Church, while truth edifies it, and therefore if we love the truth and the Church we cannot fold our arms and do nothing.

The purity of the Church (ethical and doctrinal) is as much a proper Christian quest as its unity. Indeed we should be seeking its unity and purity simultaneously.

I do not myself think a heresy trial is the right way to approach this. Heretics are slippery creatures. They tend to use orthodox language to clothe their heterodox views. Besides, in our age of easy tolerance, the arraigned heretic becomes in the public mind first the innocent victim of bigoted persecutors, then a martyr, and then a hero or saint. But there are other ways to proceed. The New Testament authors are concerned not so much about false brethren as about false teachers, who act like wolves and scatter or destroy Christ's flock. Although the contributors to *The Myth of God Incarnate* are academics, most of them are also ordained Anglican clergymen who hold a bishop's license to preach. Is it too much to hope and pray that some bishop sometime will have the courage to withdraw his license from a presbyter who denies the Incarnation? This would not be an infringement of civil or academic liberty. A man may believe, say, and write what he pleases in the country and the university. But in the church it is reasonable and right to expect all accredited teachers to teach the faith that the church in its official formularies confesses and that (incidentally) they have themselves promised to uphold.

There is a second and more positive step to take. The apostles' response to the rise of false teachers was partly to warn the churches not to listen to them or be led astray by them, and partly to arrange for the multiplication of true teachers. Thus, Paul told Titus to appoint presbyters in every town who were loyal to the apostolic teaching, so that they might be able both "to give instruction in sound doctrine and also to confute those who contradict it" (Titus 1:5, 9). It is in this connection that we must congratulate Michael Green on the speed and sagacity with which he assembled his team of authors to write the answering symposium *The Truth of God Incarnate*. Heresy cannot be finally overcome by any force except that of the truth. So there is today an urgent need for more dedicated Christian scholars who will give their lives to "the defense and confirmation of the gospel" (Phil. 1:7).

John R. W. Stott, "Cornerstone: Is the Incarnation a Myth?," *Christianity Today* 22, no. 3 (November 4, 1977): 34–35.

———

Chapter 3

FOLLOWING PAUL
IN TURKEY

For many years I have cherished the desire to follow "in the steps of St. Paul" (to quote the title of H. V. Morton's justly famous book, first published in 1936), by visiting the Pauline sites of Greece and Turkey. At last I was able to do so in early April of this year, and was fortunate to have my friends Dick and Thea Van Halsema of the Reformed Bible College as companions and guides. In 1962 they drove their whole family through these parts (described in Thea's delightful book *Safari for Seven*) and have since led several tour groups. Our most moving experience was to trace the Turkish part of the first missionary journey.

Perga in Pamphylia

Sailing from Cyprus Paul, Barnabas, and Mark landed at Perga, whose harbor in those days was located several miles up the Cestrus River, well protected from Cilician pirates. We wandered among the ruins of the city. Two rounded towers survive, which once framed the Victory Portal leading onto the twenty-one meters-wide main street. This consisted of two ways, separated by a central water channel and flanked by two rows of Ionic columns, each colonnade being paved with mosaic and lined with shops. But Paul did not linger there. Why not? And why did young John Mark desert?

We know that Paul was sick when he arrived on the Galatian plateau (Gal. 4:13, 14). I think William Ramsay was the first to suggest that he caught malaria in the low-lying swamps of Pamphylia and that his "thorn (or stake) in the flesh" referred to the stabbing headaches that resulted. Certainly his eyesight was affected, or he would never have thanked the Galatians that, if they could have done so, they would have plucked out their eyes and given them to him (Gal. 4:15). It may be that his fever led him to seek the cool of the higher ground. I have sometimes imagined that Mark did not like the look of the nasty Pamphylian mosquitoes (I searched for some, but it was the wrong season), or perhaps he was scared of the bandits who were known to lurk in the Taurus mountains ahead of them. At all events, he went back to Jerusalem, and Paul regarded it as a serious defection.

Pisidian Antioch and Iconium

We do not know if Paul and Barnabas had to walk over the Taurus mountains, or whether a chariot or horses carried them at least part of the way. In either case they had about 150 miles to cover, and a steep climb through the pass. Yet the mission in Antioch was vigorous, and specially notable as the first occasion on which Paul deliberately "turned to the Gentiles." A pair of Egyptian vultures circled over the nearby village of Yalvac as we drove through, an omen of the dereliction we were to see. For nothing is left of Pisidian Antioch except some arches of a noble first-century B.C. Roman aqueduct, in a crevice of which a pair of Black Redstarts had built their nest.

Expelled by hostile Jews from Antioch, Paul and Barnabas journeyed southeast between the Sultan and Taurus ranges about 100 miles to Iconium (the modern Konya). I wondered if they had an eye for the beauties of plain, river, lake, and mountain that filled their horizons in every direction. I think so. For when later they reached Lystra, Paul preached about "the living God who made the heaven and the earth and the sea and all that is in them" (Acts 14:15). In contrast to the disappearance of Pisidian Antioch, Konya is Turkey's fourth largest town, with some 300,000 inhabitants. Called by William Ramsay "the Damascus of Asia Minor," it is situated on the edge of a broad, well-watered plain, and is today a flourishing emporium for wheat and Turkish rugs.

Lystra and Derbe

According to Everett C. Blake and Anna G. Edmonds in *Biblical Sites in Turkey* (1977), there is still some residual uncertainty about which of two tumuli mounds covers the ruins of Lystra, and which of three or four the city of Derbe. For Lystra we visited a rather oblong mound a mile or more west of the village of Hatunsaray. A few lichen-covered stones and pieces of column littered its eastern slope, while its flat summit appeared to be occupied by moles, ground squirrels, and a fox whose heaps and holes betrayed their unseen presence. As I stood there, a pair of Hoopoes flew by down below, displaying in their undulating flight their striking plumage of black, white, and pink.

Paul was brutally stoned in Lystra, dragged out of the city, and left in the gutter for dead. The following day he left for Derbe. How could his bruised and battered body manage to travel those sixty or seventy miles? He could hardly have walked that distance, even with Barnabas's help. Perhaps they went by horse or chariot. I think they would have been refreshed (as I was) by the sight of the snow-capped peaks of Pusala Dagi on their right and Karadag ("Black Mountain") ahead of them, and by the pretty song of the Calandra Larks in the fields.

After driving through three villages of mud houses north of Karaman a brisk forty-minute walk brought us to Kerti Höyük, the most favored site for Derbe. It is another green tumulus and stands out in lovely relief against the brown earth of the ploughed fields around and the Black Mountain behind. Here Paul and Barnabas "preached the good news ... and won a large number of disciples." But there are no disciples there now, or indeed any human beings at all. Instead, as we approached the swamp that surrounds the base of the mound, twelve pairs of Ruddy Shelduck took to flight, honking in an amiable but melancholy fashion, their cinnamon bodies gleaming in the evening sunlight. Elegant Black-winged Stilts and other waders and duck had also found good feeding grounds in the Derbe marsh.

So of the four Galatian cities Paul and Barnabas evangelized, all of which were proud Greek or Roman colonies in their heyday, only one survives. The other three are deserted, unexcavated sites. Yet what humans have abandoned, birds have adopted as their home. In future I shall always associate Pisidian Antioch with Black Redstarts, Lystra with Hoopoes, and Derbe with Ruddy Shelduck, yes and the solitary pillar of Diana's Temple in Ephesus with the white Storks that had built their nest on its capital.

Paul could well have continued his journey east and south through the Cilician Gates to his hometown of Tarsus. But if this was a temptation to him, he resisted it, for he retraced his steps to Lystra, Iconium, and Antioch in order to strengthen the disciples in the midst of their persecutions. We, however, did go on to Tarsus, a city of 115,000 people, all of whom are Moslems except for two Christian families. We visited the museum, but found no reference to Paul. Would the museum director accept an exhibition display of Paul if one were presented to him, we asked? He said he would. It would certainly seem appropriate in the birthplace of one of Tarsus's most distinguished sons.

John R. W. Stott, "Cornerstone: Following Paul in Turkey," *Christianity Today* 22, no. 19 (July 21, 1978): 36–37.

Chapter 4

———

TRUTH, HERESY, AND DISCIPLINE IN THE CHURCH

L ast November I reviewed *The Myth of God Incarnate*. Four months later the initial excitement has died down. The book was not a work of profound scholarship. It will not stand the test of time. Yet it raised issues that remain. The one I take up this month is the question of heresy in the church. Those who deny the Incarnation were formerly regarded as "heretics"; now the very concept of heresy is thought by many to be outmoded, and those who would previously have had to bear that stigma are left alone (at least in some churches) to enjoy their positions of influence in peace and honor. Is this right? What can be done?

Let me begin positively. Our concern for God's truth should not make us hesitant to affirm the importance of three matters. *1. Theological exploration.* The fact that God has revealed himself in Christ and in Scripture does not rule out intellectual exploration. The theologian is no more inhibited from theological research because God has revealed himself in Scripture than the scientist is inhibited from scientific research because God has revealed himself in nature. Both are limited to the data (which, to oversimplify, are nature on the one hand, Scripture on the other), but within the limits that the data themselves impose, the Creator encourages us to use our minds freely and creatively.

If, therefore, by the myth of God Incarnate were meant the mystery of the Incarnation, we would have no quarrel with the concept. The church has always acknowledged that the Incarnation is a mystery beyond the full comprehension of human minds. A humble, reverent exploration of what God has revealed of himself in Christ is the essence of true Christological scholarship.

2. Contemporary questioning. The kinds of questions that are being asked in that book are perfectly valid. We should emphatically not wish to suppress or sidestep genuine intellectual inquiry. For example, is a development of conviction about Jesus discernible within the New Testament itself? What development took place subsequently? Can modern psychological understandings of human personality throw any light on the self-consciousness of Jesus? Is the Chalcedonian definition, which used Greek concepts of person and natures, satisfactory for our own day? This is only a random sample of legitimate questions.

3. Academic freedom. The contributors to the book all hold academic posts in Oxford, Cambridge, or Birmingham universities. Some of them occupy positions of leadership in the church as well. Their double role raises a further issue. In a secular university setting, in which the divinity department is regarded as equivalent to other departments, full academic freedom must be preserved. No subject can be protected from the most rigorous scrutiny, and all inquiry must be open-minded and open-ended. If, therefore, the contributors to *The Myth of God Incarnate* were only academics, and if their purpose in writing were only to promote academic discussion, then the publication of the book could be defended. But the book attempts to have both an academic and a popular appeal, and in consequence it falls between the two stools.

Some Necessary Distinctions

It is important to make the following distinctions. *1. The distinction between university teachers and church leaders.* It would be wrong to require any lecturer in a secular university to make an *a priori* commitment of any kind except to intellectual integrity. But clergy give a solemn, voluntary undertaking before they are ordained to uphold and expound in their teaching the fundamental doctrinal standards of their church. Their integrity, therefore, will be expressed in loyalty to these standards.

2. The distinction between questions and denials. It is one thing to question and explore a Christian doctrine because one desires one's understanding of it to be clearer, fuller, deeper, fresher, and more closely integrated with the rest of one's understanding of reality; it is another for such questioning to lead to a denial of the doctrine. Again, to pass through a temporary period of agnosticism about some doctrine is one thing; to reach a settled conviction about its falsehood is another.

3. The distinction between Scripture and tradition. Anglican evangelicals, I think, have a growing respect for tradition because we have a growing confidence in the work of the Holy Spirit. We believe that he has guided the church to express its mind in the catholic creeds of the early centuries. These creeds have continued to enshrine for all churches many essentials of biblical revelation. We think it extremely improbable that they will ever be shown to be mistaken. Nevertheless, both they and the reformation confessions, because they belong to the realm of tradition, must be left open to continuing scrutiny in the light of Scripture. Only Scripture itself, being God's Word, is not open to revision, although it calls for continuous interpretation.

Ecclesiastical Discipline

I now broach the sensitive question of church discipline. What should the church do with false teachers, and in particular with those who deny the Incarnation?

1. The fundamental issue. The real issue is neither linguistic (whether the word Incarnation is mythical, metaphorical, or literal), nor cultural (how far the biblical or Chalcedonian formulations reflect the concepts of their day). The ultimate question is absolutely plain, even to the man in the street to whom semantics, culture, and theology are all closed books. It is this: Is Jesus to be worshiped or only to be admired? If he is God, then he is worthy of our worship, faith, and obedience; if he is not God, then to give him such devotion is idolatry.

2. The necessity of the Incarnation. The first chapter of *The Myth of God Incarnate* poses the question whether there could be a Christianity without the Incarnation. This question must be answered with an unambiguous no. There is no possibility whatever of reconstructing Christianity without having at its center Jesus the God-man who is "ever to be worshiped, trusted and adored." A reconstruction of Christianity without this would be a destruction of it.

3. The denial of the Incarnation. If the worship of Jesus as God is central to Christianity, and thus the Incarnation is essential, then it follows logically that those who deny the Incarnation by not worshiping Jesus are not Christians in the sense in which the term has always been understood.

4. The special case of clergy. At their ordination clergy place themselves freely under the authority of their church, and promise to teach its doctrine. If a time comes when a clergyman can no longer conscientiously teach something central to his church's doctrine (such as the personal deity of Jesus), which he has solemnly undertaken to teach, then surely the only honorable course open to him is to resign any post he occupies as an accredited teacher of his church.

5. *The responsibility of the bishops.* What should be done if such a clergyman refuses to resign? Bishops (and their counterparts in other churches) are in a very difficult position. They are rightly concerned for the peace of the church as well as for its truth. In order to avoid a public scandal they prefer where possible to take action privately. They have no wish to make martyrs. Nevertheless in the last resort (a) if a central Christian doctrine is at stake, (b) if the clergyman concerned is not just questioning it but denying it, (c) if he is not just passing through a temporary period of uncertainty but has reached a settled conviction, and (d) if he refuses to resign, then I myself believe that the bishop or other leader concerned should withdraw his license or permission to teach in the church. I further believe that to allow such a man to continue as a practicing clergyman would damage his own conscience in addition to harming the church and lessening its credibility in the sight of the world.

The most effective way to restrain and correct error, however, is not by a resort to repressive measures but by a convincing commendation of the truth. We should not be fearful either for the truth or for the church. The living God is well able to look after both, because both are his. Only one force can overcome error, and that is the power of truth. So we evangelicals should accept our responsibility to engage in more constructive theological work ourselves. For God calls his people now as always both to defend and to proclaim his Gospel.

John R. W. Stott, "Cornerstone: Truth, Heresy, and Discipline in the Church," *Christianity Today* 22, no. 11 (March 10, 1978): 58–59.

Chapter 5

THE MYTHMAKERS' MYTH

*A Christology that meets the requirements of the
mind loses the mystery and the majesty.*

T wo and a half years have elapsed since the publication of *The
Myth of God Incarnate* (see "Is the Incarnation a Myth?"), in
which seven English academics repudiated anything approaching
the traditional doctrine of Jesus as God and man. The debate
continues. Perhaps an assessment of the present state of play is
appropriate, especially as Christmas approaches.

In February this year four contributors to *The Myth* came to
London to meet four evangelicals and one conservative Anglo-
Catholic for a day-long conference. I record here some of my own
impressions of that meeting.

Although I do not think the mythmakers' armor was dented,
at the same time, I was able to appreciate that they have at least
three genuine concerns, namely to express a Christology which
(1) safeguards a truly monotheistic faith, (2) preserves the
authentic humanness of Jesus, and (3) makes sense as "gospel"

to modern people. Yet to appreciate *The Myth* authors' good concerns (I wish we all shared them) is not to approve the conclusions to which they have come. "Tell me," I asked one of them over lunch, "do you ever worship Jesus?" "No," came his immediate response, "I don't." This, I suggest, is a simple test which the most theologically illiterate person-in-the-pew can understand and apply. For what is ultimately at stake in this debate is not the Chalcedonian Definition ("one Person in two natures," A.D. 451), nor semantic questions about "myth" and "metaphor," but whether we bow the knee to Jesus, calling upon him for salvation and worshiping him as Lord. Can those who refuse to do this be called Christians? I think not.

A more important discussion took place in July 1978 in Birmingham, England, likened, somewhat irreverently, to a "seven-a-side rugby match," for the seven *Myth* contributors met seven of their leading critics, including Professors C. F. D. Moule of Cambridge, Stephen Sykes of Durham, and Graham Stanton of London; the Roman Catholic scholar, Dr. Nicholas Lash; and Dr. Lesslie Newbigin, formerly bishop in Madras. The results of their colloquium have recently been published in a sizeable book entitled *Incarnation and Myth: The Debate Continued*, edited by Michael Goulder. The essays and responses are grouped around five major issues which Professor Maurice Wiles identifies in his opening survey: (1) Is the doctrine of the Incarnation logically coherent, or does it contain an "internal self-contradiction" so that it is actually nonsensical? (2) Can other Christian doctrines survive without the Incarnation, or is Dr. John Macquarrie right that "Christian doctrines are so closely interrelated that if you take away one, several others tend to collapse"? (3) Is the New Testament evidence for the Incarnation clear or ambiguous? (4) Can we credit Jesus with uniqueness and finality, or should we accept the claims of other religions? (5) Is the Incarnation simply a "culturally conditioned" notion of the early centuries, or can we moderns also accept it?

Summing up, Professor Basil Mitchell, the Oxford philosopher who chaired the colloquium, comments that much of the debate was more philosophical than theological. The basic issue was one of epistemology. He expresses the view that the "mythographers" (as he playfully designates the *Myth* authors) take for granted an "evolutionary world view" and see the traditional doctrine of the Incarnation as incompatible with it.

A second basic collision between the traditionalists and the radicals concerned the church's tradition. Brian Hebblethwaite, doughty defender of historic orthodoxy, affirms that "the doctrines of the Incarnation and the Trinity belong ... to the essence of Christianity," and that it is these doctrines, "expressed in all the creeds and confessions of the historic churches," which "have given Christian belief its characteristic shape down the centuries." The church must therefore maintain this faith, and both "refute" and "repudiate" the views expressed in *The Myth*. Not that "there is any one doctrine (i.e., formulation) of the Incarnation universally admitted to be orthodox" (Stephen Sykes), but rather that across the centuries there is a certain recognizable continuity, a "family resemblance." This argument from history and tradition does not impress Don Cupitt, however. He is quite ready to jettison the past. As he writes in his book *The Debate about Christ* (1979), "modern historical-critical study of Christian origins has created a new situation" and "theology written before 1800 is now of only limited relevance."

Now this is not a cavalier dismissal of *all* the past, as it may seem. If we were to ask Don Cupitt what he would substitute for the church's tradition, he would reply "the real Jesus." For "Christendom-Christianity does not work any more; the historical Jesus is the real Christ for today." If we were to press him to delineate this Jesus, he would continue: "a purely human Jesus, a first-century man of God in the Jewish tradition" (*Incarnation and Myth*, p. 42), "a prophet who brought the tradition of prophetic monotheism to completion," for this is "the primitive faith as preserved in the New Testament." So in the end, although the arguments about epistemology and tradition are important, the crucial question concerns the witness of the New Testament. Does it teach the Incarnation? Or is this doctrine a later accretion?

On this topic it is a relief to turn to Emeritus Professor Charlie Moule's characteristically cautious and lucid study, *The Origin of Christology* (1977). His main argument is that the right model for understanding the growth of New Testament Christology is not "evolution" ("the genesis of successive new species by mutations") but "development" ("growth, from immaturity to maturity, of a single specimen within itself"). Thus we should explain "all the various estimates of Jesus reflected in the New Testament as, in essence, only attempts to describe what was already there from the beginning."

Speaking now for myself, I keep coming back to three foundational arguments. First, Jesus' own self-consciousness was disclosed at least in those two favorite Aramaic words of his which the evangelists preserved in the original: "Abba" (introducing his prayers and expressing his unique sense of intimacy with the Father) and "Amen" (introducing his affirmations "I say to you," and expressing his unique sense of authority over men). Secondly, his enemies condemned him in the Jewish court for "blasphemy" (because he claimed divine prerogatives, such as the right to forgive and to judge) and in the Roman court for "sedition" (because he claimed a kingship which could be made to sound treasonable to Caesar). Thirdly, it was the universal faith of the primitive church (as Paul's earliest letters attest) to ascribe to Jesus an unrivaled cosmic lordship, the name above every name.

Though we cannot penetrate the mystery, we can worship the majesty of the Lord Christ.

John R. W. Stott, "Cornerstone: The Mythmakers' Myth," *Christianity Today* 23, no. 27 (December 7, 1979): 30–31.

Chapter 6

———

SCRIPTURE

THE LIGHT AND HEAT

FOR EVANGELISM

*Let's not consume all our energies arguing about
the Word of God, let's start using it.*

W ithout the Bible world evangelization would be not only
impossible but actually inconceivable. It is the Bible that
lays upon us the responsibility to evangelize the world, gives us a
gospel to proclaim, tells us how to proclaim it, and that it is God's
power for salvation to every believer.

It is, moreover, an observable fact of history, both past and
contemporary, that the degree of the church's commitment to
world evangelization is commensurate with the degree of its conviction about the authority of the Bible. Whenever Christians lose
their confidence in the Bible, they also lose their zeal for evangelism. Conversely, whenever they are convinced about the Bible,
then they are determined about evangelism.

As the Lausanne Covenant says, we must affirm "the divine inspiration, truthfulness, and authority of both Old and New Testament Scriptures in their entirety as the only written Word of God, without error in all that it affirms, and the only infallible rule of faith and practice." Incidentally, the expression "without error in all that it affirms" was never intended to be an evasion or loophole (as some have suggested) but rather a clarification. It acknowledges that not everything contained in Scripture is affirmed by Scripture (e.g., the speeches of Job's comforters whom God later rebuked for not having spoken of him what was right, [42:7]), and it therefore asserts the need for painstaking exegesis in order to determine what the original authors were affirming, and what God is affirming through them. We should be grateful that the International Council on Biblical Inerrancy helpfully elaborated this expression by saying in their "Short Statement" (1979) that Scripture "is to be believed, as God's instruction, in all that it affirms; obeyed, as God's command, in all that it requires; and embraced, as God's pledge, in all that it promises."

Let me develop four reasons why the Bible is indispensable to world evangelization.

Mandate

The Bible gives us the mandate for world evangelization. We certainly need one. Two phenomena are everywhere on the increase. One is religious fanaticism, and the other, religious pluralism. The fanatic displays the kind of irrational zeal which (if it could) would use force to compel belief and eradicate disbelief. Religious pluralism encourages the opposite tendency.

Whenever the spirit of religious fanaticism or of its opposite, religious indifferentism, prevails, world evangelization is bitterly resented. Fanatics refuse to countenance the rivals evangelism represents, and pluralists its exclusive claims. The Christian evangelist is regarded as making an unwarrantable intrusion into other people's private affairs.

In the face of this opposition we need to be clear about the mandate the Bible gives us. It is not just the Great Commission (important as that is) but the entire biblical revelation. Let me rehearse it briefly.

There is but one living and true God, the Creator of the universe, the Lord of the nations and the God of the spirits of all flesh. Some 4,000 years ago he called Abraham and made a covenant with him, promising not only to bless him but also through his posterity to bless all the families of the earth (Gen. 12:1–4). This biblical text is one of the foundation stones of the Christian mission. For Abraham's descendants (through whom all nations are being blessed) are Christ and the people of Christ. If by faith we belong to Christ, we are Abraham's spiritual children and have a responsibility to all mankind. So, too, the Old Testament prophets foretold how God would make his Christ the heir and the light of the nations (Ps. 2:8; Isa. 42:6; 49:6).

When Jesus came, he endorsed these promises. True, during his own earthly ministry he was restricted "to the lost sheep of the house of Israel" (Matt. 10:6; 15:24), but he prophesied that many would "come from east and west, and from north and south," and would "sit at table with Abraham, Isaac, and Jacob in the kingdom of heaven" (Matt. 8:11; Luke 13:29). Further, in anticipation of his resurrection and ascension he made the tremendous claim that "all authority in heaven and on earth" had been given to him (Matt. 28:18). It was in consequence of his universal authority that he commanded his followers to make all nations his disciples, baptizing them into his new community and teaching them all his teaching (Matt. 28:19).

And this, when the Holy Spirit of truth and power had come upon them, the early Christians proceeded to do. They became the witnesses of Jesus, even to the ends of the earth (Acts 1:8). Moreover, they did it "for sake of his name" (Rom. 1:5; 3 John 7). They knew that God had superexalted Jesus, enthroning him at his right hand and bestowing upon him the highest rank, in order that every tongue should confess his lordship. They longed that Jesus should receive the honor due his name. Besides, one day he would return in glory, to save, to judge, and to reign. So what was to fill the gap between his two comings? The worldwide mission of the church! Not till the gospel had reached the end of the world, he said, would the end of history come (cf. Matt 24:14; 28:20; Acts 1:8). The two ends would coincide.

Our mandate for world evangelization, therefore, is the whole Bible. It is to be found in the creation of God (because of which all human beings are responsible to him), in the character of God (as outgoing, loving, compassionate, not willing that any should perish, desiring that all should come to repentance), in the promises of God (that all nations will be blessed through Abraham's seed and will become the Messiah's inheritance), in the Christ of God (now exalted with universal authority, to receive universal acclaim), in the Spirit of God (who convicts of sin, witnesses to Christ, and impels the church to evangelize) and in the church of God (which is a multinational, missionary community, under orders to evangelize until Christ returns.)

This global dimension of the Christian mission is irresistible. Individual Christians and local churches not committed to world evangelization are contradicting (either through blindness or through disobedience) an essential part of their God-given identity. The biblical mandate for world evangelization cannot be escaped.

Message

The Bible gives us the message for world evangelization. The Lausanne Covenant defined evangelism in terms of the evangel.

Paragraph four begins: "To evangelize is to spread the good news that Jesus Christ died for our sins and was raised from the dead according to the Scriptures, and that as the reigning Lord he now offers the forgiveness of sins and the liberating gift of the Spirit to all who repent and believe."

Now this message for evangelism, like the mandate for evangelism, comes from the Bible. To begin, let us look at this negatively. First, it does not come from the Scriptures of other religions. We read and study these with respect. Many of us have to confess that we should be more familiar with them and more respectful toward them than we have been. What they contain of truth, beauty, and goodness we ascribe to Jesus Christ, the Logos of God and Light of the World (John 1:1–9). We are ready to quote them appreciatively when they affirm what Scripture affirms— much as Paul in Athens quoted the Greek authors Epimenides and Aratus (Acts 17:27–29). But we cannot accept that they were specially or supernaturally inspired like the Scriptures of the Old and New Testaments. Nor can they lead their readers to salvation, since they do not bear witness to Christ as the only Savior of sinners, which is the main function of the Christian Scriptures (cf. John 5:39, 40; 20:31; 2 Tim. 3:15).

Second, our message does not come from the tradition of the churches. True, a message has come down to us in the living tradition of the church, as our friends in the Roman Catholic and Orthodox churches emphasize. Further, we evangelical Christians need a doctrine of tradition that recognizes the activity of the Holy Spirit in illumining the minds of his people in every generation. Nevertheless, we cannot rely on church tradition for our message, for we cannot accept the "two-source" theory of divine revelation, namely that Holy Scripture and holy tradition are independent, equal, and authoritative sources of doctrine. Rather do we see tradition standing alongside Scripture as a fallible interpretation of an infallible revelation. We feel obliged to affirm the supremacy of Scripture over tradition, as Jesus did, when he called the traditions of the elders "the traditions of *men*" and subordinated them to the judgment of Scripture as the Word of *God* (Mark 7:1–13).

Instead, our message comes out of the Bible. As we turn to the Bible for our message, however, we are immediately confronted with a dilemma. On the one hand the message is given to us. We are not left to invent it; it has been entrusted to us as a precious "deposit," which we, like faithful stewards, are both to guard and to dispense to God's household (1 Tim. 6:20; 2 Tim. 1:12–14; 2 Cor. 4:1–2). On the other hand, it has not been given to us as a single, neat, mathematical formula, but rather in a rich diversity of formulations, in which different images or metaphors are used.

So there is only one gospel, on which all the apostles agreed (1 Cor. 15:10), and Paul could call down the curse of God upon anybody—including himself—who preached a "different" gospel from the original apostolic gospel of God's grace (Gal. 1:6–8). Yet the apostles expressed this one gospel in various ways—now sacrificial (the shedding and sprinkling of Christ's blood), now messianic (the breaking in of God's promised rule), now legal (the Judge pronouncing the unrighteous righteous), now personal (the Father reconciling his wayward children), now salvific (the heavenly Liberator coming to rescue the helpless), now cosmic (the universal Lord claiming universal dominion); and this is only a selection.

The gospel is thus seen to be one, yet diverse. It is "given," yet culturally adapted to its audience. Once we grasp this, we shall be saved from making two opposite mistakes. The first I will call "total fluidity." I recently heard an English church leader declare that there is no such thing as the gospel until we enter the situation in which we are to witness. We take nothing with us into the situation, he said; we discover the gospel only when we have arrived there. Now I am in full agreement with the need to be sensitive to each situation, but if this was the point which the leader in question was wanting to make, he grossly overstated it. There *is* such a thing as a revealed or given gospel, which we have no liberty to falsify.

The opposite mistake I will call "total rigidity." In this case the evangelist behaves as if God had given a series of precise formulas that we have to repeat more or less word for word, and certain images that we must invariably employ. This leads to bondage to either words or images or both. Some evangelists lapse into the use of stale jargon, while others feel obliged on every occasion to mention "the blood of Christ" or "justification by faith" or "the kingdom of God" or some other image.

Between these two extremes there is a third and better way. It combines commitment to the fact of revelation with commitment to the task of contextualization. It accepts that only the biblical formulations of the gospel are permanently normative, and that every attempt to proclaim the gospel in modern idiom must justify itself as an authentic expression of the biblical gospel.

But if it refuses to jettison the biblical formulations, it also refuses to recite them in a wooden and unimaginative way. On the contrary, we have to engage in the continuous struggle (by prayer, study, and discussion) to relate the given gospel to the given situation. Since it comes from God we must guard it; since it is intended for modern men and women we must interpret it. We have to combine fidelity (constantly studying the biblical text) with sensitivity (constantly studying the contemporary scene). Only then can we hope with faithfulness and relevance to relate the Word to the world, the gospel to the context, Scripture to culture.

Model

The Bible gives us the model for world evangelization. In addition to a message (what we are to say) we need a model (how we are to say it). The Bible supplies this too: the Bible does not just *contain* the gospel; it *is* the gospel. Through the Bible God is himself actually evangelizing, that is, communicating the good news to the world. You will recall Paul's statement about Genesis 12:3 that "the scripture ... preached the gospel beforehand to Abraham" (Gal. 3:8 RSV). All Scripture preaches the gospel; God evangelizes through it.

If, then, Scripture is itself divine evangelization, it stands to reason that we can learn how to preach the gospel by considering how God has done it. He has given us in the process of biblical inspiration a beautiful evangelistic model.

What strikes us immediately is the greatness of God's condescension. He had sublime truth to reveal about himself and his Christ, his mercy and his justice, and his full salvation. And he chose to make this disclosure through the vocabulary and grammar of human language, through human beings, human images, and human cultures. He used very lowly anthropomorphisms, speaking of himself as if he were a human being who rolled up his sleeves, enjoyed the smell of burning meat, or changed his mind. Through the apostles he communicated in *koinē* Greek, the common language of the office and the market place, and was even prepared to overlook, indeed use, the well-known grammatical howlers perpetrated by John in the Revelation. So complete was his adaptation to the human condition that his message never sounded alien. It was homely, simple, appropriate.

Yet through this lowly medium of human words and images, God was speaking of his own Word. Our evangelical doctrine of the inspiration of Scripture emphasizes its double authorship.

Men spoke and God spoke. Men spoke from God (2 Pet. 1:21) and God spoke through men (Heb. 1:1). The words spoken and written were equally his and theirs. He decided what he wanted to say, yet did not smother their human personalities. They used their faculties freely, yet did not distort the divine message. Christians want to assert something similar about the Incarnation, the climax of the self-communicating God. "The Word became flesh" (John 1:14). That is, God's eternal Word, who from eternity was with God and was God, the agent through whom the universe was created, became a human being, with all the particularity of a first-century Palestinian Jew. He became little, weak, poor, and vulnerable. He experienced pain and hunger, and exposed himself to temptation. All this was included in the "flesh," the human being he became. Yet when he became one of us, he did not cease to be himself. He remained forever the eternal Word or Son of God.

Essentially the same principle illustrated both the inspiration of the Scripture and the incarnation of the Son. The Word became flesh. The divine was communicated through the human. He identified with us, though without surrendering his own identity. And this principle of "identification without loss of identity" is the model for all evangelism, especially cross-cultural evangelism.

Some of us refuse to identify with the people we claim to be serving. We remain ourselves, and do not become like them. We stay aloof. We hold on desperately to our own cultural inheritance in the mistaken notion that it is an indispensable part of our identity. We are unwilling to let it go. Not only do we maintain our own cultural practices with fierce tenacity, but we treat the cultural inheritance of the land of our adoption without the respect it deserves. We thus practice a double kind of cultural imperialism, imposing our own culture on others and despising theirs. But this was not the way of Christ, who emptied himself of his glory and humbled himself to serve.

Other cross-cultural messengers of the gospel make the opposite mistake. So determined are they to identify with the people to whom they go that they surrender even their Christian standards and values. But again this was not Christ's way, since in becoming human he remained truly divine. The Lausanne Covenant expressed the principle in these words: "Christ's evangelists must humbly seek to empty themselves of all but their personal authenticity, in order to become the servants of others" (paragraph 10).

The whole question of resistance and receptivity of the gospel has been prominent in the pre-COWE study groups and will be throughout the miniconsultations. We have to wrestle with the reasons why people reject the gospel, and in particular to give due weight to the cultural factors. Some people reject the gospel not because they perceive it to be false, but because they perceive it to be alien.

Dr. René Padilla was criticized at Lausanne for saying that the gospel some European and North American missionaries have exported was a "culture-Christianity," a Christian message, that is, distorted by the materialistic, consumer culture of the West. It was hurtful to us to hear him say this, but of course he was quite right. All of us need to subject our gospel to more critical scrutiny, and in a cross-cultural situation, visiting evangelists need humbly to seek the help of local Christians in order to discern the cultural distortions of their message.

Others reject the gospel because they perceive it to be a threat to their own culture. Of course Christ challenges every culture. Whenever we present the gospel to Hindus or Buddhists, Jews or Muslims, secularists or Marxists, Jesus Christ confronts them with his demand to dislodge whatever has thus far secured their allegiance and replace it with himself. He is Lord of every person and every culture. That threat, that confrontation, cannot be avoided. But does the gospel we proclaim present people with other threats that are unnecessary, because it calls for the abolition of harmless customs or appears destructive of national art, architecture, music, and festivals, or because we who share it are culture-proud and culture-blind?

To sum up, when God spoke to us in Scripture he used human language, and when he spoke to us in Christ he assumed human flesh. In order to reveal himself, he both emptied and humbled himself. That is the model of evangelism which the Bible supplies. There is self-emptying and self-humbling in all authentic evangelism; without it we contradict the gospel and misrepresent the Christ we proclaim.

Power

The Bible gives us the power for world evangelization. It is hardly necessary for me to emphasize our need for power, for we know how feeble our human resources are in comparison with the magnitude of the task. We also know how armor-plated are the defenses of the human heart. Worse still, we know the personal reality, malevolence, and might of the Devil, and of the demonic forces at his command.

Sophisticated people may ridicule our belief, and caricature it, too, in order to make their ridicule more plausible. But we evangelical Christians are naive enough to believe what Jesus and his apostles taught. To us it is a fact of great solemnity that, in John's expression, "the whole world is in the power of the evil one" (1 John 5:19). For until they are liberated by Jesus Christ and transferred into his kingdom, all men and women are the slaves of Satan. Moreover, we see his power in the contemporary world—in the darkness of idolatry and of the fear of spirits, in superstition and fatalism, in devotion to gods which are no gods, in the selfish materialism of the West, in the spread of atheistic communism, in the proliferation of irrational cults, in violence and aggression, and in the widespread declension from absolute standards of goodness and truth. These things are the work of him who is called in Scripture a liar, a deceiver, a slanderer, and a murderer.

So Christian conversion and regeneration remain miracles of God's grace. They are the culmination of a power struggle between Christ and Satan or (in vivid apocalyptic imagery) between the Lamb and the Dragon. The plundering of the strong man's palace is possible only because he has been bound by the One who is stronger still, and who by his death and resurrection disarmed and discarded the principalities and powers of evil (Matt. 12:27–29; Luke 11:20–22; Col. 2:15).

How then shall we enter into Christ's victory and overthrow the devil's power? Let Luther answer our question: *ein wörtlein will ihn fällen* ("one little word will knock him down"). There is power in the Word of God and in the preaching of the gospel. Perhaps the most dramatic expression of this in the New Testament is to be found in 2 Corinthians 4. Paul portrays "the god of this world" as having "blinded the minds of the unbelievers, to keep them from seeing the light of the gospel of the glory of Christ ..." (v. 4).

If human minds are blinded, how then can they ever see? Only by the creative Word of God. For it is the God who said, "let light shine out of darkness," who has shone in our hearts to "give the light of the knowledge of the glory of God in the face of Christ" (v. 6). The apostle thus likens the unregenerate heart to the dark primeval chaos, and attributes regeneration to the divine fiat, "Let there be light."

If then Satan blinds people's minds, and God shines into people's hearts, what can we hope to contribute to this encounter? Would it not be more modest for us to retire from the field of conflict and leave them to fight it out? No, this is not the conclusion Paul reaches.

On the contrary, in between verses 4 and 6, which describe the activities of God and Satan, verse 5 describes the work of the evangelist: "We preach ... Jesus Christ as Lord." Since the light which the Devil wants to prevent people seeing and which God shines into them is the gospel, we had better preach it! Preaching the gospel, far from being unnecessary, is indispensable. It is the God-appointed means by which the prince of darkness is defeated and the light comes streaming into people's hearts. There is power in God's gospel—his power for salvation (Rom. 1:16).

In our day there is a widespread disenchantment with words. People are bombarded with words by advertisers, politicians, and propagandists, until they become "word-resistant." In countries where television is available, words lose their power because of the greater power of images. After all, what is a word? Only a puff of breath, and in a moment it is gone, so intangible and transient is it.

But the Bible has a different perspective. Behind every word is the person who speaks it, and the authority he possesses or lacks. God's Word has power for the sole reason that it is God who speaks it. His Word is creative ("for he spoke and it was done," Ps. 33:9), productive ("my word ... shall not return to me empty but it shall accomplish that which I purpose," Isa. 55:11), and redemptive ("it pleased God through the folly of what we preach to save those who believe," 1 Cor. 1:21). Still today God honors his Word. Whether we share it with a single individual or preach it to a congregation or broadcast it by radio or distribute it in print, through it he can put forth his saving power.

Not that we have a superstitious view of the Word of God. We do not attribute magical efficacy to the words of Scripture as if they were spells bringing a blessing or a curse. Their power is due solely to the fact that the God who once spoke these words still speaks through what he has spoken. His Spirit still uses the Word as his sword. We should never separate the Word of God and the Spirit of God.

We may be very weak. I sometimes wish we were weaker. Faced with the forces of evil, we are often tempted to put on a show of Christian strength and engage in a little evangelical saber rattling. But it is in our weakness that Christ's strength is made perfect and it is words of human weakness that the Spirit endorses with his power. So it is when we are weak that we are strong (1 Cor. 2:1–5; 2 Cor. 12:9–10).

Let us not consume all our energies arguing about the Word of God; let's start using it. It will prove its divine origin by its divine power. Let's let it loose in the world! If only every Christian missionary and evangelist proclaimed the biblical gospel with faithfulness and sensitivity, and every Christian preacher were a faithful expositor of God's Word! Then God would display his saving power.

Without the Bible world evangelization is impossible. For without the Bible we have no gospel to take to the nations, no warrant to take it to them, no idea of how to set about the task, and no hope of any success. It is the Bible that gives us the mandate, the message, the model, and the power we need for world evangelization. So let's seek to repossess it by diligent study and meditation. Let's heed its summons, grasp its message, follow its directions, and trust its power. Let's lift up our voices and make it known.

John R. W. Stott, "Scripture: The Light and Heat for Evangelism," *Christianity Today* 25, no. 3 (February 6, 1981): 26–30.

Part II

THE CHRISTIAN DISCIPLE

———

Chapter 7

WHEN SHOULD A CHRISTIAN WEEP?

S hould a Christian ever be unhappy? In some periods of church history it would have seemed absurd to ask such a question. These were the periods in which Christians cultivated an air of grave solemnity and earned for themselves a reputation for being glum and lugubrious.

At other times—including, I think, our own day—the opposite tendency has been apparent. Evangelism has been debased into the simple invitation to "come to Jesus and be happy." The signature tune of the Christian Church has been "I Am *Happy*." Christians are to appear hearty, ebullient, and boisterous. In a Christian magazine I receive, every Christian's picture (and there are many) shows him with a grin from ear to ear. Some Christians would defend this attitude by quoting such Scripture as "Rejoice in the Lord always."

But the true biblical image of the Christian is neither of these. Nor is it both together, though joy and sorrow are both part of the Christian life. "There is a time to laugh, and there is a time to weep," said the Preacher in Ecclesiastes. Moreover, we are followers of One who went about saying, "Be of good cheer. ... Go in peace," yet was called "the Man of sorrows." The Apostle Paul expressed the same paradox in 2 Corinthians 6:10—"as sorrowful, yet always rejoicing."

Human life itself can be full of joy; God has "given us all things richly to enjoy." That the Christian life, in particular, is intended to be joyful is obvious from Scripture and hardly needs to be emphasized.

The Gospel is "glad tidings of great joy," and in God's presence is "fullness of joy" (Ps. 16:11). Jesus said he wanted his disciples' joy to be full (John 15:11; 16:24; 17:13). Both joy and peace are the fruit of the Spirit, and the Apostle Paul prayed that God would fill his people with all joy and peace in believing (see Rom. 14:17; 15:13).

I do not deny any of this. On the contrary, I believe it and rejoice in it. I see it in others and have experienced it myself. There is joy—true, deep, and lasting—in the knowledge of forgiveness and the experience of fellowship, in hearing and receiving the Word of God, in seeing a sinner repent, and in God himself, who satisfies the hungry with good things.

Dr. W. E. Sangster writes in one of his books of Dr. Farmer, the organist at Harrow, who pleaded with a Salvationist drummer not to hit the drum so hard. The beaming bandsman replies: "Lor' bless you sir, since I've been converted I'm so happy I could bust the bloomin' drum." Thank God for this; it is an authentic Christian experience.

If we want to redress the balance in our own unbalanced days, however, I find myself wishing there were fewer grins and more tears, less laughter and more weeping. If Psalm 100 tells us to "serve the Lord with gladness," the Apostle Paul could describe his own ministry (which must have been full of joy in many ways) as "serving the Lord with all humility and with many tears."

Why and when should a Christian weep?

In the first place, Christians are subject to what might be called "tears of nature," that is, the tears of natural sorrow. These are not specifically Christian tears, simply human tears. They are due to the common nature we share with all humanity, and are a response to some sorrow.

For example, there is the sorrow of parting, such as Timothy felt when Paul was arrested and taken away from him and he could not restrain his tears (2 Tim. 1:4), or such as the Ephesian elders felt when Paul said goodbye to them for the last time and they wept (Acts 20:37).

There is the sorrow of bereavement, as when Jesus cried at the graveside of Lazarus (John 11:35).

There is the sorrow of our own mortality when we sense the frailty of our body and groan, longing to be finally delivered (Rom. 8:22, 23; 2 Cor. 5:2).

There are also the many trials we undergo in life, as a result of which we are "in heaviness" (1 Pet. 1:6). This kind of experience prompted the Psalmist to pray, "Put thou my tears in thy bottle" (Ps. 56:8).

Many times I have been on a railway platform when missionaries were being seen off to the field, and many times I have attended the funeral of a Christian. On such occasions I have sensed the inhibitions of Christians who have either forced themselves to suppress their feelings or turned away to hide their tears.

There is, of course, a selfish and unrestrained weeping that would be unbecoming in Christian people. Thus we are forbidden to sorrow over our Christian dead *as those who have no hope* (1 Thess. 4:13). But we are not forbidden to sorrow or to weep. Indeed, it would be unnatural not to. To regard natural sorrow as unmanly is more stoic than Christian. The Gospel does not rob us of our humanity.

In addition to these various kinds of "tears of nature," Christians are subject also to the "tears of grace." These are tears we do not share with non-Christian people, tears which (if we shed them) God himself has caused us to shed. There are at least three forms.

1. Tears of penitence.

We all know the story of the woman who stood behind Jesus weeping and began to wet his feet with her tears. These were tears of penitence for her sin and of gratitude for her forgiveness.

"But," an impatient Christian may object, "she was a fallen woman, and these were the tears of her conversion. Certainly I am glad when eyes are moist at the gospel invitation and the penitent bench is wet with tears. *This* is holy water indeed. But surely *Christians* do not weep over their sins."

Don't they? I would to God they did! Have the people of God no sins to mourn and confess? Was Ezra wrong to pray and to make confession, weeping and casting himself down before the house of God? And were God's covenant people wrong to join him in bitter weeping (Ezra 10:1)? Did Jesus not mean what he said in the Sermon on the Mount when he pronounced "blessed" those who mourn, which in the context seems to imply a mourning over their sin? Was Paul wrong as a Christian to cry, "Wretched man that I am! Who will deliver me from this body of death?" (Rom. 7:24). I know that this has often been interpreted as the cry of either an unbeliever or a defeated Christian, but from Scripture and experience I am convinced that it is the cry of a mature Christian, of one who sees the continuing corruption of his fallen nature, mourns over it, and longs for the final deliverance that death and resurrection will bring him. It is a form of that "godly sorrow" of Christian penitence about which Paul writes in 2 Corinthians 7.

David Brainerd, that most saintly missionary to the American Indians at the beginning of the eighteenth century, supplies a good illustration of this kind of penitential sorrow. For example, he writes in his diary for October 18, 1740: "In my morning devotions my soul was exceedingly melted, and bitterly mourned over my exceeding sinfulness and vileness. I never before had felt so pungent and deep a sense of the odious nature of sin as at this time. My soul was then unusually carried forth in love to God and had a lively sense of God's love to me."

2. Tears of compassion.

Tears of compassion are wept by Christian people who obey the apostolic injunction not only to "rejoice with those who rejoice" but to "weep with those who weep" (Rom. 12:15).

Of course, the non-Christian humanist can also weep tears of compassion. Indeed, some secular humanists weep tears more bitter and more copious than ours in their sorrow over the horrors and cruelties of the Viet Nam war, over starvation in Biafra, over poverty, unemployment, oppression, and racial discrimination. Are such humanists, then, more sensitive than Christian people? Are we so insulated from the sufferings of the world that we do not feel them and cannot weep over them?

But specifically Christian tears of compassion are shed over the unbelieving and impenitent, over those who (whether through blindness or willfulness) reject the Gospel, over their self-destructive folly and their grave danger.

Thus Jeremiah could cry: "O that my head were waters and my eyes a fountain of tears, that I might weep day and night for the slain of the daughters of my people" (Jer. 9:1; cf. 13:17 and 14:17).

Thus too Jesus Christ wept over the city of Jerusalem because it did not know the time of its visitation and was about to bring upon itself the judgment of God (Luke 19:41).

Thus too the Apostle Paul, during three years of ministry in Ephesus, did not cease night and day to admonish everyone with tears (Acts 20:31). And he could write also that he had a "great sorrow and unceasing anguish" in his heart on behalf of his Jewish kinsmen (Rom. 9:2).

Many more modern examples could be given of these Christian tears of compassion. Bishop J. C. Ryle has written of George Whitefield that the people "could not hate the man who wept so much over their souls." Andrew Bonar wrote in his diary on his forty-ninth birthday: "Felt in the evening most bitter grief over the apathy of the district. They are perishing, they are perishing, and yet they will not consider. I lay awake thinking over it, and crying to the Lord in broken groans." Similarly, Dr. Dale of Birmingham, who was at first critical of D. L. Moody, changed his opinion when he went to hear him. Thereafter he had the profoundest respect for him because Moody "could never speak of a lost soul without tears in his eyes."

How can we see the increasing apostasy and demoralization of the Western world today and not burst into tears?

3. Tears of jealousy.

I am referring here to the divine jealousy, which Christian people should share. Such "jealousy" is a strong zeal for the name, honor, and glory of God. It was this that caused the Psalmist to say: "My eyes shed streams of tears because men do not keep thy law" (Ps. 119:136). And it was this that led Paul to write to the Philippians of the many, whom he could mention only "with tears," who were "enemies of the cross of Christ" (Phil. 3:18).

Here were men so concerned about the law of God and the cross of Christ that they could not bear to see them trampled under foot. Those who made themselves enemies of God's law by violating it and of Christ's cross by preaching another gospel brought tears to the eyes of godly people who cared. No purer tears than these are ever shed. They contain no selfishness or vanity. They show the sorrow of a human being who loves God more than anything else in the world, and who cannot see God's love rebuffed or his truth rejected without weeping. How is it that we can walk through the secular cities of our day and restrain our tears?

In the light of this biblical evidence about the tears both of nature and of grace, I believe that we should laugh less and cry more, that if we were more Christian we should certainly be more sorrowful. We must reject that form of Christian teaching which represents the Christian life as all smiles and no tears.

Professor James Atkinson was speaking three years ago to a meeting of the Church of England Evangelical Council in London. He was describing some of the pathetically untheological conditions of the Church of England, and he did so in such a way as to make us laugh. He immediately commented: "The difference between you and me is that you laugh and I cry. Erasmus called for more Flemish wine, with no water added. Luther cried all night."

The fundamental error underlying our modern tearlessness is a misunderstanding of God's plan of salvation, a false assumption that his saving work is finished, that its benefits may be enjoyed completely, and that there is no need for any more sickness, suffering, or sin, which are the causes of sorrow.

This is just not true. God's saving work is not yet done. Christian people are only half saved. True, Christ cried in triumph "It is finished," and by his death and resurrection he completed the work he came to do. But the fruits of this salvation have not yet been fully garnered. And they will not be, and cannot be, until the end comes when Christ returns in power and glory. The ravages of the Fall have not yet been eradicated either in the world or in Christian people. We still have a fallen nature, an ingrained corruption, over which to weep. We still live in a fallen world, full of sorrow because full of suffering and sin.

Can we not see these things? The eyes that do not weep are blind eyes—eyes closed to the facts of sin and of suffering in ourselves and in the rest of humanity. To close our eyes thus is to withdraw from the world of reality, to live in Cloud Cuckoo Land, to pretend that the final victory has been won when it has not.

Thank God the day is coming when there will be no more crying, when sorrow and sighing will flee away and God will wipe away all tears from our eyes. This will take place when the kingdom of God has been consummated, when there is a new heaven and a new earth, when God's people have been totally redeemed with new and glorified bodies, when there is no more sin and no more death.

In our lives as Christians, let us rejoice in that measure of victory already gained by Christ and received by us—in the forgiveness of our sins, in Christian fellowship, and in the indwelling of the Holy Spirit. Let us rejoice too "in hope of the glory of God" (see Rom. 5:2; 12:12; 1 Pet. 1:5–8). The expectation of God's final victory is another source of joy. We know that those who sow in tears shall reap in joy.

And let us remember that meanwhile we are living in the interim period, between the beginning and the end of the salvation of God, between the inauguration and the consummation of victory. We are living between D Day and V Day—a period during which much blood was spilled and many tears were shed. Sin, suffering, and sorrow continue. Christian people are caught in the tension between what is and what shall be.

And so, although we are in heaviness through many temptations, we rejoice in the final victory of God. We are sorrowful, yet always rejoicing.

John R. W. Stott, "When Should a Christian Weep?," *Christianity Today* 14, no. 3 (November 7, 1969): 3–5.

Chapter 8

———

MUST I REALLY
LOVE MYSELF?

A chorus of many voices is chanting in unison today that I must at all costs love myself; that self-love needs to be added to love for God and neighbor as a much-neglected commandment; and that dire consequences will overtake me if I refuse—frustration, depression, hostility, inertia, and much else besides. A whole new literature is growing up around this theme. In 1976 we had *The Art of Learning to Love Yourself* by Cecil G. Osborne (Zondervan), and in 1977 *Loving Ourselves* by Ray Ashford (Fortress), *Celebrate Yourself* by Bryan Jay Cannon (Word), and *Love Yourself* by Walter Trobisch (InterVarsity).

I intended to write a column on this topic when John Piper got in first and cast his "one small vote against the cult of self-esteem," in his article *Is Self-Love Biblical?* (See the August 12, 1977, issue, page 6.) I appreciated what he wrote. But then I also appreciated the points made in the letters section in the following issue. Now that the dust has settled a bit, maybe the time has come to stir it up again. I shall begin with a negative critique, but then I shall try to affirm positively and biblically what, it seems to me, the advocates of self-love are really after.

The way that some writers are arguing, namely that we are commanded to love ourselves just as we are commanded to love God and our neighbor, is untenable for at least three reasons.

First, and grammatically speaking, the command "love your neighbor as yourself" is not a command to love both my neighbor and myself, but a command to love my neighbor as much as, in fact, I love myself. That is, self-love is not a virtue that Scripture commends, but one of the facts of our humanity that it recognizes and tells us to use as a standard. The best commentary is the Golden Rule: "Do to others what you would have them do to you" (Matt. 7:12 NIV). We know instinctively in every situation how *we* would like to be treated; so let this knowledge determine our treatment of *others*. We can be sure that this is the right interpretation partly because the Ten Commandments stipulate our duty to God and our neighbor, and partly because Jesus summarized them in terms of love for both. He said: "the first and great commandment is ...; and the second is similar ..."; he did not say "the second and third are similar."

Secondly, and linguistically speaking, the verb used is *agapaō; agapē* love (a term popularized by C. S. Lewis) always includes the ingredients of sacrifice and service. Indeed, *agapē* is the sacrifice of self in the service of another. This is extremely meaningful when we are seeking to love our God and neighbor. But how can we sacrifice ourselves to serve ourselves? The concept is nonsensical. *Agapē* love cannot be self-directed; if it is, it destroys itself. It ceases to be self-sacrifice, and becomes self-service. This may sometimes be quite proper (as in Eph. 5:28, 29), but it is then not true *agapē*. It is precisely because we should preserve a high doctrine of *agape*, portraying the love of God (his for us and ours for him) that we should resist the current fashion of self-love as inappropriate. Besides, our Lord's new commandment is not to love others *as* we love ourselves, but to love others *more* than we love ourselves, namely as he has loved us (John 13:34).

Thirdly, and theologically speaking, "self-love," that is, directing one's concern and service toward oneself, is the biblical concept not of virtue but of sin. Indeed, a mark of "the last days," of the interim between Christ's comings in which we live, is that "men will be lovers of self ... rather than lovers of God" (2 Tim. 3:2, 4). True, the Greek word here is the weaker one, and the contrast is between *philautoi* (self-lovers) and *philotheoi* (God-lovers). Nevertheless, the evils of the day are attributed to a misdirection of our love from God to self, and so also (in the context) to money and pleasure. Paul Vitz, in his courageous and perceptive book *Psychology as Religion: The Cult of Self-Worship* (Eerdmans, 1977), is biblically correct that "to worship one's self (in self-realization) ... is, in Christian terms, simple idolatry operating from the usual motive of unconscious egotism" (p. 93). He is referring to what he calls "selfist humanism."

All of this, however, does not dispose of the question. It may be no more than a game of semantics. For the advocates of self-love, however misguided they may be in their language, are concerning themselves with a topic of great theological and psychological importance, namely what a Christian's self-image should be.

It is significant that through most of his little book Walter Trobisch uses "self-love" as a synonym for "self-acceptance," and then writes: "Self-love used in the positive sense of self-acceptance is the exact opposite of narcissism or auto-eroticism" (p. 15). Right. But he also concedes the difficulty, namely that the term "self-love" can equally well mean "self-centeredness" rather than "self-acceptance." He quotes Josef Pieper: "There are two opposing ways in which a man can love himself: selflessly or selfishly" (p. 14). This being so, is it not extremely misleading to use the same expression ("self-love") for diametrically opposite concepts?

We should be able to agree that self-depreciation is a false and damaging attitude. Those who regard a human being as nothing but a programmed machine (behaviorists) or an absurdity (existentialists) or a naked ape (humanistic evolutionists) are all denigrating our creation in God's image. True, we are also rebels against God and deserve nothing at his hand except judgment, but our fallenness has not entirely destroyed our Godlikeness. More important still, in spite of our revolt against him, God has loved, redeemed, adopted, and re-created us in Christ. Anthony Hoekema is surely right, in his excellent little work *The Christian Looks at Himself* (Eerdmans, 1975), that "the ultimate basis for our positive self-image must be God's acceptance of us in Christ" (p. 102). If he has accepted us, should we not accept ourselves?

We cannot, therefore, agree with Cecil Osborne's statement that "there *must* be something truly wonderful about us if he (God) can love and accept us so readily," identifying this "something" as "that portion of himself he has planted deep within" (p. 138). Thielicke is much nearer the truth when, echoing Luther's fourth thesis, he writes: "God does not love us because we are valuable; we are valuable because God loves us."

The problem we all have in relating properly to ourselves is that we are all such mixed-up kids. We are the product on the one hand of the fall, and on the other of our creation by God and recreation in Christ. This theological framework is indispensable to the development of a balanced self-image and self-attitude. It will lead us beyond self-acceptance to something better still, namely self-affirmation. We need to learn both to affirm all the good within us, which is due to God's creating and recreating grace, and ruthlessly to deny (i.e., repudiate) all the evil within us, which is due to our fallenness.

Then, when we deny our false self in Adam and affirm our true self in Christ, we find that we are free not to love ourselves, but rather to love him who has redeemed us, and our neighbor for his sake. At that point we reach the ultimate paradox of Christian living that when we lose ourselves in the selfless loving of God and neighbor we find ourselves (Mk. 8:35). True self-denial leads to true self-discovery.

John R. W. Stott, "Cornerstone: Must I Really Love Myself?," *Christianity Today* 22, no. 15 (May 5, 1978): 34–35.

Chapter 9

—

AM I SUPPOSED TO LOVE
MYSELF OR HATE MYSELF?

The cross points a way between self-love and self-denial.

How should I think of myself? What attitude should I adopt toward myself? These are contemporary questions of great importance, questions to which a satisfactory answer cannot be given without reference to the Cross.

A low self-image is common, since many modern influences dehumanize human beings and make them feel worthless. Wherever people are politically or economically oppressed, they feel demeaned. Racial and sexual prejudice have the same effect. As Arnold Toynbee put it, technology demotes persons into serial numbers, "punched on a card and designed to travel through the entrails of a computer." Ethologists like Desmond Morris tell us that human beings are nothing but animals, and behaviorists like B. F. Skinner say that they are nothing but machines programmed to make automatic responses to external stimuli.

Further, the pressures of a competitive society make many feel like failures. And, of course, there is the personal tragedy of being unloved and unwanted. All these are causes of a low self-image.

In overreaction to this set of influences is the popular movement in the opposite direction. With the laudable desire to build self-respect, it speaks of human potential as virtually limitless. Others emphasize the need to love ourselves. In his perceptive book *Psychology as Religion: The Cult of Self-Worship* (1977), Paul Vitz cites the following as an illustration of "selfist jargon":

"I love me. I am not conceited. I'm just a good friend to myself. And I like to do whatever makes me feel good ..."

Another example is this limerick:

There once was a nymph named Narcissus,
Who thought himself very delicious;
So he stared like a fool
At his face in a pool,
And his folly today is still with us.

A Common Error

In spite of widespread teaching to the contrary, the Mosaic injunction, endorsed by Jesus, "You shall love your neighbor as yourself," is not a command to love ourselves. Three arguments may be adduced.

Grammatically, Jesus did not say that the second *and third* commandments are to love our neighbor *and* ourselves, but that the second commandment is to love our neighbor *as* we love ourselves. Self-love here is a fact we should recognize (and use to guide our conduct, as with the Golden Rule), but it is not a virtue to be commended.

Linguistically, agape love means self-sacrifice in the service of others. It cannot therefore be self-directed. The concept of sacrificing ourselves to save ourselves is nonsense.

Theologically, self-love is the biblical notion of sin. One of the marks of the last days in which we live, Paul writes, is that people will be "lovers of self" instead of "lovers of God" (2 Tim. 3:1–4).

One Key: Self-Denial and the Cross

The question is, How can we renounce both self-hatred and self-love? How can we avoid a self-evaluation that is either too low or too high? In biblical terms, how can we "think soberly" about ourselves (Rom. 12:3)? The cross of Christ supplies the answer, for it calls us both to self-denial and to self-affirmation.

Jesus' call to self-denial is plain: "If anyone would come after me, he must deny himself and take up his cross and follow me" (Mark 8:34 NIV). Now, the Romans had made crucifixion a common sight in all their colonized provinces, and Palestine was no exception. Every rebel and criminal who was condemned to death by crucifixion was compelled to carry his cross to the scene of his execution. John wrote of Jesus that "carrying his own cross, he went out to The Place of the Skull" (19:17). To take up our cross, therefore, and follow Jesus is vivid imagery for self-denial. It is to "put ourselves into the position of a condemned criminal on his way to execution" (H. B. Swete). For if we are following Jesus with a cross on our shoulder, there is only one place to which we can follow him: the place of execution. As Bonhoeffer put it, "When Christ calls a man, he bids him come and die."

To deny ourselves is to behave toward ourselves as Peter did toward Jesus when he denied him three times. The verb is the same. He disowned him, repudiated him, turned his back on him. So must we do to ourselves. Self-denial is not denying ourselves luxuries like candies, cakes, cigarettes, and cocktails (though it may include this); it is actually denying or disowning ourselves, renouncing our supposed right to go our own way. Paul was elaborating the metaphor of cross bearing when he wrote that "those who belong to Christ Jesus have crucified the sinful nature with its passions and desires" (Gal. 5:24 NIV). We have taken our slippery self and nailed it to Christ's cross.

Another Key: Self-Affirmation and the Cross

I wonder how you have reacted to the last couple of paragraphs? I hope you have felt uneasy about them. For they have expressed such a negative attitude to self that they appear to align Christians with the bureaucrats and technocrats, the ethologists and behaviorists, in demeaning human beings. It is not that what I have written is untrue (for Jesus said it), but that it is only one side of the truth. It implies that our "self" is wholly bad and must therefore be totally rejected, indeed "crucified"!

But we must not overlook another strand in Scripture. Alongside Jesus' explicit call to self-denial is his implicit call to self-affirmation (which is not the same as self-love). Nobody who reads the Gospels as a whole could possibly gain the impression that Jesus had a negative attitude to human beings himself, or encouraged one in others. The opposite is the case.

Consider, first, his *teaching* about people. He spoke of their "value" in God's sight. They are "much more valuable" than birds or beasts, he said (Matt. 6:26; 12:12 NIV). What was the ground of this value judgment? It must have been the doctrine of Creation, which Jesus took over from the Old Testament. It is the divine image in us that gives us our distinctive value. In his excellent little book *The Christian Looks at Himself* (1975), Prof. Anthony Hoekema quotes a young black who, rebelling against the inferiority feelings inculcated in him by whites, put up this banner in his room: "I'm me and I'm good, 'cos God don't make junk."

Then, second, there was Jesus' *attitude* toward people. He despised nobody. On the contrary, he went out of his way to honor those the world dishonored, and to accept those the world rejected. He spoke courteously to women in public. He invited children to come to him. He spoke words of hope to Samaritans and Gentiles. He allowed leprosy sufferers to approach him and a prostitute to anoint and kiss his feet. He ministered to the poor and hungry and made friends with the outcasts of society. In all this, his love for human beings shone out. He acknowledged their value and loved them, and by loving them he increased their value.

Third, and in particular, we must remember Jesus' *mission and death* for people. He had come to serve, not to be served, and to give his life as a ransom for many (Mark 10:45). Nothing indicates more clearly the value Jesus placed on people than his determination to suffer and die for them. He was the Good Shepherd who came into the desert to seek and save only one lost sheep, and who laid down his life for his sheep. It is only when we look at the cross that we see the true worth of human beings. As William Temple expressed it, "My worth is what I am worth to God, and that is a marvelous great deal because Christ died for me."

Resolving the Paradox

We have seen so far that the cross of Christ is both a proof of the value of the human self and a picture of how to deny and crucify it. How can this biblical paradox be resolved? How is it possible to value ourselves and to deny ourselves simultaneously?

The problem arises because we discuss and develop alternative attitudes to ourselves before we have defined this "self" we are talking about. Our "self" is not a simple entity that is either wholly good or wholly evil, one that should therefore be either totally valued or totally denied. Our "self" is a complex entity of good and evil, glory and shame, which therefore requires that we develop more subtle attitudes.

What we are (our self or personal identity) is partly the result of the Creation (the image of God), and partly the result of the Fall (the image defaced). The self we are to deny, disown, and crucify is our fallen self, everything within us that is incompatible with Jesus Christ (hence Christ's command, "let him deny himself and follow me"). The self we are to affirm and value is our created self, everything within us that is compatible with Jesus Christ (hence his statement that if we lose ourselves by self-denial we shall find ourselves). True self-denial (the denial of our false, fallen self) is not the road to self-destruction, but the road to self-discovery.

So, then, whatever we are by creation, we must affirm: our rationality, our sense of moral obligation, our masculinity and femininity, our aesthetic appreciation and artistic creativity, our stewardship of the fruitful earth, our hunger for love and community, our sense of the transcendent mystery of God, and our inbuilt urge to fall down and worship him. All this is part of our created humanness. True, it has all been tainted and twisted by sin. Yet Christ came to redeem and not destroy it. So we must affirm it.

But whatever we are by the Fall, we must deny or repudiate: our irrationality; our moral perversity; our loss of sexual distinctives; our fascination with the ugly; our lazy refusal to develop God's gifts; our pollution and spoliation of the environment; our selfishness, malice, individualism, and revenge, which are destructive of human community; our proud autonomy; and our idolatrous refusal to worship God. All this is part of our fallen humanness. Christ came not to redeem this but to destroy it. So we must deny it.

Dignity and Depravity

There is, therefore, a great need for discernment in our self-understanding. Who am I? What is my "self"? Answer: I'm a Jekyll and Hyde, a mixed-up kid, having both dignity, because I was created in God's image, and depravity, because I am fallen and rebellious. I am both noble and ignoble, beautiful and ugly, good and bad, upright and twisted, image of God and slave of the Devil. My true self is what I am by creation, which Christ came to redeem. My fallen self is what I am by the Fall, which Christ came to destroy.

Only when we have discerned which is which within us shall we know what attitude to adopt toward evil. We must be true to our true self and false to our false self. We must be fearless in affirming all that we are by creation, and ruthless in disowning all that we are by the Fall.

Moreover, Christ's cross teaches us both attitudes. On one hand, it is the measure of the value of our true self, since Christ died for us. On the other hand, it is the model for the denial of our false self, since we are to nail it to the cross and so put it to death.

John R. W. Stott, "Am I Supposed to Love Myself or Hate Myself?: The Cross Points a Way between Self-Love and Self-Denial," *Christianity Today* 28, no. 7 (April 20, 1984): 26–28.

Chapter 10

RECLAIMING THE BIBLICAL DOCTRINE OF WORK

Human-divine collaboration characterizes all honorable work.

L et me say it before you think it: a clergyman is the last person in the world to expatiate on this topic. For everybody knows that no clergyman has ever done a day's work in his life. Instead, according to the old quip, he is "six days invisible and one day incomprehensible." A few years ago a rather drunk Welsh Communist boarded the train in which I was travelling. When he learned that I was a pastor, he told me it was high time I became productive, and ceased to be a parasite on the body politic.

What is our attitude to our work? Here is a popular view:

I don't mind work
    If I've nothing else to do;
I quite admit it's true
    That now and then I shirk
Particularly boring kinds of work—
    Don't you?

But, on the whole, I think it's fair to say,
  Provided I can do it my own way
And that I need not start on it today—
  I quite like work!

What has been called "the orthodox view" of work (or so I have read in a secular book on the social psychology of industry), and has been the basis of industrial psychology and managerial practice (or so I am assured in the same book) is "the Old Testament belief that physical labor is a curse imposed on man as a punishment for his sins." The author goes on to write that this view has recently been modified. But even so it is a serious distortion of Scripture. The fall certainly turned work into drudgery, because the ground was cursed with thorns and thistles, and cultivation became possible only by the sweat of the brow. But work is a consequence of creation, not the fall; the fall has aggravated its problems without destroying its joys.

So we badly need to recover the biblical doctrine of work. In the first two chapters of Genesis God reveals himself to us as a worker. Day by day, stage by stage, his creative work unfolded. And when he created mankind male and female in his own image, he made them workers too. He gave them dominion, told them to subdue the earth, and thus made them his representatives to care for the environment on his behalf. Then when he planted a garden, he put the man he had made into the garden he had planted, in order that he might cultivate it. It is from these revealed truths about God and man that we must develop a biblical doctrine of work.

First, work is intended for the fulfillment of the worker. The two sentences of Genesis 1:26 belong together: "let us make men in our image" and "let them have dominion." It is because we bear

God's image that we share God's dominion. Therefore our potential for creative work is an essential part of our Godlike humanness, and without work we are not fully human. If we are idle (instead of busy) or destructive (instead of creative) we deny our humanity and so forfeit our self-fulfillment. "There is nothing better than that a man should find enjoyment in his work" (Eccl. 2:24; 3:22). And although employers should do their utmost to relieve the discomfort and danger of certain jobs, even such work as this can yield a measure of job satisfaction.

Secondly, work is intended for the benefit of the community. By cultivating the garden of Eden Adam will have fed and perhaps clothed his family. The Bible emphasizes productivity for service. The produce of the "land flowing with milk and honey" was to be shared with the poor, the orphan, the widow, and the alien. Paul told the thief to stop stealing and start working "so that he might be able to give to those in need" (Eph. 4:28).

Thirdly, work is intended for the glory of God. God the Creator has deliberately humbled himself to require the cooperation of human beings. He created the earth, but entrusted to humans the task of subduing it. He planted a garden, but then appointed a gardener. "You should have seen this 'ere garden," said the Cockney gardener to the person who piously praised God for the lovely flowers, "when Gawd 'ad it all to 'isself!" The fact is that creation and cultivation, nature and culture, raw materials and craftsmanship belong together. As Luther put it, "God even milks the cow through you."

This concept of divine-human collaboration applies to all honorable work. God has so ordered life on earth as to depend on us. The human baby is the most helpless of all creatures. Each infant is indeed a gift of the Lord, but he then drops it into a human lap saying, as it were, "now you take over." For years children depend on their parents and teachers. Even in adult life, though we depend on God for life, we depend on each other for the necessities of life, not only of physical life (food, clothing, shelter, warmth, and health) but of social life too (everything that goes to make up civilized society). So whatever our work, we need to see it as being—either directly or indirectly—cooperation with God in leading human beings into maturity. It is this that glorifies him. Some years ago the chief health inspector of the Port of London wrote to me that to work for his own ends did not satisfy him. "I like to think," he went on, "that I am responsible for a part of the greater field pattern whereby all serve human welfare and obey the will of our wonderful Creator."

According to God's intention, then, work might be defined as "the expenditure of manual or mental energy in service, which brings fulfillment to the worker, benefit to the community, and glory to God."

The attentive reader will observe that I have made no reference to pay, for it is "work" which I have tried to define, not "employment." We need to remember that though all employment is work, not all work is employment. Adam was not paid for working in the garden. The housewife is not paid for keeping the home and bringing up the children. And millions of people do spare time work for the church in a voluntary capacity. It is an important distinction to which I shall return next month when I enlarge on the contemporary problem of unemployment.

Unemployment is a problem of enormous magnitude. Of the total labor force 6 percent is now unemployed in Britain, 7 percent in the United States and 8 percent in Canada. And the true percentages would be higher if we included those who do not register as unemployed persons and those who are underemployed on account of "overmanning." Worst hit are young people under the age of twenty-five (44 percent of the unemployed in Britain belong to this category), the blacks, the disabled, and the unskilled. The Third World figures are much worse, however. It is reckoned that 35 percent of the work force of developing countries are unemployed (about 300 million people) as compared with an average of 5 percent in the West (some 17 million).

John R. W. Stott, "Cornerstone: Reclaiming the Biblical Doctrine of Work," *Christianity Today* 23, no. 15 (May 4, 1979): 36–37.

Chapter 11

———

CREATIVE BY CREATION

OUR NEED FOR WORK

Devising economics as if people matter.

Last month we considered the biblical doctrine of work and began to look at the growing numbers of the unemployed. Yet the problem of unemployment is not one of statistics but of people. In the Third World there is the threat to physical survival; in the West there is the psychological trauma. Industrial psychologists have likened the loss of a job to bereavement and have described its three stages. The first is shock. To be declared "redundant" (an awful word) is to receive a serious blow to one's self-esteem. "I felt immediately degraded," said one man, and thought to himself: "I've become a statistic. I'm unemployed." The second stage is depression and pessimism. By now savings are eroded, if not exhausted, and the prospects of finding a job are increasingly bleak. People lapse into inertia. Said one: "What do I do all day? I stagnate." The third stage is fatalism. In the case of the long-term unemployed, both hope and struggle decline. The spirit becomes bitter and broken. Such people are demoralized and dehumanized.

Further, the worldwide problem of unemployment is going to get worse. I have read a statement attributed to Robert McNamara, President of the World Bank, that "by the year 2,000 A.D. there will be 6 billion people unemployed." What causes this galloping problem? It is partly that when developing nations have become industrially developed, the steel and ships and commodities they produce will compete with those of the West—and in many cases displace them. It is also partly that microelectronics (silicon chips) will shortly complete the industrial revolution. The experts say that computers will take over the running of factories, the plowing of fields by driverless tractors, and even the diagnosing of diseases. Economists do not seem able to tell us how the problems of inflation and unemployment can be solved simultaneously.

In the light of the biblical doctrine of work, what Christian response should we make to the contemporary problem of unemployment? I claim no expertise, but I venture to make three suggestions.

First, we must change our attitude toward the unemployed. The so-called Protestant Work Ethic has tended not only to encourage industry but also to despise those who are losers in the struggle to survive. Well, no doubt some are shirkers, but the great majority of unemployed people want to work and are victims of the system. We need more Christian compassion towards those who suffer the trauma of "redundancy." I have recently learned that an unemployed male member of our church in London has stayed away for two whole years because he has feared that people will ask him what he is doing and, when they discover that he is not working, will make him feel a failure. Is not the failure rather ours that we have made him feel despised and rejected? It is not a stigma to be unemployed. Paul's dictum "if any one will not work, let him not eat" (2 Thess. 3:10) was addressed to the voluntary, not involuntary, unemployed; it condemns laziness not redundancy. So we need to understand, to welcome, to support, and to counsel the unemployed. Otherwise the very concept of the body of Christ becomes a sick joke.

Second, we must press for more job creation. Successive governments in Britain have done much, by methods of tax inducement, regional policies, retraining, and subsidies. But in areas of serious unemployment, Christians ought not to hesitate to lobby parliamentarians, local authorities, industrialists, employers, union officials, and others to create more employment opportunities. In England some churches and Christian organizations have themselves entered the job creation field. I have read, for example, of the Portrack Workshop in the North of England in which forty-five disabled people are making toys and remaking school desks.

Third, we must remember and act on the distinction between work and employment. What demoralizes people is not so much lack of employment (that they are not in a paid job) as lack of work (that they are not using their energies in service). I know, of course, that God intends us to earn our living, that the paycheck gives people self-respect, and that those receiving unemployment benefit feel themselves to be spongers even if they are in fact receiving their dues because they have contributed to a national insurance plan. Nevertheless, I reaffirm my point that, as a means to self-esteem, work significance is more important than work earnings. To employ people to dig holes and fill them up again gives them pay but not self-respect; to help them to work significantly gives them self-respect, even if the work is unpaid. Unemployed people can still use their time and energy creatively.

This distinction will become increasingly important, because all of us will be engulfed in the coming social revolution. Many think that the only way to anything approaching full employment will be "work sharing." That is, shorter hours with no overtime (perhaps a 35-hour, or even a 30-hour, week), longer holidays, and earlier retirement would spread the same employment opportunities over a larger number of employees. The net result will be that everybody has more leisure. But how will they spend it? God's fourth commandment is not only to rest one day a week, but to work six days. How can people work six days on a 30-hour week?

We need to develop more opportunities for creative leisure, for this is an authentic form of "work" (even if unpaid) and a welcome relief from interminable hours of destructive television viewing. Do-it-yourself improvements to the home, servicing your own car, working with wood or metal, dressmaking, pottery, painting, sculpting or writing, and community service like prison visiting and sick visiting, working with mentally or physically handicapped people, teaching illiterates to read—these are a few examples, but the list could be greatly extended. Some will doubtless dismiss this as a middle-class reaction to the problem, which would be inappropriate for the so-called working classes, especially in cities and ghettoes. Maybe. Yet I would appeal to the biblical truths that mankind by creation is creative, that we cannot find ourselves or serve God if we are idle, and that we must find a creative outlet for our energies. Therefore, if people do not have facilities either to learn or to practice skills, and cannot find these facilities, should not the church pioneer by providing them?

It is only when we continue to spend whatever energies we have in some form of service that we can bring fulfillment to ourselves, blessing to others and glory to God.

John R. W. Stott, "Cornerstone: Creative by Creation: Our Need for Work," *Christianity Today* 23, no. 17 (June 8, 1979): 32–33.

Chapter 12

WHAT MAKES LEADERSHIP CHRISTIAN?

Look for these five distinctives.

Many people today are warning us that the world is heading for disaster, but few are offering advice on how to avert it. Technical know-how abounds, but wisdom is in short supply. People feel confused, bewildered, alienated. We are like "sheep without a shepherd"—and our leaders often appear as "blind leaders of the blind."

There is a great need for clear-sighted, courageous, and dedicated leaders in the home, the church, the community. Management books refer to "B.N.L.'s" ("born natural leaders"), men and women endowed with strong intellect, character, and personality. But as Bennie E. Goodwin, a black American educator, has written: "Although potential leaders are born, effective leaders are made." And Christian leadership, to use the words of Oswald Sanders, is "a blending of natural and spiritual qualities," or of natural talents and spiritual gifts.

What, then, are the marks of leadership in general, and of Christian leadership in particular? How can God's gifts be cultivated and leadership potential developed? And what is needed to blaze a trail that others will follow?

Let me suggest five essential ingredients.

Vision

"Dreams" and "visions," dreamers and visionaries, sound somewhat impractical and remote from the harsh realities of life on earth. Yet the biblical proverb holds true: "Where there is no vision, the people perish."

Of course, more prosaic words are used today. Management experts tell us we must set both long- and short-term goals. Politicians publish election manifestos. Military personnel lay down a campaign strategy. But whether they call it a "goal," a "manifesto," or a "strategy," it is a *vision* nevertheless.

So what is vision? It is an act of seeing—an imaginative perception of things, combining insight and foresight. More particularly (and in the sense in which I am using the word), it is a deep dissatisfaction with what *is* and a clear grasp of what *could be*. It begins with indignation over the status quo, and it grows into the earnest quest for an alternative. Both are quite clear in the public ministry of Jesus. He was indignant over disease, hunger, and death, for he perceived these things as alien to the purpose of God. Hence his compassion.

Indignation and compassion form a powerful combination, and they are indispensable to vision—and therefore to leadership. History abounds with examples, both biblical and secular. Moses was appalled by the cruel oppression of his fellow Israelites in Egypt. He remembered God's covenant with Abraham, Isaac, and Jacob, and was sustained throughout his long life by the vision of the Promised Land. Nehemiah heard in his Persian exile that the wall of the Holy City was in ruins and its inhabitants in great distress. The news overwhelmed him, until God put into his heart what he could and should do. "Come, let us rebuild the wall of Jerusalem," he said. And the people replied, "Let us start rebuilding" (Neh. 2:17–18 NIV).

Moving to New Testament times, the early Christians were well aware of the might of Rome and the hostility of the Jews. But Jesus had told them to be his witnesses "to the ends of the earth," and his vision transformed them. Saul of Tarsus, for example, had been brought up to accept as inevitable and unbridgeable the chasm between Jews and Gentiles. But Jesus commissioned him to take the gospel to the Gentile world, and Paul was "not disobedient to the heavenly vision." Indeed, the vision of a single, new, reconciled humanity so captured the apostle's heart and mind that he labored, suffered, and died in its cause.

Today, we see with our mind's eye the three billion unevangelized peoples of the world, people who have had no real opportunity to hear or respond to the gospel—the poor, the hungry, and the disadvantaged; people crushed by political, economic, or racial oppression. We see these things—but do we care? We see what is—but do we see what could be? The unevangelized could be reached with the good news of Jesus, the hungry could be fed, the oppressed liberated, the alienated brought home. We need a vision of the purpose and power of God.

Industry

The world has always been scornful of dreamers. "Here comes that dreamer!" Joseph's older brothers said to one another. "Come now, let's kill him. ... Then we'll see what comes of his dreams" (Gen. 37:19ff.). The dreams of night tend to evaporate in the cold light of morning.

So dreamers have to become thinkers, planners, and workers, and that demands industry or hard labor. Men of vision need to become men of action. It was Thomas Carlyle, the nineteenth-century Scottish writer, who said of Frederick the Great that genius means first of all "the transcendent capacity of taking trouble." And it was Thomas Alva Edison who defined genius as "1 percent inspiration and 99 percent perspiration."

Adding industry to vision is a hallmark of history's great leaders. It was not enough for Moses to dream of the land flowing with milk and honey; he had to organize the Israelite rabble and lead them through the dangers and hardships of the desert before they could possess the Promised Land. Similarly, Nehemiah was inspired by his vision of the rebuilt Holy City. But first he had to gather materials to reconstruct the wall and weapons to defend it.

Thus dream and reality, passion and practicality, must go together. Without the dream the campaign loses its direction and its fire; but without hard work and practical projects the dream vanishes into thin air.

Perseverance

It is one thing to dream dreams and see visions. It is another to convert a dream into a plan of action. It is yet another to persevere when opposition comes. And opposition is bound to arise. As soon as the campaign gets under way, the forces of reaction muster: entrenched privilege digs itself in more deeply, commercial interests feel threatened and raise the alarm, cynicism sneers at the folly of "do-gooders," and apathy becomes transmuted into hostility.

But a true work of God thrives on opposition. Its silver is refined and its steel hardened. Of course, those without the vision, those who are merely being carried along by the momentum of the campaign, will soon capitulate. So it is that the protesting youth of one decade become the conservative establishment of the next. But not so the real leader. He has the resilience to take setbacks in stride, the tenacity to overcome fatigue and discouragement, and the wisdom to "turn stumbling blocks into stepping stones." The real leader adds the grace of perseverance to vision and industry.

In the Old Testament, Moses is again the outstanding example. On about a dozen distinct occasions the people "murmured" against him, and he had the beginnings of a mutiny on his hands. When Pharaoh's army was threatening them, when the water ran out or was too bitter to drink, when there was no meat to eat, when the scouts brought back a bad report of the strength of Canaanite fortifications, when small minds became jealous of his position—these were some of the occasions on which the people complained of his leadership and challenged his authority. A lesser man would have given up and abandoned them to their own pettiness. But not Moses. He never forgot that these were *God's* people by *God's* covenant who by *God's* promise would inherit the land.

In the New Testament, the man who came to the end of his life with his ideals intact and his standards uncompromised was the apostle Paul. He too faced bitter and violent opposition. He had to endure severe physical afflictions—beatings, stonings, imprisonment. And he suffered mentally, for his footsteps were dogged by false prophets who contradicted his teaching and slandered his name.

He also experienced great loneliness. Toward the end of his life he wrote, "At my first defense ... everyone deserted me" (2 Tim. 1:15; 4:16 NIV). Yet Paul never lost his vision of God's new, redeemed society, and he never gave up proclaiming it. In his underground dungeon, from which there was to be no escape but death, he could write: "I have fought the good fight, I have finished the race, I have kept the faith" (2 Tim. 4:7). The apostle persevered to the end.

In recent centuries perhaps no one has exemplified perseverance more than William Wilberforce. When the Abolition of Slavery Bill was passed in both Houses of England's Parliament in July 1833, this political leader saw the successful culmination of 45 years of single-minded struggle on behalf of African slaves. Sir Reginald Coupland wrote that, in order to break the apathy of Parliament, a would-be social reformer "must possess, in the first place, the virtues of a fanatic without his vices. He must be palpably single-minded and unself-seeking. He must be strong enough to face opposition and ridicule, staunch enough to endure obstruction and delay." These qualities Wilberforce possessed in abundance.

Mind you, perseverance is not a synonym for pigheadedness. The true leader is not impervious to criticism. On the contrary, he listens to it and weighs it and may modify his program accordingly. But he does not waver in his basic conviction of what God has called him to do. Whatever the opposition aroused or the sacrifice entailed, he perseveres.

Service

We must not assume that Christian and non-Christian understandings of leadership are identical. Nor should we adopt models of secular management without first subjecting them to critical Christian scrutiny. Jesus introduced into the world an altogether new style of leadership, and expressed the difference between the old and the new in these terms:

"You know that those who are regarded as rulers of the Gentiles lord it over them, and their high officials exercise authority over them. Not so with you. Instead, whoever wants to become great among you must be your servant, and whoever wants to be first must be slave of all. For even the Son of Man did not come to be served, but to serve, and to give his life as a ransom for many" (Mark 10:42–45 NIV).

Among the followers of Jesus, leadership is not a synonym for lordship. Our calling is to be servants not bosses, slaves not masters. True, a certain authority attaches to all leaders, and leadership would be impossible without it. The apostles, for example, were given authority by Jesus, and exercised it in both teaching and disciplining the church. Even Christian pastors today, although they are not apostles and do not possess apostolic authority, are to be "respected" because of their position "over" the congregation (1 Thess. 5:12ff.), and even "obeyed" (Heb. 13:17).

Yet the emphasis of Jesus was not on the authority of a ruler-leader but on the humility of a servant-leader. The authority by which the Christian leader leads is not power but love, not force but example, not coercion but reasoned persuasion. Leaders have power, but power is safe only in the hands of those who humble themselves to serve.

What is the reason for Jesus stressing the leader's service? Partly, no doubt, because the chief occupational hazard of leadership is pride. The Pharisaic model would not do in the new community Jesus was building. The Pharisees loved titles like "Father," "Teacher," "Rabbi," but this was both an offense against God (to whom these titles properly belong) and disruptive of the Christian brotherhood (Matt. 23:1–12).

However, Jesus' main reason for emphasizing the leader's servant role relates to the intrinsic worth of human beings—the presupposition underlying his own ministry of self-giving love, which is an essential element in the Christian mind. If human beings are godlike beings, then they must be served not exploited, respected not manipulated. As Oswald Sanders said: "True greatness, true leadership, is achieved not by reducing men to one's service but in giving oneself in selfless service to them."

Herein also lies the peril of seeing leadership in terms of projects and programs. People must take precedence over projects. And people must be neither "manipulated" nor even "managed." Though the latter is less demeaning than the former, both words are derived from *manus,* meaning *hand,* and expressing a "handling" of people as if they were commodities rather than persons.

In all this Christian emphasis on service, the disciple is only seeking to follow and reflect his teacher. For though he was lord of all, Jesus became the servant of all. Putting on the apron of servitude, he got down on his knees to wash the apostles' feet. To him, service was an end in itself.

Now Christ tells us to do as he did, to clothe ourselves with humility, and in love to serve one another. No leadership is authentically Christlike that is not marked by the spirit of humble and joyful service.

Discipline

Every vision has a tendency to fade. Every visionary is prone to discouragement. The Christian ideal of humble service sounds fine in theory, but seems impractical in reality. So the leader may catch himself soliloquizing: "It is quicker to ride roughshod over other people; you get things done that way. And if the end is good, does it really matter what means we employ to attain it? Even a little prudent compromise can sometimes be justified, can't it?"

Leaders are made of flesh and blood, not plaster or marble or stained glass. Even the great leaders in the Bible had fatal flaws. They too were fallen, fallible, and frail. Righteous Noah got drunk. Faithful Abraham was despicable enough to risk his wife's chastity for the sake of his own safety. Moses lost his temper. David broke five commandments (committing adultery, murder, theft, false witness, and covetousness) in that single episode of moral rebellion over Bathsheba. Jeremiah's lonely courage was marred by self-pity. John the Baptist, whom Jesus described as the greatest man who had ever lived, was overcome by doubt. And Peter's boastful impetuousness was doubtless a cloak for his deep personal insecurity. If those heroes of Scripture failed, what hope is there for us?

Enter discipline—the final mark of a Christian leader. Not only self-discipline in general (in the mastery of passions, time, and energies), but in particular the discipline with which one waits on God. The leader knows his weakness. He knows the greatness of his task and the strength of the opposition. But he also knows the inexhaustible riches of God's grace.

Many biblical examples could be given. Moses sought God, and "the Lord would speak to Moses face to face as a man speaks with his friend." David looked to God as his shepherd, his light and salvation, his rock, the stronghold of his life, and in times of deep distress "found strength in the Lord his God." The apostle Paul, burdened with his "thorn in the flesh," heard Jesus say to him, "My grace is sufficient for you," and learned that only in his weakness was he strong.

But our supreme exemplar is the Lord Jesus himself. It is often said that he was always available to people. He was not. There were times when he sent the crowds away. He refused to allow the urgent to displace the important. Regularly he withdrew from the pressures and the glare of his public ministry in order to seek his Father in solitude and replenish his reserves of strength.

Only God "gives strength to the weary and increases the power of the weak." Those who "hope in the Lord" and wait patiently for him "will renew their strength. They will soar on wings like eagles; they will run and not grow weary, they will walk and not be faint" (Isa. 40:29–31). Only those who discipline themselves to seek God's face will keep their vision bright. Only those who live before Christ's cross have their inner fires constantly rekindled. Those leaders who think they are strong in their own strength are the most pathetically weak of all people; only those who know and acknowledge their weakness can become strong with the strength of Christ.

A Final Caution

In grabbing hold of the quality of leadership, we need to repent of two particularly horrid sins. The first is *pessimism,* which is dishonoring to God and incompatible with Christian faith. To be sure, we do not forget the fallenness, indeed, the depravity, of man. We are well aware of the pervasiveness of evil. We are not so foolish as to imagine that society will ever become perfect before Christ comes and establishes the fullness of his rule. Nevertheless, we also believe in the power of God—in the power of God's gospel to change individuals, and in the power of God's people (working like salt and light) to change society. We need, then, to renounce both naïve optimism and cynical pessimism, and replace them with the sober but confident realism of the Bible.

The second sin we need to repent of is *mediocrity,* and the acceptance of it. I find myself wanting to say, especially to young people: "Don't be content with the mediocre! Don't settle for anything less than your full God-given potential! Be ambitious and adventurous for God! God has made you a unique person. He has himself created you, and he does not want his work to be wasted. He means you to be fulfilled, not frustrated. His purpose is that everything you have and are should be stretched in his service and in the service of others."

This means that God has a leadership role of some degree and kind for each of us. We need, then, to seek his will with all our hearts, to cry to him to give us a vision of what he is calling us to do with our lives, and to pray for grace to be faithful—not necessarily successful—in obedience to that heavenly vision.

Only then will we be able to say with Paul, "I have fought the good fight, I have finished the race, I have kept the faith," and hear

Christ say those most coveted of all words, "Well done, good and faithful servant!"

John R. W. Stott, "What Makes Leadership Christian?," *Christianity Today* 29, no. 11 (August 9, 1985): 24–27.

Chapter 13

———

THE UNFORBIDDEN FRUIT

Why power, knowledge, orthodoxy, faith, and
service are not the mark of a true Christian.

One biblical text has been especially significant to me over the years. I have quoted it in prayer daily, I think, for 20 years. I have come to see it as of key importance to anyone concerned about holiness. I refer to Galatians 5:22–23, the great verses about the fruit of the Spirit: "But the fruit of the Spirit is love, joy, peace, patience, kindness, goodness, faithfulness, gentleness and self-control. Against such things there is no law" (all Scripture quotations NIV). From these verses come five affirmations about love.

The first is that love is the pre-eminent Christian grace. It is quite true that the apostle lists nine qualities that he calls the fruit, or the harvest, of the Spirit, but love has pride of place; it is the first fruit of the Spirit.

We hear a great deal about the Holy Spirit today. He is no longer the neglected member of the Trinity. Many people claim rather spectacular manifestations of the Holy Spirit. I sometimes think that he is positively embarrassed by the publicity he is given today. But the first fruit of the Spirit is not power, but love.

People have other ideas about the hallmark of the follower of Christ. When asked what is the chief distinguishing mark of the child of God, some reply, "Truth, orthodoxy, correct belief, loyalty to the doctrines of Scripture, the so-called catholic creeds, and the Reformation confessions."

To some degree they are right, of course. Revealed truth is sacred. Biblical doctrine is vital. We must contend earnestly for the faith that has been once for all delivered unto the saints. Nevertheless, though all that is true, Paul says elsewhere, "If I ... fathom all mysteries and all knowledge ... but have not love, I am nothing" (1 Cor. 13:2). Love is greater than knowledge.

Other people reply that the authentic mark of the true believer is faith, because we are justified by faith only. Luther was right when he said that justification by faith is the principal article of all Christian doctrine. Sixteenth-century English Reformer Thomas Cranmer said, "This doctrine whosoever denieth is not to be counted for a true Christian man." Not bad for an Episcopalian! Or I could turn to a modern evangelical statement: "Justification by faith is the heart and hub, the paradigm and essence of the whole economy of God's saving grace." That is true: *sola fide,* by grace, by faith alone. The watchword of the Reformation should be our watchword, too.

Nevertheless, "If I have a faith which can move mountains, but have not love, I am nothing" (1 Cor. 13:2). Paul, the great champion of grace and faith, says love is greater than faith.

Others reply, "No, the authenticating mark of the true believer lies in the realm of religious experience." Often it is an experience of a particular and vivid kind, which they sometimes insist must be reproduced in everybody else.

To some degree, they are right. Religious experience is very important. A first-hand, personal relationship with God the Father through Jesus Christ by the Holy Spirit is an essential part of being a true Christian believer. The Holy Spirit does witness with our spirit that we are the children of God. There is such a thing as joy unspeakable and being full of glory. Nevertheless, "If I speak in the tongues of men and of angels and if I have the gift of prophecy [claiming direct revelation from God] and have not love, I am nothing" (1 Cor. 13:2). Love is greater than religious experience.

Those of a very practical bent say that the authentic mark of a true believer is service, especially service to the poor and the needy. Once again, they are right in what they affirm, because without good works of love, service, and philanthropy, faith is dead. Since Jesus came not to be served but to serve and to give his life in service, we must give our lives in service, too, if we are authentic followers of Jesus. Since he was the champion of the poor, we must be champions of the poor as well. We can thank God for the recovery in recent days of the temporarily mislaid social conscience of evangelicals.

Nevertheless, "If I give all I possess to the poor and surrender my body to the flames"—presumably in martyrdom—"but have not love, I gain nothing" (1 Cor. 13:3).

Paul's priority is quite clear. Love is the greatest thing in the world. It is no accident that the first and greatest two commandments are to love the Lord our God with all our being and then to love our neighbor as ourselves. For God is love in his own innermost being. Father, Son, and Holy Spirit are united eternally in self-giving, reciprocal love.

Moreover, God has set his love upon us, and he has come in the person of his Son and given himself in love, even to death on the cross. The Holy Spirit pours God's love into our hearts. And he who loves calls us also to love. There is no holiness without love. That is the first thing I learned from my text.

Second, love brings joy and peace. The fruit of the Spirit is love, joy, and peace; the sequence is very significant.

Human beings have always pursued happiness, joy, and peace. Thomas Jefferson was so convinced that the pursuit of happiness is an inalienable human right that he wrote it into the Declaration of Independence and called it a self-evident truth.

But Christians have this to add: those who pursue happiness never find it. Because joy and peace are extremely elusive, happiness is a will-o'-the-wisp, a phantom, and even if we reach out our hand to grasp it, it vanishes into thin air. God gives joy and peace not to those who pursue them but to those who pursue *him,* and strive to love. Joy and peace are found in loving and nowhere else.

We must bear witness to this today, when self-realization has become the rage and the human-potential movement continues to gather momentum. One of its fathers was Carl Rogers, the influential past president of the American Psychological Association. Much of Rogers's message focused on the need to actualize the potential of the self, to live with unconditional self-regard. Others carried on the emphasis, such as Thomas Harris in his *I'm O.K., You're O.K.* Such perspectives helped the idea take hold that Jesus taught us to love *ourselves* and that the second commandment, to love your neighbor as yourself, is a *command* to love self.

When you stop and think about it, however, this is not so. Self-love in Scripture is the synonym of sin and not the path to freedom. Besides, to love your neighbor is *agape* love. *Agape* has to do with sacrificing yourself to serve another, whether God or a person. If *agape* is sacrificial, how can it be self-directed?

How can I sacrifice myself to serve myself? The very concept is nonsense.

No, Jesus said we find ourselves when we lose ourselves. We live when we die to our own self-centeredness. We are free when we serve. When we love, joy and peace follow as natural consequences. Love is the pre-eminent Christian grace, and it brings joy and peace in its train.

Third, love issues in patience, kindness, and goodness, according to Paul. Love, in other words, is not romance. It is certainly not eroticism. Love is not even pure sentiment or emotion. It is sacrificial service. As Dostoevski rightly said, "Love in action is much more terrible than love in dreams."

Love is active, constructive, serving, sacrificial. The word *love* sounds very abstract, but it manifests itself in concrete attitudes and actions. Negatively, its quality is patience, longsuffering, bearing long with aggravating and demanding people. Longsuffering is an essential attribute of love. There are many demanding and aggravating people in our Christian congregations.

If patience is a negative quality, kindness and goodness are the positive complements. Kindness is wishing good to people, and goodness is doing good to people. As Paul writes elsewhere, all three are the outworkings of love because love is patient, love is kind, and by love we serve one another.

It is no good making protestations of love for the human race. We have to get involved with real people and be patient, kind, and good.

Fourth, love is balanced by self-control. The last three fruits of the Spirit are faithfulness, gentleness, and self-control. All three contain different nuances of self-mastery. Faithfulness is keeping our promises and fulfilling our responsibilities. Gentleness or meekness is not the same as weakness; gentleness is taming our strengths and harnessing our energies. Self-control is disciplining our instincts and mastering our passions.

The Buddha once said that if one person conquers in battle a thousand times a thousand, while another conquers himself, the latter is the greatest of all conquerors. But how much do we know about self-conquest, self-mastery, and self-control?

We cannot rightly give ourselves in love until we have learned to control ourselves. Our self has to be mastered before it can be offered in the service of others. I find it significant, then, that the fruit of the Spirit begins with self-giving and ends with self-control.

———————

Finally, the fifth and last affirmation is that love is the natural result—the fruit—of the supernatural work of the indwelling Holy Spirit.

Paul's words on the fruit come in the middle of the section in Galatians in which he contrasts the flesh and the Spirit. The works of the flesh are immorality, anger, and self-centeredness, while the fruit of the Spirit is love, joy, peace, and so on.

Paul means by *the flesh* not this soft, muscular tissue that covers our bony skeleton, but our fallen human nature that is depraved, tainted, and twisted with self-centeredness. By *the Spirit* Paul means the Holy Spirit himself who comes to dwell within us when we are born again, the Spirit who is able by his indwelling presence and power to subdue our fallen human nature, and produce in its place the fruit—his fruit, which is love, joy, and peace.

Here within us, as we know from experience and Scripture, are two irreconcilable forces. They engage us in a fierce tug of war. The flesh pulls us down and the Holy Spirit pulls us up.

Which prevails in this contest depends on the attitude we adopt toward either side. According to Galatians 5:24, we are to crucify the flesh with its affections and desires. Paul is not being literal, of course, but he means that we are ruthlessly to reject the claims of our fallen nature to rule over us. According to the next verse, we are to walk in the Spirit, keep in step with the Spirit, and surrender day by day to his indwelling power and control. Crucify the flesh, Paul says, and walk in the Spirit.

I remember reading about a California shepherd who had a couple of sheep dogs. When somebody who was hiking in the mountains fell in with the shepherd, he noticed that the two sheep dogs were always fighting. He said to the shepherd, "Which of your two dogs usually wins?" The shepherd replied, "The one I feed the most."

Our new nature will gain the ascendancy over the old only insofar as we feed the new and starve the old. That's not the metaphor Paul uses here. He prefers an agricultural metaphor. Indeed, if he speaks in Galatians 5:22 of the harvest of the Spirit, he writes in 6:8 that we are to *sow* to the Spirit, and then we reap what we *sow*. Whether we reap the fruit of the Spirit depends on whether we sow to the Spirit.

———————————

The seeds we sow to the Spirit that produce this harvest are what the Puritans used to call a disciplined use of the means of grace. That is daily prayer and meditation on the Scriptures, regular public worship and attendance at the Lord's Supper, reading Christian books, making Christian friends, and getting engaged in Christian service. It is by a disciplined use of these means of grace that we grow in grace, and the Holy Spirit within us is able to produce the beauty of holiness.

One of my great heroes, Charles Simeon, taught me something here. Simeon was the vicar (or senior pastor, you might call him) at Holy Trinity Church in Cambridge for 54 years during the last century. He had an enormous influence upon generations of students in Cambridge University, and he really changed the face of the Church of England.

When he began his ministry, he was a very angular gentleman by nature and disposition—hot tempered, proud, and impetuous. One of his biographers writes that on his first visit to the English missionary leader Henry Venn, Venn's oldest daughter, Nellie, wrote, "It is impossible to conceive anything more ridiculous than Mr. Simeon's look and manner. His grimaces, the faces he pulls, were beyond anything you could imagine. So, as soon as he left, we all got together in the study and set up an amazing laugh."

But their father summoned his daughters into the garden. And although it was early summer, he asked them to pick one of the green peaches. When they showed surprise, he said, "Well my dears, it is green now, and we must wait. But a little more sun and a few more showers, and the peach will be ripe and sweet. And so it is with Mr. Simeon." As the Holy Spirit got to work within him, his character and conduct were beautifully refined and changed.

Of course, there is only one person in the whole long, checkered history of the world in whom the fruit of the Spirit was ripened to perfection—Jesus of Nazareth. If the fruit of the Spirit is love, he loved as no one has ever loved before or since.

Love, joy, and peace were characteristics of the life of Jesus. He was patient and kind and full of good works. He was reliable, meek, and gentle in heart, and he had perfect self-control. When he was insulted he never retaliated, so complete was his mastery of himself.

In a real sense, the fruit of the Spirit is Christlikeness. Paul wrote in 2 Corinthians 3:18 that "we … are being transformed into his likeness with ever-increasing glory, which comes from the Lord, who is the Spirit." Christlike holiness is God's purpose for you and me. It has been my personal goal for many decades, and I hope it will remain my goal until I die. Paul would have us all pray to be filled with the Spirit, for the fullness of the Spirit leads to the fruit of the Spirit.

John Stott, "Meditation: The Unforbidden Fruit," *Christianity Today* 36, no. 9 (August 17, 1992): 34–36.

Part III

—

THE MISSION OF
THE CHURCH

Chapter 14

———

CHRISTIANS AND MUSLIMS

Some barriers are cultural rather than theological.

T here are between 600 and 700 million Muslims in the world, and Islam has been more resistant to the Gospel than any other ethnic religion. Indeed, Muslims regard Islam as superior to Christianity: "As Christianity superseded Judaism, so Islam has superseded Christianity," they say. Now too there is a resurgence of Islamic faith, even in the West. In the United States, for example, the Muslim Students' Association claims 117 campus groups, while in England the Ahmadiyya sect is investing about two million dollars on a program to "evangelize" Britain, including "committed Christians."

At the same time, especially in situations of social change, there is among Muslims a new openness to the Gospel. We await with great expectation, therefore, the outcome of the North American Conference on Muslim Evangelization that was to be held October 15 and 21 in Colorado Springs. Jointly sponsored by the North American Lausanne Committee and by World Vision International, and directed by Donald McCurry, it was to bring together 150 key men and women deeply concerned to bring the Gospel to Muslims.

In the Middle East the largest Christian contact with Muslims is that of the ancient Orthodox Churches. But, generally speaking, these churches do not see themselves as having an evangelistic task. "We have coexisted beautifully with Islam for 1300 years," an Orthodox Archbishop said to me a few months ago. He hoped that such peaceful coexistence would continue. But it was being disturbed by "Protestants" (a big enough umbrella to cover even Jehovah's Witnesses), who were distributing propaganda tracts in the villages; it had to be explained to the Ministry of the Interior that they were "agents from the other side" (i.e. Israel). The Orthodox Churches were letting their light shine, but not preaching. "Are any Muslims coming to Christ through this light?" I asked.

"Many buy and read Bibles, and want to become Christians, but it is forbidden."

"You mean that baptisms are forbidden? But are there no secret conversions?"

"No, definitely there are no conversions at all; the government does not allow conversions."

"I expect the Archbishop means that the government allows no open conversions," I persisted, "but surely the government cannot legislate for the work of the Holy Spirit?" My point was not conceded, however.

An exception to this Orthodox nonexpectation of Muslim evangelization is Dr. Charles Malik, well known to readers of CHRISTIANITY TODAY as a former contributor and as a past president of the United Nations General Assembly. He has recently retired from the chair of philosophy in the American University of Beirut. "I am a Trinitarian Christian," he had said to the architect designing his house, "and I wish this to be reflected in the building." He is a Chalcedonian Christian, too. So one side of his home is fitted with a series of three windows, each with three panels, while the windows on another side contain both a central cross and two stone supports symbolizing the two natures of Christ.

We sat on the terrace in the hot sunshine, beneath the Chalcedonian windows, drinking Turkish coffee and listening uneasily to the intermittent gunfire in the middle distance. Malik spoke with passionate conviction about the necessity of defending Christianity in Lebanon. "There is nothing like it anywhere in Africa or Asia, this long Christian tradition rooted deeply in the soil of our Lebanese villages. Surely Western governments are not so bankrupt of wisdom that they will allow a Christian culture to be destroyed for the sake of Arab oil?" I then asked him how he could see the Muslim world penetrated for Jesus Christ. "There must be missionaries," he replied, "humble, suffering missionaries, to live there, to witness there, to suffer there, and to die there. There is no other way."

I think I detect among evangelicals a new sensitivity, both theological and cultural, in our attitudes to the evangelization of Muslims. The bad old days of bitter polemic against Mohammed and Islam are, I hope, over. Even direct confrontation between Bible and Koran, between Jesus and Mohammed, is not likely to prove the most fruitful approach. Instead there is a humble desire to build bridges. Bishop Kenneth Cragg writes of "the Christian potential of the Koran," and of the "convertibility" of those elements in Islam that are not incompatible with the Gospel. He wants to persuade Muslims that "Christ is the conclusion of their own logic." Another brother, a national of a Middle Eastern country, although determined not to compromise any biblical essentials, has yet developed "seven fundamental principles" that he sees as common to Judaism, Christianity, and Islam. These include the great truths that God created and loves man, that man is separated from God by sin, that sin can be removed only by faith not by works, and that Jesus is the Savior who died and rose to redeem us. Each of his seven propositions is supported by appropriate quotations from Towrah (the law), Zabur (the Psalms), Injeel (the New Testament), and Qur'an.

The highest barriers that keep Muslims from faith in Jesus are cultural rather than theological, however: "People reject the gospel not because they think it is false, but because it strikes them as alien. They imagine that in order to become Christians they must renounce their own culture, lose their own identity and betray their own people" (Pasadena Statement, 1977). The very word Christian is associated in a Muslim's mind with all that he abominates most—the memory of those brutal Crusades, the materialism and moral decadence of the West, and our (to him) incredible espousal of Zionist imperialism. It is inconceivable to him that he should ever betray his Islamic inheritance. To become a Christian would be treason as well as apostasy, and would deserve the death penalty. So the question is whether a whole new way of presenting the Gospel can be developed. Can we show that "however much new converts feel they need to renounce for the sake of Christ, they are still the same people with the same heritage and the same family" (Willowbank Report), and that "conversion does not unmake, it remakes" (Kenneth Cragg)? Is it possible to conceive of converts becoming followers of Jesus without so forsaking their Islamic culture that they are regarded as traitors? Can we even contemplate Jesus mosques instead of churches and Jesus Muslims instead of Christians? It is with radical questions like these that the October conference was to grapple.

Neither theological bridges nor cultural sensitivity alone will win Muslims to Jesus Christ, however. The only way to a Muslim's heart is love. "We Christians have lived alongside Muslims in this country for over 1,000 years," an Egyptian Christian said to me in slightly broken English, "but we still hate and despise their religion. We ought rather to show our Christianship by our active love."

Hassan Dehqani-Tafti, himself a convert from Islam and now Anglican Bishop in Iran, has expressed it admirably in his autobiography *Design of My World* (1959): "Words alone cannot bring the Muslim to the foot of the Cross. ... Christians must show in their lives how Christianity is in truth the incarnation of the love of God. Most of the Muslims I know who have followed Christ have done so because of the sacrificial life and sustained love of some Christian friend. You cannot bring the Muslim to Christ unless you love him personally."

John R. W. Stott, "Cornerstone: Christians and Muslims," *Christianity Today* 23, no. 5 (December 1, 1978): 34–35.

Chapter 15

THE BATTLE FOR WORLD EVANGELISM

Dear Brother Arthur [Johnston]:

I greet you warmly in Christ. You and I are good friends, and have many concerns in common.

In your recently published *Battle for World Evangelism* (Tyndale) you have been somewhat critical of the Lausanne Committee in general, and of me in particular. I hope that this open response may be a helpful way to ventilate the issues further, although you will appreciate that I write only for myself and not for the Lausanne Committee.

I understand your book to have a double purpose, namely (1) to trace the tragic decline of commitment to evangelism in the ecumenical movement during this century, and (2) to warn the Lausanne movement against a similar process. Your topic is important. I genuinely applaud your personal dedication to biblical truth and world evangelization. Let me spell out the reasons why on balance I am glad your book has been published.

First, you are entirely right to deplore the ecumenical betrayal of the unevangelized millions, and to attribute it to the loss of biblical authority and the consequent growth of universalism and syncretism. Strangely enough, I myself in 1974 wrote a similar though much shorter sketch, "The Rise and Fall of Missionary Concern in the Ecumenical Movement 1910 to 1973," which was published in *Vocation and Victory*, an international Festschrift in honor of General Erik Wickberg of the Salvation Army. And I think you know that at both the fourth and fifth Assemblies of the World Council of Churches at Uppsala and Nairobi, respectively, I pleaded publicly for a return to biblical evangelism.

Second, watchdogs are valuable, in the church as in the home. We need them to warn us of approaching danger, and we would be foolish to ignore their warnings. The Lausanne Covenant itself calls for "both watchfulness and discernment to safeguard the biblical Gospel."

Third, your paramount concern is that evangelicals will continue to submit to Scripture. You write: "The complete truthfulness and final authority of Scripture provides the essential parameters for evangelicals." In this the Lausanne Committee is, of course, in complete agreement with you.

Fourth, I welcome your candor. In fact, I constantly long for more evangelical openness. Nothing is lost and everything is gained by candid and charitable dialogue with one another.

At the same time, it seems to me that we also need both precision and penitence. I confess to having been upset by your tendency to generalize and to make dark innuendoes about "the evangelical left," "the conciliar elements within the Lausanne Committee," supposed departures from biblical inspiration, and espousals of unbiblical tradition. This kind of vagueness only spreads suspicion.

Next, you disapprove of the penitent note in the covenant. But why? Frankly, I miss this note in your book. You write as if ecumenicals are always wrong, and evangelicals always right, and as if any idea that comes from Geneva must *ipso facto* be misguided. Surely, however, we need to admit that we evangelicals have also had our blind spots, for example, on slavery and race. You rightly urge vigilance against liberalism; I want also to urge vigilance against prejudice. You think I react too positively to Geneva; I think you react too negatively. Should we not be willing to *listen* to anybody who wants to speak to us, while *agreeing* with them only if they agree with Scripture?

Let me stay a bit longer on this vital question of Scripture. In your evaluation of paragraph two of the covenant, you seem to me to blow hot and cold. You begin by saying that it "reasserted the authority and inspiration of Scripture" and you generously describe its statement as "beautiful, powerful and relevant," so that "evangelicals need not be apologetic or ashamed because of it." You also rightly say that the covenant must be interpreted in the light of the Congress as a whole, and not in isolation from it. But then you express two criticisms. The first is that nothing is said about the supremacy of Scripture over tradition. In this I agree with you. I think the covenant would have been helpfully strengthened by such an addition; in fact, I wish you had yourself proposed it, since you were there as a participant. Second, you express hesitations about the clause "without error in all that it affirms." But this was intended as a clarification, not as a loophole, and it was one of the alternatives submitted to the drafting committee by a respected group of theologians from what you would describe as "the evangelical right."

I come now to the question of Christian social responsibility on which you concentrate. You write that this "has always been a concern among evangelicals," since "the Scriptures obviously teach both evangelism and socio-political responsibilities." Fine. You then go on to emphasize the primacy of evangelism. You correctly point out that the Lausanne Covenant itself affirms this, namely, that "in the church's mission of sacrificial service evangelism is primary." So at its first meeting the Lausanne Committee faithfully echoed these words in the definition of its purpose, adding that "our particular concern must be the evangelization of the 2,700 million unreached people of our world." You are unfair and inaccurate to criticize us for disloyalty in this matter. As a member of both the committee and the executive I can say from personal knowledge that we have consistently striven to develop an agenda that reflects a primary commitment to world evangelization.

At the same time, speaking for myself, I think that this distinction between evangelism and social action is often artificial. Although some individual Christians are called to specialist ministries (some as evangelists, others as social workers, and so forth), the Christian community as a whole should not have to choose, any more than Jesus did. In many missionary situations such a choice would be inconceivable. The evangelist could not with integrity proclaim the good news to the victims of flood or famine while ignoring their physical plight, or to Latin American Indians, Filipino peasants, or ghetto blacks while ignoring their exploitation or deprivation.

What then is the proper relation of evangelism to social action? This is the theological question that Lausanne left unresolved and that still needs to be pursued. Your own repeated emphasis is that social action is the *consequence* of evangelism. Let me concede this for a moment. What is the implication of it? Supposing we go out exclusively to evangelize, and that under the blessing of God converts are won. Presumably they, being the "consequence" of our evangelism, are now free to become involved in social service. But then we ourselves are in the position of those converts, for we ourselves are the consequence of other people's evangelism. Why then should we not also, on your own premise, engage in social action? I think the logic of your argument brings us closer to one another than you realize.

You quote other evangelical leaders to the effect that service is both the "means" or "bridge" to evangelism (i.e., it is useful because it confronts people with the Gospel) and the "fruit" of evangelism (i.e., it issues naturally from conversion). Thus explained, service leads both *to* and *from* evangelism. I accept both these truths, but do not feel able to stop there. It seems to me that Scripture itself goes further, and indicates the kind of "partnership" between evangelism and service that you say you cannot accept. Certainly the "words" and "works" of Jesus belonged indissolubly to one another. In one sense his works made his words visible, were a visual proclamation of the Gospel of the Kingdom, and elicited faith. Christian good works of love have the same nature and effect. You say that the Gospel is completely self-authenticating, and I know what you mean. I, too, believe in the gracious authenticating work of the Holy Spirit. But does not the Gospel lack credibility whenever Christians contradict it by their lives?

In another sense, the works of Jesus were just plain compassion, irrespective of their evidential value. Must we not follow the example of Jesus? I do not build my case entirely on John 20:21, as you imply, but also on the "great commandment" to love our neighbor, which you do not mention.

Brother Art, you say that I have "dethroned evangelism as the only historical aim of mission": I would prefer to say that I have attempted to "enthrone love as the essential historical motivation for mission." If we see our brothers or sisters in need (whether spiritual or social), and have the wherewithal to meet their need, but fail to do so, how can we claim that God's love dwells in us?

I express my sincere love for you in Christ, and my earnest desire to continue this discussion.

Ever your friend and brother,

JOHN R. W. STOTT

Chapter 16

———

TRANSCENDENCE
NOW A SECULAR QUEST

I t used to seem rather pedantic to talk about "transcendence." The word belonged to learned lectures by theologians who drew careful distinctions between "transcendence" and "immanence," between God beyond us and God among us. Nowadays, however, especially since the craze for transcendental meditation, "transcendence" has become part of everybody's vocabulary.

The old materialism no longer satisfies. It prevailed too long anyway. J. H. Woodger, professor of biology in London University (1947–1959), so wise that his friends have always called him "Socrates," once said to me: "I work in an atmosphere so materialistic that the word 'spirit' is never mentioned, unless prefaced by the adjective 'methylated'!" Against this kind of materialistic secularism many young people are rebelling today. Theodore Roszak gave us an excellent documentation of the youthful revolt against the technocracy in *The Making of a Counter Culture* (1969). I do not think he claims to be a Christian. So I was all the more struck that when he wanted to express the folly of imagining that scientific technology could satisfy human beings, he felt obliged to resort to the words of Jesus: "What does it profit a man if he gains the whole world and loses his own soul?"

During the last few years increasing numbers of university students have been deserting the faculties of science and technology and enrolling instead in courses on philosophy, history, and literature. They know that reality cannot possibly be confined in a test tube, or smeared on a slide for microscopic examination, or apprehended with cool scientific detachment. They are convinced that there is another dimension to human experience which they like to call "transcendence" and that reality is "awesomely vast" (Roszak's expression). So they seek it, often in strange and even perilous places, through mind-expanding drugs, through yoga, transcendental meditation and the "higher consciousness," through sexual adventures, through art, music, and science fiction, and through experiments with the occult.

None of this should surprise us, who look to the Bible for our understanding of life and who love to quote Augustine's assertion that the human heart is restless until it finds its rest in God. It is true that ever since the first disobedience in the Garden of Eden fallen human beings have been running away from God. Indeed, we are worse than fugitives; we are rebels who defy his authority and resist his love. And yet we are restless in our rebellion. Instinctively we know that the God we are trying to avoid is our only home. So at times we "feel after him." We seek to find him whom we are simultaneously seeking to escape. Such is the paradox of our fallenness.

One of the most popular fields of exploration is that of the paranormal, in the form either of psychic phenomena or of astrology or of UFOs. And science fiction cashes in on this cult. I gather that Erich von Daniken, author of *The Chariots of the Gods*, has even outsold Dr. Spock. It is claimed that 34 million copies of his books have been sold in thirty-five languages.

The science fiction example I would like to develop is Steven Spielberg's motion picture *Close Encounters of the Third Kind* (1977). Film critics have described it as mere entertainment, without any hidden meaning. But personally I attribute its popularity to its offer of a secular experience of transcendence. Its message could be summarized as follows:

1. "We are not alone in the universe." We are not condemned to live in what Bertrand Russell called "cosmic loneliness," for there are other and superior beings in space.

2. They are friendly, awe-inspiring in their power, but friendly, and even taking the initiative to make contact with us (a secular equivalent to "grace").

3. Bourgeois suburbanites, preoccupied with material security, dismiss believers as mad. They are excluded from the transcendent by their incredulity.

4. The establishment also, symbolized by the Army, not only disbelieve themselves, but do their utmost to keep other people from believing.

5. Little children, however, like four-year-old Barry, grasp the transcendent with wide-eyed delight. For it is "revealed to babes." They respond to it with joy and eagerness, and have no fear.

6. Simple believers too, like Roy Neary, the film's hero, refuse to be put off. Roy feels himself "invited," even "compelled," towards the rendezvous which, significantly enough, is a kind of "holy mountain." Nothing will deter him from reaching it.

7. The scientists also discover the truth by their open-minded investigation. They fall to their knees in wonder, almost in worship.

8. In the end, when the glorious space ship descends, the "close encounter" with this Other Reality is an overwhelming experience of rapture, a secular form of "beatific vision." Spielberg describes it on the last page of his book in these words: "Neary walked forward ... leading the way deep into the fiery heart of the mystery." Then slowly "the great phantom starship began to lift off ... through layer after layer of clouds until this great city in the sky became the brightest of the brightest stars." The book's last words are "the indisputable proof."

This claim to a secular experience of transcendence constitutes a powerful challenge to the quality of our Christian public worship. Does it offer people what they are seeking—the element of mystery, the sense of the numinous, in biblical language "the fear of the Lord," in modern language "transcendence," so that we bow down before the Infinite God in that mixture of awe, wonder, and joy which we call "worship"?

"Not often," I'm afraid the honest answer would have to be. We evangelicals do not know much about worship. Evangelism is our specialty, not worship. We have little sense of the greatness of Almighty God. We tend to be cocky, flippant, and proud. And our worship services are often ill-prepared, slovenly, mechanical, perfunctory, and dull.

We need to listen again to the biblical criticism of religion. The Old Testament prophets were scathing in their denunciations of formalism and hypocrisy. And Jesus reapplied their critique to the Pharisees of his day: "These people draw near to me with their lips, but their hearts are far from me." This indictment of the Lord and his prophets is uncomfortably relevant to us. Much of our public worship is ritual without reality, form without power, religion without God.

What is needed, then? At least these three things: (1) Such a humble, faithful reading and preaching of God's Word that the human readers and preachers are forgotten, and the voice of the living God himself is heard and he addresses his people. (2) Such a reverent, believing administration of the Lord's Supper that there is a "real presence" of Jesus Christ in the midst, the risen Lord himself, really and objectively present, coming to meet his people in accordance with his promise, ready to make himself known to them and to give himself to them, so that they may "feed on him in their hearts by faith." (3) Such a sincere offering of prayer and praise that believers say with Jacob at Bethel, "Surely God is in this place ... this is the house of God and the gate of heaven," while unbelievers coming in fall down and worship God exclaiming "God is really among you" (Gen. 28:16, 17; 1 Cor. 14:25).

In brief, one of the tragedies of contemporary Christendom is that just when people are disillusioned with materialism and are seeking a spiritual dimension to life, we seem unable to satisfy their hunger. So they turn to drugs, sex, yoga, mysticism, astrology, and science fiction, instead of to the Christian church in whose worship true transcendence should always be experienced.

John R. W. Stott, "Cornerstone: Transcendence: Now a Secular Quest," *Christianity Today* 23, no. 12 (March 23, 1979): 36–37.

Chapter 17

FREEING A STALWART
PEOPLE FROM FATALISM

*Religion is hardly an appropriate word for the Eskimo
system of belief—there is no worship of God.*

I t was commercial interests that first turned European eyes
toward the white wilderness of the Canadian Arctic. The trade
routes between Europe and Asia, which took ships around the
southern tips of the African and American continents, were long
and hazardous. If a Northwest Passage above Canada could be
found, it would almost halve the distance. After the failures of
Christopher Columbus in 1492 and of John Cabot in 1497, a whole
series of further expeditions was launched.

Now in the latter part of the twentieth century the possible commercial use of the Northwest Passage is again being
canvassed. It was the discovery of oil in Alaska that led to the
conversion of the *Manhattan* into a giant ice-breaking tanker
of 150,000 tons, fitted with highly sophisticated, computerized
equipment. The huge costs of construction and of antipollution
insurance have led at present to pipelines as an alternative means

of transporting oil and gas to the south. But we may yet hear more of the Northwest Passage before the century ends.

Nevertheless, Christian interest in the Arctic focuses less on fossil fuels and mineral deposits than on the people who for centuries have maintained their brave struggle for survival against cold and starvation. We tend to call them "Eskimos" (a corruption of a contemptuous Indian term meaning "raw flesh eaters"), but they call themselves "Inuit," signifying just "the people," the plural of "inuk," a "person." Although they are divided into numerous subcultures, speak different dialects and refer to themselves and each other by picturesque expressions like "people of the muskox," "people of the rich fishing grounds," and even "people of the back of the earth," yet they are one people. Most scholars seem to agree that their ancestors came from northern China, some migrating northwest through Mongolia to Siberia and Lapland, and others northeast across the Bering Strait to Alaska, Arctic Canada, and Greenland. There are thought to be about 85,000 Eskimos living today, 40,000 in Greenland, 25,000 in Alaska, 18,000 in Canada, and the remaining 2,000 in Siberia.

The traditional religion of Eskimos has been a form of animism. Although, according to Roger P. Buliard, a Roman Catholic missionary among them for 15 years, in their ancient faith "God was regarded as primary," he was remote and uninterested in human affairs, "leaving mundane matters entirely in the hands of lesser authorities," i.e., the spirits (*Inuk*, 1950, p. 273). "Religion" is hardly an appropriate word to use for their system of beliefs and practices, however, for it contains no worship of God—only the appeasement of spirits. These spirits are thought to be in control of everything. They inhabit birds, beasts, and fish; they animate inanimate objects like rocks and ice; they direct the weather; and they influence the whole of human life, especially birth and death. Moreover, they are mostly malicious.

Hence, they have a felt need for an *angakuk* (medicine man or shaman). Indeed, Eskimo animism is really a combination of shamanism (placating the spirits by magic) and fetishism (gaining protection by wearing amulets or charms), together with a set of social taboos. Yet all this elaborate procedure for gaining power over the spirits leaves the Inuk ultimately powerless. He "simply accepts things as they are," explains Raymond de Coccola, another Roman Catholic missionary, "and lets them go at that. If they do not work out for him, he will dismiss misfortune with one word: *Ayorama*, 'that's destiny, that's life, there isn't anything I can do about it.' "

The earliest expression of Christian concern for the Eskimos that I have come across was Pope Gregory's instruction in A.D. 835 that the Greenlanders be evangelized. Norse missions began soon afterwards, and in A.D. 999 Leif, the son of Eric the Red, arrived in Greenland, preached the gospel, and baptized the king and other leaders. The first bishop was consecrated in the year 1121. Hans Egede, a Danish Lutheran pastor, came to Greenland in 1718, and the Moravian Brethren came in 1733.

Anglican involvement in the Arctic may be traced back to August 1578 when Robert Wolfall, Chaplain to Admiral Sir Martin Frobisher's third expedition, administered the Lord's Supper on Baffin Island. The 400th anniversary of this first Anglican Communion on the North American continent was celebrated last year by a special synod of the Diocese of the Artic. The first Anglican missionary, however, was the first chaplain to the Hudson's Bay Company (1820), John West, a convert of John Wesley. In 1876 the Rev. E. J. Peck, often called "the Apostle to the Eskimos," arrived from England to pioneer for 48 years the

Christian mission in the eastern Arctic around Hudson Bay. He believed in indigenous principles, and encouraged the Eskimo churches to become self-reliant and self-propagating. Today the Anglican Diocese of the Arctic, which stretches some 2000 miles from Inuvik at the Mackenzie River Delta to Northern Quebec, has about 30 clergy, of whom 12 are Inuit.

I myself have now had the opportunity on four occasions to travel north of the Arctic Circle, and in particular to visit Bathurst Inlet, whose lodge at the mouth of the Burnside River has been created by the enterprise of former R.C.M.P. Glenn Warner and his wife Trish. Only after my arrival did I learn to my surprise that the small Inuit community, who call themselves the *kringaunmiut* or "people of the nose mountain" (from the shape of the rocky peak behind their camp), were all Anglicans! Since this discovery, having been appointed their "Honorary Chaplain," I have had the privilege of seeking to minister the gospel to them by word and sacrament. This last July I was there again. Since my previous visit in 1976 there were two more healthy Eskimo babies to baptize, and there was another marriage to bless.

Pray that God will bless these fine Inuit people, and enable them to fight under Christ's banner against sin, the world, and the devil as manfully as they fight against the rigors of the Arctic winter.

John R. W. Stott, "Cornerstone: Freeing a Stalwart People from Fatalism," *Christianity Today* 23, no. 23 (October 5, 1979): 42–43.

Chapter 18

———

THE BIBLICAL SCOPE OF
THE CHRISTIAN MISSION

*We see in Scripture the reflections of our own
prejudice rather than the disturbing message.*

T he Christian mission is inconceivable without the Christian
Scriptures. It is the Bible that supplies the mandate, the
inspiration, the direction, and the power for our witness and
service in the world. Without the Bible we would have neither
the authority nor the inclination to engage in Christian mission.
With the Bible, on the other hand, we are stripped of every excuse
for opting out of it.

Above all, we need the wholesome wholeness of the biblical
perspective. Only the Bible can correct our skewed vision, redress
our imbalance, broaden our narrow interests, and liberate us
from the petty preoccupations in which we imprison ourselves.
Consider the breadth of biblical mission.

First, the Bible relates to *the whole world*. It is true that
Scripture lays much emphasis on God's covenant of grace, and
on his steadfast love for his covenant people. Yet Yahweh, the God
of Israel, is no tribal deity like Chemosh, the god of the Moabites,

and Milcom, the god of the Ammonites. He is the living God, the Creator and Sustainer of the universe, the Ruler of the nations, and the Lord of history. So even in the Old Testament, in which God's judgment on the nations is pronounced, the salvation of the nations is also promised. Johannes Blauw was doubtless correct in his book, *The Missionary Nature of the Church* (1962), that the Old Testament perspective was not so much one of "mission" (Israel going out to win the nations) as of "universalism" (the nations being included one day). He added that a "centripetal missionary consciousness" (the nations flowing to Jerusalem) was replaced by a "centrifugal missionary activity" (the disciples going out to the nations) only after the Resurrection when "all authority" in heaven and on earth was given to the risen Lord Jesus.

Once this biblical emphasis has gripped our minds, we shall find it impossible to stay in our cozy little ecclesiastical nests. The Bible is hostile to narrow parochialism. It flings us out into God's world. It gives us a new global consciousness.

Secondly, the Bible presents *the whole gospel*. We must, therefore, allow the Bible to correct our evangelical reductionism. I have two particular tendencies in mind. The first is to keep looking for what is sometimes called "the irreducible minimum of the gospel." Of course we have a responsibility to make the gospel as simple and straightforward as we can; the Holy Spirit is not the author of muddle and confusion. It is "when any one hears the word of the kingdom *and does not understand it"* that the devil comes and snatches it away (Matt. 13:19). But to simplify the gospel and to reduce it are two different processes. Who wants an "irreducibly minimum gospel" when the apostle Paul declared "the whole counsel of God" and on that account could affirm his innocence of his hearers' blood (Acts 20:26, 27)? We need to soak our minds in the full biblical gospel from creation to consummation.

Our other tendency is to fix the gospel in terms congenial to our own culture and resist the desire of other Christians to restate the same biblical gospel, but in terms more meaningful to their culture. We have to liberate the gospel from both reductionist and cultural bondage. For it is the gospel itself, the biblical good news in its glorious fulness, which is God's power for salvation to every believer. To tamper with the gospel either by shrinkage or by overlay is to weaken its saving power.

Thirdly, the Bible summons us to *a whole mission.* "Holistic" is the popular modern word for this concept, although I confess I have always found the term harsh in sound and ugly in aspect. Yet I guess it is correct in meaning. For if "atomistic" is the tendency to reduce a whole to its parts, "holistic" is the tendency to unite the parts into a whole.

Now there are many possible ways of stating and defending the wholeness of the mission to which God summons us in the Bible. One way derives from his own character (that he is the God of social justice as well as of personal salvation), another comes from the nature of the human beings he has made (that the neighbor we are to love and serve is a physical and social as well as a spiritual person), a third is from the concept of salvation or the kingdom of God (which combines total blessing with total demand, and insists that saving faith always expresses itself in serving love), a fourth arises from the model of Christ's mission (that he combined words and works in his public ministry, his works embodying his words and his words interpreting his works), and a fifth proceeds from the responsibility of the church (that it is to be the world's salt and light). Wherever we look, then— at God or Christ, at human beings, salvation, or the church—we see this healthy fusion of soul and body, word and deed, faith and works, witness and service, light and salt, the individual and the community, evangelism and social action. We must not separate what God has joined.

Fourthly, the Bible addresses *the whole church,* each local manifestation of it and each individual member of it. That the local church is to be a mission community is, according to the New Testament, plain beyond doubt. A good example is the Thessalonian church. Consider the sequence of events Paul outlines in the first chapter of his letter: "our gospel came to you" (v. 5) so that "you received the word" (v. 6), and then "the word of the Lord sounded forth from you" (v. 8). Thus, the gospel came to you, you received it, and you passed it on. In consequence, it came to others, who received it, and passed it on. This is the way God means the good news to spread: from church to church.

Moreover, the gospel "is at work in you believers" (2:13). It changed their lives. They turned from dead idols to serve the living God and to wait for his Son from heaven (1:9, 10). So complete was their transformation that it was not only "the word of the Lord" which sounded forth from them, but the news of their "faith in God" (1:8). They embodied the gospel; Paul assumed that every church member would be involved in this transformation and therefore in this mission.

The whole church taking the whole gospel on a whole mission to the whole world. Nobody can read the Bible and miss this "wholesome wholeness" of the Christian mission in its four dimensions. And yet, some of us manage to do that very thing. Such are our personal and cultural blind spots that we tend to see in Scripture the reflections of our own prejudice rather than the disturbing message of God. It has been so down the Christian centuries, and still is today. The most diligent readers of the Bible are not necessarily the most conscientious doers of its message. We need then to pray, both for ourselves and for others, that God will break through our defensive system in such an irresistible incursion that he causes us to hear, to grasp, and to obey.

John R. W. Stott, "Cornerstone: The Biblical Scope of the Christian Mission," *Christianity Today* 24, no. 1 (January 4, 1980): 34–35.

Chapter 19

SAVING SOULS AND
SERVING BREAD

*Must specialized ministry drive wedges
between evangelism and social action?*

S ix months have passed since the World Council of Churches Commission on World Missions and Evangelism Melbourne Conference, "Your Kingdom Come," and the Lausanne Committee for World Evangelization Pattaya Consultation, "How Shall They Hear?" Both were concerned with the church's mission in the world. Melbourne listened attentively to the cries of the poor and the oppressed. The LCWE Consultation on World Evangelization (COWE), on the other hand, concentrated on how to evangelize the world's unreached peoples.

The distinction between the two conferences, between concern for the poor and concern for the lost, should not be over-pressed, however. At neither conference was there a total disjunction between these two Christian responsibilities. At COWE one miniconsultant focused on refugees, and another on the urban poor. Similarly, Melbourne did not altogether disregard the necessity of evangelism, as some have unjustly said. Its

Section II declared that "the proclamation of the gospel to the whole world remains an urgent obligation for all Christians," and its Section III that we have a "special obligation to those who have never heard the good news of the kingdom."

Nevertheless, the difference in emphasis remains. The Melbourne documents pulsate with indignation over human injustice and with longings to liberate the oppressed, whereas their call for world evangelization lacks a comparable passion. As for COWE, its almost exclusive preoccupation with evangelism led to the issue of "A Statement of Concerns," which originated with Third World evangelical leaders but was quickly signed by a widely representative group of more than 200 others. Although it recognized the useful work done since Lausanne by the committee's Strategy and Theology groups, it went on to criticize it for seeming to have gone back on the Lausanne Covenant's commitment to both evangelism and sociopolitical involvement, and for not being "seriously concerned with the social, political and economic issues ... that are a great stumbling block to the proclamation of the Gospel."

The LCWE's executive, to whom the "Statement of Concerns" was addressed, invited three of its leading signatories to meet them and elaborate their criticisms, and was able to assure them that it had no intention of going back on the Lausanne Covenant. Indeed, the Thailand Statement (overwhelmingly endorsed by the participants on the last day, with only one dissenter) includes these sentences: "Although evangelism and social action are not identical, we gladly reaffirm our commitment to both, and we endorse the Lausanne Covenant in its entirety. It remains the basis of our common activity, and nothing it contains is beyond our concern, so long as it is clearly related to world evangelization." It then goes on to reaffirm the covenant's declaration that "in the church's mission of sacrificial service evangelism is primary," and explains the reason for this primacy in the following terms: "This is not to deny that evangelism and social action are integrally related, but rather to acknowledge that of all the tragic needs of human beings none is greater than their alienation from their Creator and the reality of eternal death for those who refuse to repent and believe."

Meanwhile, can anything be done to dissipate the current confusion? My friend David Hesselgrave (see "Tomorrow's Missionaries," July 18 issue), while saying that he thinks it permissible to opt for my wide definition of "mission" as "everything the church is sent into the world to do," asks whether I mean to involve "missionaries" in this "everything," and invites me to be explicit on this point. I am happy to oblige.

It seems to me important to distinguish between polarization and specialization. That is, although we should not polarize on this issue—some Christians defining mission in terms of evangelism and others in terms of social action—we must accept the reality that God calls some to specialize in the former, and others in the latter. The early church first recognized this when the apostles affirmed that their special calling was pastoral (the ministry of the Word and prayer), while the seven were appointed to the social work of caring for the widows (Acts 6). Paul's doctrine of the body of Christ, with all members gifted for different ministries, confirms and universalizes this truth.

Nevertheless, how can legitimate specialization be prevented from driving wedges yet more deeply between evangelism and social action? I have three suggestions to make.

First, in general terms, in spite of our specialist callings, every Christian is sent into the world as both a witness and a servant.

Whenever we see someone in need, whether that need is spiritual or physical or social, if we have the wherewithal to meet it, we must do so; otherwise we cannot claim to have God's love dwelling in us (1 John 3:16). Often people have more than one need, and if we love them with God's love we shall do our utmost to relieve their needs. It is then, too, that they are most likely to believe. Verbal witness is not enough. As Jesus said, it is when people "see our good works" that our light shines most brightly and will give glory to our heavenly Father (Matt. 5:16).

Second, each local church should be involved in both evangelism and social action. Since God calls and gifts different people for different ministries, it seems a logical deduction that those with similar gifts and callings should coalesce into specialist study and action groups and be encouraged to concentrate on their particular God-given ministries. At the same time, they should be given regular opportunities to report back to the whole congregation, so that the body of Christ may know what its different members are up to and may support them with encouragement and prayer.

Third, what about missionaries? It is agreed that they neither can do everything (for lack of time and energy), nor should give themselves to any ministry for which they have not been gifted and called, nor should they meddle in the politics of their host country (unless specifically requested by national Christians), since they are guests and aliens in it. Nevertheless, because missionaries have come to identify with another country, all its people's needs and aspirations should arouse their sympathetic concern. They cannot close their eyes to local poverty or hunger, disease or drought, bad farming or exploitation. What, then, should they do if these needs remain unmet, and if they remain convinced of their own continuing calling to evangelism? Should they not do, in principle, what the apostles did in Acts 6, namely take steps to ensure that others are appointed to do the social work to which they have not been called?

My personal belief is that we should develop many more mission teams, so that evangelists, teachers, doctors, agriculturalists, social workers, and relief and development experts can work together in the name of Jesus Christ, offering a humble, holistic service to the whole neighborhood to which they have been called.

John R. W. Stott, "Cornerstone: Saving Souls and Serving Bread," *Christianity Today* 24, no. 19 (November 7, 1980): 50–51.

Chapter 20

REVIVING EVANGELISM
IN BRITAIN

C hristians in Britain during the seventies became increasingly concerned about the secularization of their country, and began to give serious thought to reevangelization. First, a number of evangelicals met in 1975 to consider inviting Billy Graham for another crusade. Second, Archbishops Donald Coggan of Canterbury and Stuart Blanch of York, who had just issued their "Call to the Nation"—posing questions of what kind of society we wanted and what kind of people would be needed to shape it—were being urged by some to go beyond a national call to a national mission. Third, the British Council of Churches' Executive, catching wind of these thoughts, expressed their "conviction that the time is ripening for a concerted national effort in evangelism."

These three streams coalesced in October 1976 when the archbishop of Canterbury called together for consultation a group of denominational, ecumenical, and evangelical leaders, with a Roman Catholic representative. During 1977 the churches were consulted and responded positively. In 1978 the "Nationwide

Initiative in Evangelism" was thus launched, with the archbishop of Canterbury as chairman of its council of reference. Dr. Donald English, a young evangelical Methodist who had recently been conference president, was chosen as chairman of the Initiative committee, and evangelicals invited to serve on it included Gordon Landreth, secretary of the Evangelical Alliance, and Tom Houston, director of the Bible Society.

One of the factors that influenced Christian leaders towards the Initiative was the widespread sense of growing convergence among evangelical and ecumenical spokesmen in their understanding of mission and evangelism. Dr. M. M. Thomas, as moderator of the World Council of Churches Central Committee, drew attention to this publicly in the course of his report to the Fifth Assembly in Nairobi in 1975. Referring to the recent conferences in Bangkok (ecumenical), Lausanne (evangelical), Rome (Catholic), and Bucharest (Orthodox), he expressed the view that "their theological convergence is very striking." This was further confirmed when the Nairobi Assembly's Section I produced its report "Confessing Christ Today" and when almost simultaneously Pope Paul issued *Evangelii Nuntiandi,* his apostolic exhortation on "Evangelization in the Modern World."

People began to study and compare these documents, especially the Lausanne Covenant (1974), "Confessing Christ Today" (1975), and *Evangelii Nuntiandi* (1975). At the suggestion of the British Council of Churches, four journals (Roman Catholic, Anglican, Methodist, and Evangelical) each agreed to commission somebody to explore the signs of convergence and divergence in the documents, to publish all four evaluations, and so to promote debate. I was asked to contribute the article in *Third Way* and concluded it with "Ten Affirmations on Evangelism." These related to the church sent into the world, the mission of evangelism and social action, the biblical origin of the gospel, Christ crucified and risen, the offer of salvation, the demand of conversion, costly discipleship, the mobilization of God's people, the renewal of the church, and the power of the Holy Spirit. Each affirmation was supported by appropriate quotations from the three foundation documents; the similarities were remarkable.

At the same time, many evangelicals remained uneasy. Indeed, I was uneasy myself. The similarity was there to be seen. Yet the method used in demonstrating it was suspect. To begin with, it concentrated on the convergence and overlooked the divergence. For example, *Evangelii Nuntiandi* gives an extremely broad definition of evangelism, refers to "Christian Tradition and the Church's Magisterium" as sources of the defined faith alongside the biblical revelation, omits any clear exposition of *sola* fide, and concludes with an unfortunate reference to the Virgin Mary as the "Star of Evangelization" into whose "hands and heart" the church's evangelistic task is entrusted. In brief, my tabulation of agreements was a highly selective "lowest common denominator" approach.

How real and substantial, then, was the convergence? And how solid a foundation did it offer for common evangelistic witness in Britain today? These questions continued to nag me. Since evangelism, at its simplest and most basic, is the sharing of the good news, united evangelism is impossible without prior agreement about the good news to be shared. For evangelicals this is a matter of conscience. It was certain, I argued, that evangelicals would never cooperate with the National Initiative in Evangelism unless and until they were convinced that it held fast to the apostolic gospel. So we needed a "crisp, positive, comprehensive and Christ-centered" statement, which would both reassure our tender evangelical consciences and at the same time help the churches to recover something of the gospel's glory.

———————————

In 1979 the Initiative committee invited 15 theologians from different traditions to undertake this task. Bishop Lesslie Newbigin was asked to be chairman, with me as his vice-chairman. We spent our first meeting getting to know and respect one another by sharing our personal experiences and beliefs. We described frankly how we had come to faith in Christ, what good news we wanted to share with others, and why we felt evangelism to be urgent. As we listened to one another, we were surprised to discover a further convergence: the same Spirit had disclosed to us the same Lord. We were able to proceed with our task in a greater spirit of mutual confidence.

For our second meeting we divided into four small groups which discussed respectively "the Bible and Evangelism," "God and the World," "Jesus and Salvation," and "the Church and the Kingdom." The first group was able to produce an agreed report, but the other three could only issue personal statements and responses in which some quite sharp differences of approach and emphasis were exposed. At our third meeting we studied and discussed these reports. I confess I found this a depressing meeting, for at a number of important points we seemed to be at an impasse, with no apparent way forward.

So I came to our fourth and last meeting with a "now or never" stance of its importance. Was it really going to be impossible for us to produce an honest statement that plotted substantial areas of agreement? I took with me a short, sharp declaration in five paragraphs, which I felt would be an irreducible minimum. Martin Conway, the British Council of Churches' Secretary for

Ecumenical Affairs, had drafted a somewhat longer statement of "Ten Theses." Yet the two revealed a considerable degree of overlap. So the working group asked us to conflate them, which we did, and then they spruced up our conflation.

―――――――――

What is now published as "The Gospel We Affirm Together" does not claim to be a comprehensive confession of evangelical theology. It will not satisfy those who insist on the inclusion of every jot and tittle of evangelical orthodoxy before we can engage in any common work or witness. Yet the essence of the biblical gospel is recognizably there—God as Creator, Lord and Father; Jesus Christ as the conqueror of sin and death by his cross and resurrection; the Bible as the unique and irreplaceable witness to Christ, through which God both spoke and speaks; the church as Christ's penitent people who have received from him a new life and entered his new society; the Holy Spirit as sovereign in his works of power; the kingdom of God as his rule already present in Jesus, whose resurrection is the pledge of God's final triumph; and evangelism as the common responsibility and joy of all Christian people.

Lacking, from an orthodox Protestant viewpoint, is sufficient precision at three crucial points. Though Jesus is termed God's "son," his deity is not spelled out. Though the Bible's "irreplaceable witness" and "unique authority" are declared, its status as the church's only rule of faith and practice is not. Though the statement includes references to God's grace, the necessity of "turning in penitence to Christ," and the reception from him of a new life, the freeness of salvation as God's gift through faith is not clearly enough affirmed.

Still, those who can subscribe to this sevenfold affirmation with a good conscience should surely be able with an equally good conscience to join hands in spreading its message to others. At the NIE Assembly at the end of September, its content seemed to be acceptable; the questions raised about it concerned rather how we can now communicate it to Britain's alienated masses.

John R. W. Stott, "Cornerstone: Reviving Evangelism in Britain," *Christianity Today* 24, no. 21 (December 12, 1980): 40–41.

Chapter 21

———

THE PROBLEMS
AND PROMISE FOR
EVANGELISM IN INDIA

*After two centuries of missionary effort, less than
3 percent of India's 670 millions is Christian.*

I t is not difficult to be a lover of India. The gentleness and sim-
plicity of its people with their spiritual sensitivity and hunger
for God, its handsome men, elegant sari-clad women, and viva-
cious children with wondering eyes and ready laughter—these
are some of the characteristics that endear Indians to those of
us who have the good fortune to know any.

The Christian good news reached India very early. Although
the claim of Syrian Christians that Saint Thomas came to India in
the first century lacks solid historical evidence, yet trade between
Palestine and India is known to have flourished at that time, and
one of the signatories of the decrees of the Council of Nicea in
A.D. 325 was "John. Bishop of Persia and Great India."

The Portuguese explorers, who opened up trade with Europe,
also paved the way for the Jesuit missionaries, and Francis Xavier

arrived in 1542. Protestant missions date from the eighteenth century, and the modern missionary movement may be said to have begun with William Carey, who arrived in Bengal in 1793.

In spite of two centuries of Protestant missionary effort, however, less than 3 percent of India's 670 millions profess to be Christians, and two-thirds of these are Roman Catholics or Orthodox. Why has the headway been so slow?

The first reason is doubtless the peculiar character of Hinduism in both its intellectual and moral aspects. Intellectually, it is a totally inclusive faith, absorbing everything and rejecting nothing. It would gladly embrace Jesus Christ also—if only he would renounce his exclusive claims. But any talk of his uniqueness or finality is deeply offensive to Hindus. Mohandas Gandhi was a perfect example of this attitude. I have visited Sevagram, the ashram where he lived between 1936 and 1946, and seen the small, glass-fronted bookcase in which he kept his Bhagavad Gita, Koran, and Bible. He loved these three books equally, he said. He greatly admired Jesus, particularly his Sermon on the Mount, but strenuously denied that he was unique.

To this intellectual obstacle a moral one is added, namely the dreadful doctrine of *karma,* that every human being must eat the fruit of his own wrongdoing, if not in this life then in *samsara,* the endless cycle of future reincarnations. "A Hindu will never admit that he needs a Savior," a Christian professor of theology once said to me, "not because he does not acknowledge that he is a sinner, but because he believes he can save himself—by *karma,* by *bhakti* (religious devotion), or by ceremonial washing." This is why the Hindu reformer Vivekananda said that "it is a sin to call a person a sinner." To such people, steeped in the illusion of self-salvation, the cross is a stumbling block—until in despair (as one convert expressed it to me) they are driven by their own Hindu scriptures, which say there is no forgiveness, to Jesus who says there is, since he died to secure it and offers it to us freely.

A second hindrance to the spread of the gospel has been imperialism, and the Western appearance of the Christianity many missionaries planted. "Everywhere," wrote Roland Allen in 1912, "Christianity is still an exotic." Similarly, Stanley Jones, the American Methodist missionary, championed what he called the "naturalization" of Christianity in India. He ended his book *The Christ of the Indian Road* (1925) with an illustration drawn from an Indian marriage custom: "The women friends of the bride accompany her with music to the home of the bridegroom ... that is as far as they can go. Then they retire, and leave her with her husband." Just so, he argues, the missionary's "joyous task" is to introduce Christ to India and then to retire. "We can only go so far—he and India must go the rest of the way."

Yet western missionaries have not always displayed this modesty. In Bishop Lesslie Newbigin's words in *The Finality of Christ* (1969), they have sometimes confused the *tradenda* (the fundamentals of the faith which must be handed down) with the *tradita* (traditions which we have received, but are not indispensable), and have passed on the latter with the former, "a whole mass of stuff ... everything from harmoniums to archdeacons." It is only with slowness and hesitancy that the Indianization of Christianity is taking place.

The third hindrance to the evangelization of India I am reluctant to mention, because I cannot do so without implied criticism of my Indian brothers and sisters. But it is they who have expressed this matter to me, and I am only passing on their own convictions. It concerns the lack of moral discipline in the

churches, and the toleration in church members of such acknowledged evils as caste discrimination, corruption, and litigation.
These are public sins, which cause a public scandal. Until there
is repentance and renewal, one cannot expect the church to be
an effective agent of the gospel.

In spite of these three hindrances, there are many encour-
agements today.

It is wonderful to watch the development of indigenous Indian
missions, especially the Indian Evangelical Mission formed by
the Rev. Theodore Williams, and the Friends' Missionary Prayer
Band, whose founder-president is Dr. Sam Kamalesan. The FMPB
now has 155 missionaries (mostly in the unevangelized regions
of North India), 31 candidates in training, and the stated goal of
440 missionaries by the end of 1982. All these Indian missionaries
are supported by Indian money. Moreover, they are finding great
receptivity to the gospel in many Hindu villages. In one area of
South India, which has previously been totally resistant to the
gospel, and in which there is no church building for miles around,
100 baptisms are now taking place each month.

————————

The resolve to evangelize is not limited to the missionary agencies, however. The 1977 All India Congress on Mission and
Evangelization at Devlavi addressed its call to "all Christians in
India." Pointing out that 98 percent of evangelistic effort was being
directed towards the existing Christian community, it called for
a redirection of concern and action towards the responsive seg-
ments of the unreached 97 percent of the population. The All India
Conference on Evangelism and Social Action followed in 1979. Its
Madras Declaration called for the gospel to be visibly demonstrated
in Christian action against poverty, injustice, and corruption.

So there is a mood of confident expectancy among evangelical Christians in India today. The Rev. P. T. Chandapilla, general secretary of the Federation of Evangelical Churches of India, spoke to me in Madras in January about the importance of the growing evangelical compassion for the poor and the necessity of good works of love to authenticate our gospel preaching. It is in this context that "We are seeing the greatest turning to Jesus Christ which India has ever seen," he said, "especially in the tribal belts. For India there is no other option left."

John R. W. Stott, "Cornerstone: The Problems and Promise for Evangelism in India," *Christianity Today* 25, no. 7 (April 10, 1981): 80.

Part IV

THE CHURCH AROUND
THE WORLD

Chapter 22

———

A VISIT TO LATIN AMERICA

Six weeks' exposure to Latin America, even though it was a second visit and involved brief stops in seven countries, hardly constitutes a foundation on which to base an informed judgment. At the same time, it may not be inappropriate for me to voice some impressions.

There is no doubt that Latin Americans regard themselves as an oppressed people. Although their deliverance from the colonial rule of Spain and Portugal was achieved some 150 years ago, they do not feel economically or politically free. For example, Professor José Miguez Bonino begins his *Doing Theology in a Revolutionary Situation* (1975) with a historical analysis, which argues that Christianity entered Latin America in two distinct but equally oppressive stages, namely "Spanish colonialism (Roman Catholicism) and North Atlantic neocolonialism (Protestantism)." "The basic categories for understanding our history," he writes later, "are not development and underdevelopment but domination and dependence." Not that the domination is entirely from outside, however. Dom Helder Camara, Roman Catholic Archbishop of Recife in Brazil, is a courageous protester against continuing political and economic oppression

145

by Latin America's own right wing oligarchies and military governments: "It is a serious matter that, while external colonialism is ended ... the worst form of colonialism continues, I mean internal colonialism."

Now evangelical Christians have no business to ignore this situation, to declare that it is no concern of ours, and to attempt to defend our pietism by the quotation of texts wrenched from their total biblical context. God made man in his own image. He still does, in spite of the distortion of his image by the fall, and he sets himself against anything that undermines the full humanity of man. We should have no quarrel with liberation theologians, therefore, who see "humanization" as a proper goal for Christian aspiration; our quarrels with them are rather that they sometimes equate that process with the biblical understanding of salvation, tend to espouse both utopianism and universalism, and often resort to dubious exegesis to support their position. But when will evangelicals develop their own biblical theology of liberation? It is of little value to denounce if we have nothing better to offer.

Granted the Latin American consciousness of oppression, the visitor is bewildered by the variety of competing solutions that are being proposed. Maximum publicity is given to the minority who advocate violent revolution. If liberation from the Spanish *conquistadores* was won by violence, they argue, only violence today can wrest power from North American multinational corporations and Latin American oligarchies. Che Guevara remains a cult hero for many students. More challenging for Christians is the example of Camilo Torres, who was a Roman Catholic priest; a little over a decade ago he joined the Colombian guerrillas and was shot in action. "I took off my cassock to be more truly a priest," he declared, and "the Catholic who is not a revolutionary is living in mortal sin." Two things struck me as I read his writings. The first is his extraordinary naiveté. He imagined that Colombia was ripe for revolution and that, given leadership, the people would rise and seize power. But he lived in a dream world of his own; his policies lacked realism. More important, they lacked a biblical base. His justification for violent revolution was founded, paradoxically, on the command to love our neighbor. For "only by revolution," he reasoned, "by changing the concrete conditions of our country, can we enable men to practise love for each other," that is, by bringing food, clothing, and education to the majority. But he made no attempt to reconcile his advocacy of violence with the non-violent teaching and example of Jesus.

It is with relief that one turns to the writings of Dom Helder Camara, whom one might describe as the Martin Luther King of Latin America. "My personal conviction," he said, "is that of a pilgrim of peace ... personally, I would prefer a thousand times to be killed than to kill." This is not because he has a weak social conscience, however. He bases his nonviolence partly on the requirements of the Gospel, and partly on the demands of realism. "Non-violence means believing more passionately in the force of truth, justice, and love than in the force of wars, murder, and hatred," he writes.

I also admire Archbishop Camara's discerning mind. He avoids blanket condemnations. What deeply troubles me in the contemporary debate is both the uncritical hostility to capitalism of many Latin Americans and the equally uncritical hostility to communism of many North Americans. Must we be so ingenuous in our use of slogan words? Dr. Miguez has been outspoken against capitalism, but in personal conversation with him in Costa Rica he explained that his attack is on "profit as an end in itself," whereas the proper goal for production should be "the satisfaction of human need." What evangelical can possibly disagree with this, without thereby enthroning greed rather than altruism as his motivation? Personally, I want to continue defending the freedom for creative human enterprise for which capitalism stands, but only if such freedom is responsibly controlled and is not made the excuse either for the spoliation of God's creation or for the exploitation of human beings made in his image.

What about socialism? Of course evangelicals reject the appalling brutalities committed in its name, and the materialistic philosophy and crushing of personal initiative with which it has been associated. But is that the end of the matter? Good Pope John XXIII dared to write in his encyclical *Pacem in Terris* (1963) that we should recognize in socialism "good elements worthy of approval." Evangelicals are foolish to turn a blind eye to the genuine idealism and solidarity with the poor and oppressed that undoubtedly motivate many young socialists. Significantly, when Ecuadorian Bishop Leonidas Proaño addressed a large gathering of Marxist students in Quito about the authentic, compassionate, and radical Jesus of the Gospels, the students responded, "If we had only known *this* Jesus, we would never have become Marxists."

So is there any solution to Latin America's problems? I am still convinced that there is more hope in evangelization than in any other single Christian option. We are under the authority of the Lord Jesus who has commissioned us. And nothing is more humanizing than the Gospel. Through it men and women begin to be remade in the image of God. Moreover, the Gospel of God's love supplies the most powerful of all incentives to rescue people from everything that dehumanizes them. But this assumes that we are proclaiming the true and full New Testament Gospel. We must not use the Gospel to administer fresh doses of opium to the people, inducing them to acquiesce meekly to the status quo by promising them joy and justice in the sweet bye-and-bye.

I think Dr. René Padilla is right when he insists that "there are no global solutions." He does not say this despairingly, however, but because he believes (as I do) that God's way is to supply in his new society a model of human community as sign of his kingdom, and to encourage his people to be innovative. For example, Christian social action can include such enterprises as Christian cooperatives like those initiated by John Perkins for his people in Mississippi, a Christian medical center operated voluntarily by Christian doctors and medical students in their spare time as in the Dominican Republic, community development schemes as at Huaylas in Peru, the literacy and development programs sponsored by Alfalit in several countries, Gregorio Landero's combination of evangelistic and social work on the coast of Colombia, the improvement of agricultural techniques for Indians as in Northern Argentina, and even the founding of a bank by Christian graduates as in Venezuela. One ardently hopes that Christian missions in Latin America will increasingly seek to promote such projects alongside evangelization; without the accompanying good works the Gospel lacks credibility.

John R. W. Stott, "Cornerstone: A Visit to Latin America," *Christianity Today* 21, no. 23 (September 9, 1977): 49–50.

Chapter 23

"UNHOOKED" CHRISTIANS

I n one of Latin America's larger cities a group of Christian students, disenchanted with the local churches, has dropped out. Now they meet on their own and call themselves *cristianos descolgados,* literally "unhooked" (like a picture taken down from the wall) or "unattached Christians." Talking some time ago to a pastor who knew them well, I asked the causes of their disillusion. He said that they lack serious biblical and expository teaching and social concern, that they've seen a blatant gap between what was taught and what was lived, and that the laity, especially young people, have not been allowed to participate in or even contribute to church programming.

In another Latin American city a crowd of students had just returned from a camp. The Lord had met with them and they glowed with enthusiasm. Several of their friends had been converted. They were so excited that they had even (mistakenly, as I believe) baptized these converts in a river. Now the anticlimax had set in. "Why can't we form our own university church?" they asked. I had a hard time persuading them to stay in their local churches and to seek to be instruments of reform in God's hands.

This kind of disaffection is doubtless part of the worldwide revolt against institutional authority. But it is serious among Christians precisely because the Church ought not be the kind of oppressive structure or privileged establishment against which modern youth feel bound to revolt. In the secular world leaders "exercise authority," Jesus said, but added, "it shall not be so among you." He came to create a different kind of community, and he initiated a new style—leadership by service.

So the young, with their strong loathing for the inauthentic, quickly detect any dichotomy between the Church and its founder. Jesus has never ceased to attract them. They see him as the radical he was, impatient with the traditions of the elders and the conventions of society, a merciless critic of the religious establishment. They like that. But the Church? Somehow it seems to them to have lost the "smell" of Christ. So many vote—with their feet. They get out.

Is it possible, then, to spell out what the Church's priorities should be? Here is my own list. First, we need a preaching and teaching ministry that faithfully expounds the text of Scripture at the same time it relates to the burning issues of the day. Evangelical preaching tends to be biblical but not contemporary, liberal preaching contemporary but not biblical. Why must we polarize? It is the combination of the two that is so powerful. It is a rare phenomenon.

Secondly, we need a warm, caring, supportive fellowship. Young people hunger for the authentic relationships of love. Hobart Mowrer, emeritus professor of psychiatry in the University of Illinois and well known critic of Freud, though by his own profession neither a Christian nor a theist, once described himself as having "a lover's quarrel with the Church." Asked what he meant by this, he replied that the Church had failed him when he was a teenager and continued to fail his patients today. How? "Because the Church has never learned the secret of community," he said. Unfair perhaps, because some churches *are* genuine communities. But it was his opinion, which was born no doubt of bitter experience. I think it is the most damaging criticism of the Church I have ever heard.

Thirdly, we need worship services that express the reality of the living God and joyfully celebrate Jesus Christ's victory over sin and death. Too often routine supplants reality, and the liturgy (if any) becomes lugubrious. I think public worship should always be dignified, but it is unforgivable to make it dull. "The longer I live," said the late Archbishop Geoffrey Fisher, "the more convinced I am that Christianity is one long shout of joy." He was right. And the joy of worship needs to be more uninhibited than is customary, at least in some of our more stolid historic denominations.

Fourthly, we need an outreach into the secular community that is imaginative, sensitive, and compassionate. The true eccentricity of the Church is seen when it turns toward the world. Such an outgoing concern would combine evangelism and social action and would overcome the sterile polarity that has developed between the two. It would insist that if faith without works is dead, then good news without good works lacks credibility. It would also involve a renunciation of "clericalism," that is, the clerical suppression of the laity. Instead, all the members of the body of Christ would be active, their different ministries determined by their different gifts.

As I have thought about these four major signs of spiritual renewal in the Church, I have been struck that they were exactly the characteristics of the newborn Church on the day of Pentecost.

Those first spirit-filled Christians "devoted themselves to the apostles' teaching and fellowship, to the breaking of bread and the prayers. … And the Lord added to their number day by day those who were being saved" (Acts 2:42, 47 RSV). Wherever the Holy Spirit is present in power, the Church is always characterized by an apostolic doctrine, a loving fellowship, a joyful worship, and a continuous evangelism.

John R. W. Stott, "Cornerstone: 'Unhooked' Christians," *Christianity Today* 22, no. 1 (October 7, 1977): 36–37.

Chapter 24

ENGLISH-SPEAKING
WEST AFRICA

I t is surely impossible for any American or European Christian to visit West Africa without feeling embarrassed and even ashamed. There hideous slave-trade brought untold misery to the whole region for some 250 years. It is conservatively estimated that between thirty and forty million slaves were sold to the European colonies, and that as many perished on the voyage across the Atlantic. Dr. Kenneth Scott Latourette was not exaggerating when he referred to this as a "colossal evil." Nor was Malcolm X when he called it "the world's most monstrous crime." True, Christians took the initiative to get the trade abolished and the slaves freed, but before this both horrors had been tolerated for too long.

Then there is the colonial record. In her Reith Lectures published as *The Colonial Reckoning* (1961) Margery Perham, an expert in African affairs, paid tribute to those good things that the colonial powers bequeathed (from roads to schools and law courts). She conceded that the first imperial motivations were selfish (trade, security, and power), and that the philanthropic concept of serving the interests of the ruled rather than of the rulers developed much later, and then slowly. "When at last Africans woke to self-consciousness," she wrote, "it was to discover that as long as history recorded they had been ignored, enslaved, subjected, despised or patronized by the rest of the world." Africans felt themselves "humiliated rather than oppressed" and the quest for liberation was (and still is) less a cry for political independence than for human dignity.

In a chastened and humble mood I spent September visiting the five English-speaking countries of West Africa, beginning in Nigeria, continuing through Ghana, Liberia, and Sierra Leone, and ending in the little country of the Gambia. My responsibilities included pastors' conferences, student work, and some public meetings. Although the Anglican churches were in most cases involved in the planning, I was sponsored by the Scripture Union that, along with the Pan-African Fellowship of Evangelical Students (PAFES), has had a remarkable influence on the up-and-coming Christian leadership of the region.

Indigenization

In one of his books Dr. Lesslie Newbigin, formerly Bishop of Madras, playfully chides the early missionaries in South India for exporting all the paraphernalia of Western church life, "from archdeacons to harmoniums." The same could be said of West Africa. The anomalies are rather grotesque. Gothic spires rise above the coconut palms; some Anglican bishops don robes that are not only European, medieval, and Roman in origin but also in tropical heat and humidity a cruel punishment to wear. The continuing use of the Prayer Book liturgy of 1662 compels African tongues to get round archaic words like "vouchsaf' st," which we Anglo-Saxons can scarcely manage any longer. Hymns and choruses too—both words and music—are still mostly Western (at least in the older mission-founded churches), though Africa Christian Press has published *Living Songs* that includes some translations from local languages. It was a particular joy in Ghana to hear and watch the young people when at last they sang one of their native Twi songs. Only then did they become themselves. With loud voices and rhythmic body movements, accompanied by drums, handclapping, tambourines, and even the tapping of a knife on (of all things) an empty Coca-Cola bottle, they gave themselves up to worship, their eyes and teeth gleaming with uninhibited joy.

The main impetus toward the formation of the African Independent Churches has been a protest against alien cultural forms and the quest for an authentically African expression of Christian faith and life. Dr. David Barrett of Nairobi in his book *Schism and Renewal in Africa* (1968) has documented 6,000 of these churches; indeed it is reckoned that about one-fifth of Africa's total Christian community belongs to them. Peter Barker, literature secretary of the Christian Council of Ghana, has compiled a brief survey and directory of Christianity in Ghana, which is shortly to be published as *Five Hundred Churches*. Of these he shows that about 450 are "independent" or "spiritual" churches. Many have chosen picturesque titles like Nigeria's well known "Cherubim and Seraphim Church," or "the Church of the Lord Aladura" or "God is our Light Church." Some are distinctly heretical, and others make observers apprehensive because of their tendency to syncretism and their accommodation to such superstitious practices as jujus and medicine men. All of them raise serious questions about schism and the fragmentation of the church. Yet the majority of them seem to be genuinely Christian, confessing Jesus Christ as God and Savior, and we can only applaud their determination to develop genuinely African forms of Christianity.

Evangelization

European missionaries arrived in West Africa during the eighteenth century. Most of the repatriated slaves who began a new life of freedom in Liberia and Sierra Leone were Christians. And in the middle of the nineteenth century freed slaves in Barbados even formed "The West Indian Association for the Furtherance of the Gospel in Western Africa." Their first two missionaries landed in 1855 in what is now the Republic of Guinea. Yet from those beginnings one has to say with sorrow that the Gospel has not spread as widely or as rapidly as it should have. The exact Christian percentage of each country is hard to discover, but it ranges from about 53 per cent in Ghana to only 2 per cent in the Gambia, whose remaining 98 per cent is almost entirely Muslim.

During recent years, however, partly stimulated by the Berlin and Lausanne Congresses, a new zeal for the evangelization of the region has been emerging. "New Life for All" (an African version of Latin America's "Evangelism in Depth") began in Nigeria and has spread to other countries. Ghana, for example, now has four full time traveling secretaries who are promoting this program. Ghana also had its own congress on evangelism earlier this year, and several leading evangelicals are busy forming a "Christian Outreach Fellowship" to stimulate evangelism both in their own country and beyond. Nigeria had its first congress on evangelism in August of 1975, attended by 831 participants, and is now planning its second for August of 1978. They hope to attract up to 1,500 people and to follow the congress with "Operation Good News," which will aim to bring the Gospel to every Nigerian before the end of 1980.

Perhaps the most encouraging news of all is that ECWA (the Evangelical Church of West Africa, which, since 1893, has grown out of the labors of the Sudan Interior Mission) now has not only 1,400 churches in Nigeria but 260 missionaries belonging to its

"Evangelical Missionary Society." So far these are all working in Nigeria and its neighboring countries, but soon they are to begin work among the Muslim Nigerians of the Sudan, that is, among some of the tens of thousands who make the pilgrimage to Mecca annually but fail to complete the return journey.

Finally, we have to face the hindrances to evangelism in West Africa today. All the churches complain of the scourge of nominalism. "People are baptized and confirmed," Bishop Rigal Elisée of the Gambia said to me, "but that means nothing; what we need to understand most is how are we converted." Alongside nominalism go low moral standards, especially immorality at home and corruption in business. A third obstacle to effective witness is the disunity of the church, caused by tribalism and denominationalism. I have already mentioned the bewildering proliferation of independent churches. Also older Protestant churches have failed to come together. The proposed union in Nigeria between the Anglican, Methodist, and Presbyterian churches ended in December of 1965, only weeks before its inauguration; a similar plan ended in Ghana only days before. Since then hardly any fresh initiatives have been taken. Nevertheless, each country has its Christian Council that facilitates cooperation, and there are several united theological seminaries.

Evangelicals also are showing increasing signs of working more closely together. The third General Assembly of AEAM (the Association of Evangelicals of Africa and Madagascar) was held at the beginning of August in the Ivory Coast. The late lamented Byang Kato has been succeeded as General Secretary by another Nigerian, Tokunboh Adeyemo, who plans to return to Africa in December after completing his doctoral research at Dallas Theological Seminary. In Francophone Africa BEST (the Bangui Evangelical School of Theology) opened in October with about thirty students, and the African Evangelical Theological

Society has been launched by AEAM's theological commission. All this is encouraging news. My own prayer is that more and more evangelicals will offer themselves to God as instruments in his hand for the reformation and renewal of all West Africa's churches. Without this, the work of evangelization will continue to be impeded.

John R. W. Stott, "Cornerstone: English-Speaking West Africa," *Christianity Today* 22, no. 5 (December 9, 1977): 38–39.

Chapter 25

———

CHURCH AND STATE
IN ENGLAND

REFLECTIONS ON JUBILEE YEAR

Queen Elizabeth's triumphant Jubilee Year has just ended. It began on June 7 last year with a service of thanksgiving in St. Paul's Cathedral amid all the traditional pageantry that we British people love. Critics of the institution of monarchy are still vocal, but nobody can doubt the Queen's personal popularity. She is universally admired for her dedication, hard work, Christian faith, probity, and family life.

She is also the "supreme governor" of the Church of England, a title dating back to the sixteenth century. Pope Clement refused to annul Henry VIII's marriage to Catherine of Aragon. So Henry asserted the royal supremacy in the church in place of the papal supremacy.

During and after the Reformation period views on church-state relations ranged from the "Erastian" (that the church must be completely subordinate to the state) to the "theocratic" (that Christ had put both spiritual and temporal powers into the hands of the church). In sharp contrast to these the First Amendment proclaims the total religious neutrality of the United States Congress.

Here then are three positions that possibly deserve the description "extreme"—Erastianism (the state controlling the church), theocracy (the church controlling the state), and neutralism (the entire separation of the two). Must we choose between these alternatives? Or is there another way? Is it possible for church and state to be not separated but related in such a way that each serves, but neither controls, the other? I believe there is.

Distinctions and Definitions

In order to pursue this possibility it is important to distinguish between a "state" church, an "established" church, and a "national" church. In a state church the head of state is recognized as the church's chief authority; all citizens pay the church tax (unless they deliberately contract out); the state examines, appoints, and pays the clergy; and it settles ecclesiastical disputes. The European Lutheran churches are state churches. The Church of England, however, is not, since the state levies no church tax. An established church is so called because it has been "established by law" as the nation's official religion, is given certain privileges, and may be subject to a measure of state control. A national church is so called because it accepts a Christian responsibility—evangelistic, pastoral, and prophetic—to the whole nation.

Now both the Church of England (Anglican) and the Church of Scotland (Presbyterian) are at the same time established and national churches. Yet the Scottish model is the better and more biblical of the two, since the Church of Scotland is entirely free of state control and emphasizes national mission more than establishment, and therefore responsibility more than privilege. My thesis is that the Church of England has for more than half a century been moving in the Scottish direction and may before long catch up.

Criticisms of "Establishment"

There are two elements of the English model of establishment that are obnoxious to Christians with biblical sensitivity. They concern the control that the state exercises and the privilege it bestows.

Any kind of state intervention in, or control of, the church is intolerable. And gradually during this century the Church of England has been freeing itself from such control. In 1919 it was given a measure of self-government (from the "Parochial Church Council" to the "National Assembly"), and in 1969 full synodical government. Nevertheless, Parliament still retained its veto on church legislation (using it in 1928–29 to reject the revised Prayer Book). In 1974, however, the parliamentary veto was abolished, and the church was given authority to order its worship and interpret its doctrine, provided that it stayed within the doctrinal limits set by the 1662 Prayer Book.

Also in 1974 General Synod asked to be given the "decisive voice" in appointing bishops who had previously been appointed by the Queen on the advice of her prime minister, though after widespread behind-the-scenes consultation. Two years later Synod accepted the proposal that in future, whenever an episcopal vacancy occurred, a small, representative church committee would submit two names to the Prime Minister, who would no longer do any nominating himself. An overwhelming majority voted in favor of this (390–29), even if many did so not because they considered it an ideal arrangement but because they believed it was the best concession they could get without provoking a constitutional crisis. It at least gave the church the sole right to nominate (if not to elect or appoint) its own bishops.

The second distasteful element in the present establishment is that of privilege, in both social and ecumenical terms. Perhaps the best example is the fact that the twenty-six most senior bishops are ex officio members of the House of Lords. One is certainly thankful to have such a Christian voice in Parliament's upper house. But why should the Church of England have a privilege that is not granted to any other group in the country and that is denied to the other churches?

Reciprocal Duties of Church and State

According to the Lausanne Covenant, "it is the God-appointed duty of every government to secure conditions of peace, justice and liberty in which the church may obey God, serve the Lord Christ, and preach the gospel without interference" (para. 13). The biblical basis for this assertion is found in Romans 13 and First Timothy 2. The complementary duty of the church is to pray for the state and its leaders, obey its laws (within the limits set by Christian conscience), pay its taxes, be exemplary in citizenship, seek the nation's good, be the guardian of its conscience, and the pastor of its people.

These reciprocal responsibilities are likely to be accepted only in countries that have enjoyed a considerable Christian influence. In other situations the state oppresses and persecutes the church, as in Communist lands today. Where the state protects the church, however, and even establishes it, it is not inevitable that Christianity will become a civil religion and its leaders civil servants. A notable example to the contrary is Bishop George Bell who in the House of Lords during World War II outspokenly condemned the British government's indiscriminate bombing of German cities.

An acknowledgment or establishment of the church by the state can benefit both of them if they develop a partnership in which each recognizes its and the other's distinct God-given roles, and seeks to fulfill its own without trespassing into the other's. In the case of the Church of England this involves the resolve to complete the process of taking control of its affairs, to forfeit its unwarranted privileges, and as the national church, to exercise more conscientiously its evangelistic, pastoral, and prophetic responsibilities.

I find myself in agreement with paragraph K7 of the Nottingham Statement (April 1977): "We hope that our church will not seek to renounce, but to share with other Protestant churches, the ancient constitutional ties that establish her as the church of this realm. We value these, not for privilege but for service, not for the church but for the nation."

John R. W. Stott, "Cornerstone: Church and State in England: Reflections on Jubilee Year," *Christianity Today* 22, no. 7 (January 13, 1978), 36–37.

Chapter 26

THE LAMBETH CONFERENCE

T he eleventh conference of the bishops of the worldwide Anglican (Episcopal) Church concluded on August 13. The first (1867) was attended by 76 bishops, but this one brought 440 together plus 25 observers from other churches and 20 consultants of whom I had the privilege of being one.

This decennial assemblage of bishops is called the Lambeth Conference because the earliest conferences were held at Lambeth Palace, the official London residence of the Archbishop of Canterbury. But this year for the first time the conference was held out of London, at the University of Kent, overlooking Canterbury Cathedral in which Archbishop Thomas Becket was murdered in 1170. For the first time too the conference has been residential, permitting three weeks of communal living.

The Anglican Communion has recently been described by Edward Norman, Dean of Peterhouse, Cambridge, as "that ecclesiastical ghost of the deceased British Empire." It is a rather harsh judgment, however. For there are hardly any "colonial bishops" left. Instead, the twenty-five "provinces" into which this church of some 65 million Anglicans is divided are all autonomous, with an almost entirely indigenous leadership. Approximately one-third of the bishops who converged on Canterbury last month came from the Third World, about 150 from Africa, and 50 from Asia. We specially rejoiced that 20 bishops came from Uganda. President Amin flew them out in a special plane, with a large security escort and an invitation to the Archbishop to hold the next Lambeth Conference in Uganda.

It was typical of Donald Coggan, the president of the conference, being the man of God that he is, to emphasize that the overriding purpose was "prayer and waiting upon God." In his sermon during the opening service in Canterbury Cathedral he issued a mild rebuke to his brother bishops that "we have stopped listening to God," and went on to describe his ideal for a bishop as "one who is open to the wind of the Spirit, warmed by the fire of the Spirit, on the look-out for the surprises of the Spirit." So each day's program began before breakfast with a service according to the liturgy of one of the provinces and after breakfast with a devotional lecture.

Only then did we turn to the day's business, either in plenary sessions or divided into three sections or subdivided into thirty-three groups. These studied topics as varied as mission and ministry, politics, violence, conservation, social ethics, technology, the family, and ecumenical relations. Some people have mistakenly tried to draw an analogy between Vatican II and Lambeth XI, and in consequence their expectations have not been fulfilled. For the Lambeth Conference is a consultative, not a legislative body. Its only authority is moral and persuasive.

One of the thorniest issues before the conference was that of women priests (i.e., presbyters). On the one hand 150 women have already been ordained to the presbyterate (in Hong Kong, U.S.A., Canada, and New Zealand), and half the member churches have agreed to it in principle. On the other, the ordination of women has caused deep division, including a small schism in the American Episcopal Church, while both Roman Catholic and Orthodox Churches had plainly warned that an affirmative vote would jeopardize the continuance of Anglican talks with them. How, they asked, could one church, acting unilaterally, overthrow a universal tradition that had been unbroken for 1,900 years? In the end a confessedly compromise resolution was passed, securing 316 votes, with only 37 against and 17 abstaining. In it the conference recognizes the autonomy of its member churches, and encourages them to continue in communion and dialogue with each other; declares its "acceptance" both of those member churches that now ordain women and of those that do not; and emphasizes for the benefit of the Catholic and Orthodox Churches that this "holding together of diversity within a unity of faith and worship is part of the Anglican heritage." Many people were disappointed by the lack of theological debate. It was said that the arguments on both sides had by now been well rehearsed. But Archbishop Marcus Loane of Sydney reminded the bishops that the 1958 Lambeth Conference had declared the arguments "inconclusive," and that in his conviction they had still not been resolved. He pleaded with the conference not to dismiss the theological issues as if they were of no account. But his warning, and that of those who counseled a five-year moratorium, went unheeded.

Although a whole day was set aside for debate on this important question, I am glad to say that the bishops did not spend all their time on domestic matters. For the overall topic was "Today's Church and Today's World." When the conference first convened, Lady Jackson (alias Barbara Ward) and the Reverend Professor Charles Elliott delivered notable lectures on conservation and economics. In response, the bishops approved a statement that challenges many modern assumptions and values. They plead for a new kind of society in which technology becomes the servant of the people, the economy is based on stewardship rather than waste, changed attitudes toward work and leisure are developed, the necessity of a redistribution of wealth and trade is faced, and progressive world disarmament is achieved. They passed another resolution on "war and violence," and a third on "human rights and dignity," which was originally put forward by some of the African bishops but was later universalized.

I was disappointed that comparatively little was said about mission and evangelism. True, one group's report has a full statement about the relations between worship and mission, about evangelistic witnessing ("the spontaneous overflow of hearts filled with Christ"), about the urgent need for cross-cultural missionaries ("there are still millions of people in the world who have never heard of Jesus Christ or had an adequate opportunity to respond to him"), about social action, and about the need for the church to be radically renewed, since "mission without renewal is hypocrisy." But the resolutions themselves, which alone carry the authority of the whole conference, almost ignore the subject. Bishop Festo Kivengere proposed an amendment to a resolution on dialogue, stating that "dialogue can never be a substitute for proclamation," and calling on member churches "to respond with greater obedience to our Lord's unfulfilled commission." But it was narrowly defeated. Strange. I cannot believe that Anglican bishops have now washed their hands of evangelism; it is more charitable to guess that they had not fully understood the purport of Bishop Festo's amendment.

John R. W. Stott, "Cornerstone: The Lambeth Conference," *Christianity Today* 23, no. 1 (October 6, 1978): 34–35.

Chapter 27

EVANGELICALS IN NORWAY

G ottfried Osei-Mensah and I were privileged to be guest speakers at the Norwegian Lausanne Conference near Oslo over the first weekend of September. This visit to Norway was for me an occasion of special pleasure because my ancestors were Vikings. Since *Stut* is Norwegian for a bull, it is presumed that they were cattle-breeders who on one of their raids in the North of England decided to stay. I am thankful not only to have piratical blood in my veins, but also that my pagan Norse forebears were introduced to Christ in England.

There is another link between Norway and England of which I enjoyed reminding my Norwegian friends, namely that while Norsemen were plundering England, the English were evangelizing Norway. True, the first Scandinavian converts had been won by Anskar, "the apostle of the north" (A.D. 801–865). But it was King Olaf Tryggvasson and King Olaf Haraldsson, both originally Viking chiefs, who after their conversion at the beginning of the eleventh century, invited English clergy to evangelize and teach their people. Canute (1016–1035), king of England and Denmark (which then included Norway), completed the process of Christianizing Norway. Consequently, Kenneth Scott

Latourette could write, "The Church in Norway was the offspring of the English Church."

In the sixteenth century, King Christian II of Denmark and Norway championed the Reformation and the clergy quickly became Lutherans. Yet the religious revivals of the eighteenth and nineteenth centuries constituted a kind of second reformation. Its key figure was Hans Hauge (1771–1824). He was a farmer who had a profound evangelical conversion experience in 1796 and then, as Norway's equivalent to John Wesley, traveled widely, preached and wrote about personal repentance and holiness, and also pioneered Christian social projects. Others followed him. It was a grass roots, lay movement from the beginning and led in due course to the formation of the Norwegian Missionary Society (1842), the Lutheran Inner or "Home" Mission Society (1868), and the Norwegian Lutheran Mission (1891). These organizations have all remained within the State Church, while at the same time jealously guarding their independence and preserving a decentralized structure. Between them they have several thousand local groups.

The Free Churches became legal in 1845 but have remained comparatively small. Five of them (Lutheran Free, Methodist, Baptist, Mission Covenant, and Free Evangelical Assemblies) have about 8,000 adult members each, totaling 40,000, which is also the number of Pentecostals. Still, 95 per cent of Norway's citizens remain members of the State (Lutheran) Church. The charismatic movement, which has brought renewal to a number of churches, is viewed as being in continuity with the earlier pietistic revivals and has been enriched and kept from excesses by good Lutheran theology.

Why is evangelicalism stronger in Norway than in the other Scandinavian countries? And why is it that at the fourth and fifth assemblies of the World Council of Churches at Uppsala and Nairobi, respectively, the most forceful theological analysis of ecumenical positions came from the Norwegian delegation, who also on both occasions threatened to withdraw? The answer surely lies in the Free Faculty of Theology, which this year celebrates its seventieth anniversary. In 1908 faithful evangelicals were shocked by the governmental appointment to the University Theological Faculty of a New Testament professor who denied the deity of Jesus. This symbol of liberal infiltration into the church convinced many of the need to start again. So Professor Sigurd Odland resigned his post in the University and founded with others the Free Faculty of Theology. It opened with eight students, but today has about 1,000, some 600 of whom are studying for the pastorate and other church ministries. This means that four-fifths of the State Church clergy train at the Free Faculty. Not that its evangelicalism has escaped question. A few years ago the greatly respected Carl Wisløff retired three years earlier than he need have done in protest against what he judged to be liberalizing tendencies in the Free Faculty.

What about the state connection? It has a long history. It is also defended by senior evangelical leaders on the ground that it preserves the unity of the church and the freedom of conservatives. Certainly it has not muzzled the church. For example, during the terrible five-year Nazi occupation of Norway, courageous leadership of the resistance movement was given by Bishop E. Berggrav of Oslo. In the last decade church-state tension has steadily increased. The government has introduced legislation on Christianity in state preschools that challenges the teaching of Christian values, and on sex discrimination that has led to the ordination of about twenty women priests; this is felt by many to have been an unwarranted imposition by the state. A yet more direct clash took place in 1975 when a bill to make abortion available more or less on demand was strenuously opposed by all ten bishops. When the bill was passed, Bishop Per Lønning resigned. As government pressure on the church grows, so also does the demand—especially among younger clergy—for church freedom. "We need more space for breathing in the Christian way," Bishop Haakon Andersen said to me. "It is only a matter of time," added a theologian of the Free Faculty, whose lecture was reported in the press.

The Lutheran Church of Norway has been one of the pioneers in evangelical student work. Informal Scandinavian student groups were meeting already at the end of the nineteenth century, and in 1895 the Scandinavian Student Christian Movement (SCM) was formed. Theological problems soon arose, and in 1924 the Norges Kristelige Student og Gymnasiastlag (*Laget* for short) came into being, with an evangelical constitution. Its members' evangelistic zeal was evident from the start. They were concerned about their contemporaries who deserted the Oslo churches each weekend in order to go hiking (in the summer) and skiing (in the winter) in the mountain area nearby. So in 1933 they got busy hauling logs and themselves built "The Chapel of the North Forest," which now has residential as well as canteen facilities. Every Sunday evening the students organize their own evangelistic services there, and many have been won for Christ.

In 1934 the first international student conference was held in Oslo. The main speaker was Ole Hallesby who was the acknowledged evangelical leader in Norway from 1920 to 1960, and whose books *Prayer, Conscience,* and *Why I Am a Christian* have been read with great profit by generations of students. "It is God's hour," he said at the conference; "it is an unspeakable privilege to move forward at God's time." He was referring to the possibility of an international evangelical student movement. Further international conferences were held almost annually, and then after the war the International Fellowship of Evangelical Students (IFES) was formed in 1946, with Hallesby as its first honorary president.

In my travels in different parts of the Third World, I have constantly been impressed by the fine quality of the missionaries sent out from Norway. Their numbers are extremely impressive too. From a country of 4 million people, of whom only 2 per cent are regular churchgoers (though 12 to 15 per cent are thought to be converted Christians), no fewer than 1,536 missionaries are at present serving, the largest number (703) being in sixteen countries of Africa. The thirty-eight Norwegians who came to the Lausanne Congress returned with much enthusiasm, and within just over six months had formed the Norwegian Lausanne Committee under the chairmanship of Bishop Erling Utnem. Because of his ill health he has been succeeded by Sigurd Aske who, introducing the Conference for Christian Leaders in early September, said that the Lausanne Covenant had given them "a path to follow amid a world of theological uncertainty and ecumenical pluralism."

As a lost son of Norway, who had temporarily returned to his fatherland, I felt proud to have connections with such a vigorous Christian community.

John R. W. Stott, "Cornerstone: Evangelicals in Norway," *Christianity Today* 23, no. 3 (November 3, 1978): 39–40.

Chapter 28

———

THE CHRISTIAN
CHURCH IN BURMA

*"Tell the missionaries that there are now twice
as many Christians as when they left."*

In May 1978 the Burmese government published 10,000 Bibles. Christians there are grateful for this gesture and interpret it as a token of religious freedom. Further, the Burmese government permitted U Aung Khin, General Secretary of the Burma Christian Council, to attend an ecumenical conference in Singapore last November. This lifting of a fifteen-year travel ban raises everybody's hopes that soon more Burmese Christians, isolated from fellow believers for so long, will be able to taste again the joys of the international Christian fellowship.

Although a few Roman Catholic missionaries visited Burma from the seventeenth century onwards, it was through the devoted labors of Adoniram Judson (1788–1850) that the Christian faith took root in Burmese soil. A graduate of Brown University and Andover Seminary, Judson reached Rangoon in 1813. Soon after his arrival, he wrote in his journal that he and his wife Ann partook of the Lord's Supper together, just the two of them, believing "the command as binding and the privilege as great as if there were more." Although Judson was a gifted linguist and worked long hours every day at language study, it was six years before he felt able to preach in Burmese. Meanwhile, he had been witnessing to individuals. His son Edward in the *Life* (1883) describes the resistance that he encountered to the Gospel of salvation, since Buddhism teaches that "there is no God to save, no soul to be saved, and no sin to be saved from."

On 27 June 1819, however, a thirty-five-year-old man named Moung Nau was the first Burmese convert to be baptized. "O may it prove the beginning," Judson wrote, "of a series of baptisms in the Burman Empire which shall continue in uninterrupted succession to the end of time!" His prayer was answered in his lifetime, for when he died in 1850 he left more than 7,000 baptized Burmans and Karens in sixty-three churches. Edward wrote, "He had laid the foundations of Christianity deep down in the Burman heart where they could never be washed away." Today there are about 400,000 Baptists in Burma, while nearly 400 students are receiving theological education.

Yet the price Judson paid was considerable. By unremitting self-discipline he translated the whole Bible into Burmese, wrote tracts, a catechism and a grammar, and completed the English-Burmese section of a dictionary. He was widowed twice, lost several children, suffered long separations from his family and was afflicted with much illness. Then in 1824, at the outbreak of the first Anglo-Burmese war, because he was suspected of being a spy, he had to endure eleven months in the death-prison of Ava (the ancient capital), in chains, filth, heat, and stench, and ten more months of custody after that. In thirty-seven years of missionary service he returned home to the United States only once.

The Anglican mission in Burma started forty years after Judson's arrival. The Society for the Propagation of the Gospel (SPG) sent out J. E. Marks, a fine Jewish Christian, whose vision for Christian education led him to establish in Rangoon St. John's College (for boys) and St. Mary's College (for girls) in 1864 and 1866 respectively. The somewhat Anglo-Catholic tradition of the SPG is balanced by the evangelical emphasis of the Bible Churchmen's Missionary Society (BCMS), which in 1924 sent A. T. Houghton to Mohnyin in Upper Burma, where he began Anglican work among the Kachins and the Shans.

Last year both Baptists and Anglicans enjoyed centenary celebrations. The Kachin Baptist Convention recruited 300 young people as volunteer missionaries, trained them for forty days and then sent them out in teams of ten to fifteen on a three-year commitment. It is claimed that as many as 90,000 Baptists converged on Myitkyina for the festivities, and that one day in a nearby river no fewer than 6,200 converts were baptized in possibly the largest baptismal service ever held in the history of the church.

The Anglicans also are active in evangelism. All expatriate missionaries had left Burma by the end of 1966. But up in Kachin State some of the clergy could say with smiling faces last year: "Tell the missionaries that there are now twice as many Christians in our area as when they left." They have a three-year program of lay training and evangelism. Each year after harvest three centers are visited by a team of five clergy including the local bishop. They stay for ten days of intensive teaching and training, followed by a week of practical experience, after which local teams visit the surrounding villages. About 250 were trained in this way during the first year.

The Burmese people belong to several diverse tribes, and their territory is part of the Indo-Chinese peninsula, with India on their northwestern border, and China and Laos to the northeast.

So the government's fear of insurgency is readily understandable. But they need have no fear of the Christians, who now number about a million, or 4 per cent of the population, and whose only revolutionary program is the love and peace of Jesus Christ. The remarkable spirit of Adoniram Judson lives on today among Burmese Christians. Francis Wayland, author of the original *Memoir* (two volumes, 1853), wrote of his "inherent love of excellence," while his son Edward declared that "prompt and straightforward obedience to Christ was the keynote of his life." Perhaps more important even than his uprightness and obedience, however, was his faith. Asked one day whether the prospects were bright for the speedy conversion of Burma, he replied "as bright as the promises of God."

John R. W. Stott, "Cornerstone: The Christian Church in Burma," *Christianity Today* 23, no. 9 (February 2, 1979): 30–31.

Chapter 29

CHALLENGING THE
CHRISTIANS DOWN UNDER

*Creeping secularization, cultural pluralism, and the
aboriginal population are high on the agenda.*

A well-known evangelical preacher in a well-known evangelical church in the United States, who was about to visit Australia to speak at a Christian convention, was being farewelled by his congregation. "Lord," prayed a venerable deacon, his gray beard twitching with emotion, "protect our beloved pastor from those wild Australians." His sentiment accorded well with the myth, cherished by many Americans, that Australia is an untamed country of bush and billabong, inhabited by koalas and kangaroos and jolly swagmen.

Although the present reality is vastly different, Australians are still coming to terms with their history. "One of the ghosts in our past which still haunts us," said Manning Clark, the historian, in his 1976 Boyer Lectures, is "the bloody encounter between the white man and the black man," while the other is "the use of cheap convict labor to plant civilization in Australia."

Today at least three major challenges face Australian Christians. The first is secularism. Although the 1976 census reveals that 78 percent of the population still profess to be Christians, there was a "mass swing of the sixties and seventies away from God and church" (see Leon Morris, "Christians in Australia," Jan. 19 issue). The weekly church attendance of Protestants is now less than 20 percent, while in the 21- to 24-year age group it is only 9 percent.

This creeping secularization is due less to an intellectual rejection of the gospel than to the apathy that materialism brings. Although there is some poverty—especially among working class migrants—the majority of Australians are very comfortably well off. It was Donald Horne who in 1976 coined the expression "the lucky country." The label has stuck, but in a sense in a different way from that intended by its originator. He meant that Australia had become a modern industrial country more by good luck than by good management. But what Australians usually mean when they use the expression of themselves is that their country's vast natural resources guarantee their affluence, and its sunshine their health and enjoyment.

The second challenge is that of cultural pluralism. Before World War II virtually all Australians were of British descent. People referred to Britain as "the old country" and described a trip there as "going home." But after the war there was a planned influx of Italians, Dutch, Germans, Yugoslavs, Poles, Austrians, and especially Greeks (Melbourne is now the third largest Greek-speaking city in the world, after Athens and Thessaloniki), while more recently immigrants have been arriving from Turkey, Egypt, Lebanon, Latin America, and the Chinese dispersion. So the original homogeneous Anglo-Saxon culture no longer exists. In its place a multicultural society is emerging, in which the different ethnic groups are learning to respect each other. I know no better statement of the ideal of "integration" than that given in 1969 by Roy Jenkins when he was British Home Secretary. He defined it "not as a flattening process of assimilation, but cultural diversity, in an atmosphere of mutual tolerance." Thus the church has new opportunities to reach out to the growing numbers of Muslims and Chinese.

The third challenge is the Australian aboriginal population. It is thought that the Aborigines migrated to Australia from Asia some 20,000 years ago. When the European colonists arrived, there were probably 300,000 of these simple people, hunters and food gatherers, divided into more than 600 tribal groups, speaking more than 200 languages, and regarding the whole continent as theirs. The decimation of the aboriginal population was appalling. Many died of European diseases, while others were ruthlessly slaughtered, until by the mid-1930s there were only about 60,000 "full blood" Aborigines left. (The aboriginal population has more than doubled since then, and it is estimated that it may be back to 300,000 by the end of the century.)

The Aborigines were also dispossessed of their land. "Unlike other British colonial territories, Australia was claimed and occupied without negotiation of a treaty, without any act of purchase and without any payment of compensation." So writes Frank Engel, former general secretary of the Australian Council of Churches, in a recent paper.

Worse even than the Aborigines' loss of life and land was their loss of morale. "It is my thesis," wrote the aboriginal author Kevin Gilbert in *Living Black*, "that Aboriginal Australia underwent a rape of the soul so profound that the blight continues in the minds of most blacks today."

Most of the churches have missions to the Aborigines, and have a reasonable record of bringing them education and health care in addition to the gospel, and of helping to champion their rights and preserve their identity. It is thought that perhaps 75 percent of them are now nominally Christians. Only a few Christian Aborigines have been ordained to the pastorate, however, although the number is growing. The Aboriginal Evangelical Fellowship was founded earlier in this decade and draws about a thousand to its annual convention. As yet, however, there is little liaison between them and white evangelicals.

For three weeks in May, Billy Graham conducted his third crusade in Sydney; 95 percent of the churches cooperated in the Crusade. The statistics are astonishing. Eleven thousand people enrolled in the counseling classes, and more than 2,500 prayer groups were formed. On April 22, 30,000 Christians visited a million homes. Then, in spite of unseasonable cold and rain, huge crowds came to the Randwick Racecourse each night, growing to 85,000 on the final Sunday afternoon. At each meeting more than 1,000 responded to the invitation, a high proportion of whom had no church affiliation; thousands of small nurture groups are now caring for them. Mass media coverage was overwhelming, and landline radio relays were arranged in 130 centers. A team of associates held satellite crusades in other cities, and nearly 1,000 clergy and church workers enrolled in the week-long School of Evangelism, which it was my privilege to address on three mornings. Church leaders have spoken of the powerful impact the crusade has had not only on Sydney but throughout the nation. "My visit to Australia," said Billy Graham as he left, "has been one of the most satisfying experiences of my entire ministry."

John R. W. Stott, "Cornerstone: Challenging the Christians Down Under," *Christianity Today* 23, no. 20 (August 17, 1979): 30–31.

Chapter 30

BRAZIL:

THE SPIRITUAL CLIMATE

*The biggest surprise is the spell spiritism
has cast over the country.*

"Latin America is a region of untold natural wealth and untold human misery." Such is the evaluation of Derek Winter, former Baptist missionary in Brazil, in his *Hope in Captivity* (1977). Similarly, a UN report a few years ago described two-thirds of the population as "physically undernourished to the point of starvation in some regions," while illiteracy varied in different countries between 20 percent and 60 percent, and millions had no medical care at all.

Brazil shares these problems, with its industrial achievements and modern cities on the one hand and its inhuman "favelas" (slums) on the other. And Brazil dominates the South American continent, for it encompasses nearly half the land mass of Latin America and is larger than the United States without Alaska. It is in the context of this enormous social need that the Christian churches are called to witness and to serve.

The biggest surprise awaiting the Christian visitor to Brazil is the spell spiritism has cast over the country. Its origin goes back to the African slaves who were imported in the middle of the sixteenth century to work on the sugar plantations. Today 15 percent of the population are negroes, and two of the most popular spiritistic cults—Macumba and Umbanda—are clearly Afro-Brazilian. Other types give evidence of Hindu influence, especially Kardecism (named after the Celtic poet Alan Kardec), which teaches Karma and reincarnation. The greatest tragedy, however, is not spiritism's mixture of African and Asian religions, but its identification of the deities of African traditional religion with Christian saints, and the weakness of the Roman Catholic Church in tolerating such syncretism.

The popularity of spiritistic cults has been variously explained. Some trace it to the hunger for transcendence many churches are failing to satisfy; others to the desire for physical healing, personal blessing, or business success that spiritism promises; while the many educated people who have embraced it appreciate its offer of a complete world view, without too many embarrassing ethical demands, and even claim that it is the logical completion of Judaism, Christianity, and Islam. It presents one of the biggest challenges to Christianity in Brazil, for there are said to be about half a million active mediums, 15 million professed members, and (according to some) a fringe following of up to 50 million, which is approaching half the population of the country.

Ever since Pedro Alvaras Cabral took possession of Brazil in 1500 in the name of the king of Portugal, however, it has been overwhelmingly Roman Catholic in its nominal allegiance. Today at least three different forms of Catholicism compete with one another—traditional, charismatic, and revolutionary. Traditional Catholicism continues to give Protestants big problems. True, the era of physical violence to Protestant churches, pastors, and members has passed. Also without doubt there is some sincere Catholic devotion to Christ. Yet popular syncretism and super- stition remain rife, particularly in relation to the virgin Mary and the saints, and are deeply distressing to the evangelical con- science. One fears that Pope John Paul II on his forthcoming visit, because of his outspoken veneration of Mary, will not speak out (as he should) against those attitudes and practices that under- mine the sufficiency of Jesus Christ. Instead, perhaps the growing movement of Catholic charismatics, whose personal commit- ment to Christ appears to be very real, will register their protest against everything that is derogatory to his unique glory.

Liberation theology, a largely Roman Catholic phenomenon, is said to have given birth to "a new breed of Christians." It has to be understood against the background of the colossal social prob- lems of Latin America. The Roman Catholic bishops expressed themselves on these problems at their two most recent meet- ings, namely at Medellín in Colombia (strongly) and at Puebla in Mexico (less strongly), and in 1970 the Brazilian bishops, meet- ing in Brasilia, urged their government to initiate social reforms, give the opposition a voice, and investigate allegations of torture. Blanket approvals and disapprovals of liberation theology are equally inappropriate; what is needed is a critical evangelical assessment. I will make only three basic points.

First, we should have no quarrel with the goal of human lib- eration. On the contrary, with our biblical doctrine of the created dignity of human beings, everything that dehumanizes should arouse our indignant opposition, and everything that humanizes, our enthusiastic support. Our criticism is that liberation theolo- gians tend either to emphasize humanization at the expense of salvation or even to equate the two.

Second, we should welcome these theologians' insistence on "praxis," that is, on active Christian involvement on behalf of all needy and oppressed people. For, as Paul put it, "faith works through love." We should therefore agree with Professor José Miguez Bonino in his *Doing Theology in a Revolutionary Situation* (1975) that "love ... demands efficacy. It is not content to express and demonstrate, it intends to accomplish" (p. 114). Our criticism concerns the form this commitment will take. I for one accept neither that Marxism is "the unavoidable historical mediation of Christian obedience" (Miguez, p. 98), nor that revolutionary violence is the way to secure justice for the oppressed.

Third, the evangelical debate with liberation theologians needs to focus on the hermeneutical question. They are right to urge us to scrutinize more critically our cultural presuppositions, since our theologians often mask our ideologies. But I do not find them equally suspicious of their own hidden ideological presuppositions, and sometimes their biblical exegesis appears to be totally unprincipled.

Although the Dutch invaded Brazil in the second quarter of the seventeenth century, Protestantism in general reached Latin America between 1870 and 1890. Church historians criticize its arrival for having been just as "colonial" as the introduction of Portuguese Catholicism in the sixteenth century: the European Protestant churches brought their ecclesiastical culture with them. Moreover, those churches that have clung to their traditions and have failed to become authentically Brazilian are in steady decline today. The two Protestant church groups that continue to experience growth are the Baptists and (especially) the Pentecostals. The Brazilian Baptist Church registered an 8.8 percent growth in 1978, has doubled its membership in eight years to about half a million baptized members, and hopes to double it again by 1982, its centenary year. This denomination has more than 4,000 churches, and 72 missionaries in other lands.

Most of us are aware of the phenomenal explosion of the Pentecostals, but may not have inquired into its causes. They attribute it, of course, to the work of the Holy Spirit. But since he uses means, it is not improper to ask what these have been, particularly in relation to the alternatives of Catholicism, spiritism, and Marxism.

First, Latin American Pentecostalism has been described by Lalive D'Epinay as a "haven of the masses." Certainly most of its members are peasants and workers, socially marginalized people who have found security and significance in their church. Second, Brazilian Pentecostalism is very evidently not a foreign import, but genuinely indigenous and exuberantly Latin, as its worship and music testify. Third, both Catholicism and spiritism have accustomed Brazilians to an easy acceptance of the supernatural, and Pentecostals take it for granted that exorcism and healing are readily available through the power of the Holy Spirit. Fourth, the doctrine of the Body of Christ is so central to their beliefs that they encourage lay ministries and expect every church member to be active in evangelism.

Although there have been seemingly endless splits, which to me are regrettably schismatic, yet these have also enabled charismatic leaders to develop their own spheres of service (as in the African Independent Churches) and so have contributed to church growth. Our prayer should be that, in addition to evangelists, God will give conscientious pastors and teachers to these churches, so that their members may become stable, holy, and mature in Christ.

My visit to Brazil last January was sponsored by the Aliança Biblica Universitaria do Brasil, the Brazilian Inter-Varsity movement. Founded officially in 1963, it has active groups in the universities and high schools of more than 60 cities. It seeks to minister to students caught in the conflict between the old world and the new. They and the Christian graduates or "professionals" constitute a fine resource for the future Christian leadership of their country.

John R. W. Stott, "Cornerstone: Brazil: The Spiritual Climate," *Christianity Today* 24, no. 7 (April 4, 1980), 32–33.

Chapter 31

___

PROTESTANT UNITY
IN YUGOSLAVIA

*Rivalry among the many ethnic factions has
historically spilled over into the churches.*

66 **Y**ugoslavia is the despair of tidy minds." With these unprom-
ising words—discouraging to those who struggle to understand it—Trevor Beeson begins his chapter on the country in
Discretion and Valour (1974). He describes it as a "minefield" for
would-be commentators, however sensitive and well informed.
I have tried to heed his warning: after a brief visit I can share
only the tentative gleanings of my reading, looking, and listening.

Artificially created in 1918 out of territories that were previously Austrian, Hungarian, Italian, and Turkish, Yugoslavia is
now a "Socialist Federal Republic." The historical rivalry between
the Serbs (42 percent) and the Croats (22 percent), and between
10 other ethnic groups, continues unabated. It is unfortunately
exacerbated by religious differences. Most of the inhabitants of
Serbia, Bosnia and Hercegovina, Montenegro and Macedonia are
traditionally Orthodox, while Croatia and Slovenia are strongly
Roman Catholic: to diverge from these traditions is regarded as

disloyalty to one's cultural heritage. In addition, large areas of the south are predominantly Moslem. Throughout the country, 11 percent of the people are Moslems, while official figures put self-styled atheists as high as 12 percent.

Being part of Eastern Europe (though regarded as "Western" by the Soviet bloc), Yugoslavia is of course committed to communism. Yet President Josip Broz Tito, who won the eternal gratitude of Yugoslavs (movingly expressed in the nationwide tributes at his funeral) by leading their freedom fighters in the repulse of the Germans in 1944, also boldly rejected the Moscow line in 1948. Since Stalin's death in 1953, under Tito's continuing leadership the country has enjoyed reforms in the direction of a mixed economy and, generally, an increasing measure of religious freedom.

The history of relations between church and state in Yugoslavia is complex, and the tide of religious freedom has ebbed and flowed. At first, in keeping with their Marxist ideology, the Communist leaders proclaimed their conviction that religion would wither and die. Yet the first constitution of 1946, while affirming the separation of church and state, and prohibiting all political activities by the church, guaranteed freedom of belief and worship. The oppression of the Roman Catholic church in the late forties and early fifties had strong political overtones. The tension between Yugoslavia and Italy was exacerbated by the Vatican's "interference" in the affairs of the Roman Catholic church. Diplomatic relations between Yugoslavia and the Vatican, ruptured in 1952, were resumed only in 1970 after the Protocol of 1966 reaffirmed both the state's guarantee of religious freedom and the church's renunciation of political activity. An organization called "Christianity Today" was founded in 1967 with a view to promoting the spirit of Vatican II.

In the early seventies, government fears that Croat nationalism and Communist revisionism were threatening the national unity led to a renewal of repressive activity, from which the church also suffered. But now the pendulum has swung again. Although there is still some antireligious propaganda in the schools and the army, and the public expression of religious faith is restricted to religious buildings (except for baptisms, weddings, and funerals), yet the profession, practice, and propagation of Christianity is unhindered. Bibles and Christian literature are on sale even in secular bookshops, and Christians are not being harassed.

Protestant Christians at less than 1 percent of the population are what Stella Alexander in *Church and State in Yugoslavia Since 1945* (1979) rightly calls "only a minute proportion of the inhabitants of Yugoslavia." They include Lutherans, Reformed, Baptists, Pentecostals, Methodists, and Christian Brethren. In spite of their small numbers the Protestant churches have not enjoyed very cordial relationships with each other. There has often been competition instead of cooperation.

It was thus an earnest of good things to come that about 150 pastors and church leaders (two or three times as many as had been expected) participated in a seminar during the weekend after Easter. Coming from six denominations, all parts of the country, and many age and language groups, they constituted an extremely varied gathering. Indeed, this was the first interdenominational pastors' conference ever to be held in Yugoslavia. (One or two of those present had scarcely met since the Lausanne Congress.) The seminar took place at the Baptist Theological School in Novi Sad, 50 miles northwest of Belgrade. Its conveners were Stjepan Orčić, the principal of the school, Dr. Branko Lovreć, a Baptist layman who is a physician turned editor and publisher, and Peter Kuzmić, the young director of the Biblical Theological Institute (Pentecostal) in Zagreb. In addition, it had the good will of Dr. Josip Horak, dean of the Theological Faculty in Zagreb (founded in 1976), although he was not able to be present, while

Bishop Struhárik of the Slovak Lutheran church and Bishop Csete of the Reformed church both sent personal representatives.

The theme of the weekend was "Aspects of the Church Today." Expository biblical studies were given on Christ's will for his people (John 17), the marks of a Spirit-filled church (Acts 2), evangelism (1 Thess. 1), ideals of pastoral ministry (1 Thess. 2), unity and diversity (Eph. 4), and the church in society (Matt. 5 and 6). Groups then discussed this biblical teaching in relation to their local situations. The seminar was entirely free of acrimony and tension. Instead, the Holy Spirit gave an extraordinary degree of love, joy, and peace. Leaders who had been critical of one another, and not even on speaking terms, were seen worshiping together, laughing together, and embracing one another.

On the final day, the groups expressed a unanimous wish to continue such meetings, and to establish an evangelical fellowship that would both express their common evangelical identity (agreeing on the primary biblical doctrines, while respecting each other's viewpoints on secondary matters) and facilitate cooperation. This was only a beginning, of course, but it was unanimously decided to send to all evangelical pastors in Yugoslavia the proposed basis and aims of the fellowship, together with a summary of the group reports, and to invite both individuals and local churches to join. We need to pray that God himself, who so manifestly began this good work after Easter, will bring it to full maturity. I counted it a great privilege to be present at what others described as a "historic" meeting, and I got a considerable kick out of hearing myself referred to in Serbo-Croat as "Bratta Stotta" (brother Stott) by the middle-aged and as "Tatta Stotta" (daddy Stott) by the young people.

John R. W. Stott, "Cornerstone: Protestant Unity in Yugoslavia," *Christianity Today* 24, no. 13 (July 18, 1980): 38–39.

Chapter 32

———

POLAND'S POWER OF
THE PROLETARIAT

The major weakness of Protestantism is fragmentation.

For more than a millennium, ever since Mieszko I became a Christian in the year 966, Poland and Roman Catholicism have been practically synonymous. "Probably no country in the world," writes Trevor Beeson in his *Discretion and Valour* (1974), "is more tenaciously Catholic. *Polonia semper fidelis* was the motto of the old Polish gentry and bourgeoisie, and neither passage of time nor radical political change requires this motto to be modified." The election of a Polish pope may require it rather to be underlined. The knowledge that a Pole reigns from the Vatican has given a great lift to Polish Catholic morale.

More than 95 percent of the population are Roman Catholics by baptism, and it is claimed that more than 75 percent attend church regularly. Communism's failure to win the mind and soul of Poland is largely due to cultural heritage and national identity. For Communism smacks of Russia, as Protestantism smacks of Germany, and both countries are traditional enemies; to be a loyal son or daughter of Poland one must be a Roman Catholic.

Moreover, the church has been able to retain considerable educational authority over its people. Young people are expected to receive religious instruction for an hour or two a week at one of 18,000 "catechetical points" throughout the country. Even many party leaders' children conform to this pattern. Nor is there any sign that Roman Catholic influence is diminishing. New churches are being built, and 10,000 men are in training for the priesthood in the 27 diocesan seminaries or for one of the orders in the 35 special seminaries. In addition, there are four Academies of Catholic Theology and two full-blown Catholic Universities.

If we ask what kind of Catholicism prevails in Poland, an equivocal answer has to be given. On the one hand, Pope John Paul II's June 1979 message in Warsaw centered on Christ. Without Christ, he boldly affirmed, it is not possible for man to understand or to fulfill himself. Also, a few charismatic prayer groups are meeting, and the "Oasis" movement encourages young people to read the Bible, pray, and serve. On the other hand, traditional Catholic piety continues, and an official church document refers to the "Marian character of Polish Catholicism." The principal Marian shrine is at Czestochowa, southwest of Warsaw, and contains the world's most famous image of the virgin. Since 1656 the Virgin Mary has been proclaimed "the Queen of Poland." When the Pope visited the shrine in 1979, the Christ-centered Christianity he had expressed in Warsaw seemed to become Mary-centered again. Our Protestant conscience is troubled, and our evangelical theology affronted, by this unbiblical devotion to Mary.

How do Protestants fare in Poland, then? They constitute a tiny minority of about 100,000 Christians, or less than one-third of 1 percent of the population. The major weaknesses of Protestantism, according to a paper by Karol Karski, were from the beginning elitism and fragmentation. The latter continues. Even in cities in which several Protestant denominations maintain small and struggling churches, there is little fellowship or cooperation between them. And of course the Roman Catholics both notice this and take advantage of it. At least, however, Protestants have since 1945 enjoyed a certain brotherly association through the Polish Ecumenical Council, although they are outnumbered by the Orthodox and Old Catholic Churches.

Poland's largest and most ancient non-Roman church, dating from the fourteenth century, is the autocephalous Orthodox church, with nearly a half-million members, especially Ukrainians. The two Old Catholic churches, which do not acknowledge the papal primacy, are the "Mariavites" of Russian origin and the "Polish Catholic Church": they have nearly 60,000 members between them. The Lutherans now number about 80,000, the Evangelical Reformed church about 4,500, the Methodists 4,000, and the Baptists 3,000, while the United Evangelical Church (a federation formed in 1947 of two Pentecostal churches, the Christian Brethren, the Evangelical Christians, and the Churches of Christ) has a membership of about 9,000 baptized adults. The Polish Ecumenical Council maintains close links with the Christian Theological Academy in Warsaw, which came into being in 1954, and enjoys a direct continuity with the earlier Evangelical Theological Faculty at Warsaw University. It has Orthodox, Old Catholic, and Evangelical sections, which have independent programs but unite for some lectures and worship services, so that virtually all the non-Roman ministerial candidates (120 at the moment, from 10 churches) are trained in it.

The dominant Roman Catholic church is obliged to live with, but does not acquiesce in, the present system of inequity. For how can it be just for the Roman Catholic 95 percent of the country's 35 million people to be controlled by the 3 million who are registered as Communist party members? To be sure, the church enjoys more liberty in Poland than in any other East European country. Roman Catholic chaplains are still appointed to army units, hospitals, and prisons. Nevertheless, the church is still inhibited in a number of ways. Its children are indoctrinated in the schools and taught a rewritten history of Poland; it has no access to the news media; its ecclesiastical appointments have to be endorsed by the state; and all its manuscripts have to be submitted to government censorship.

Yet there is a large degree of free speech. In answer to my question about religious freedom in Poland, Dr. Witold Benedyktowicz, superintendent of the Methodist Church and president of the Polish Ecumenical Council, replied: "We can do everything, except perhaps street preaching, which in any case is not a Polish tradition. We can also say anything from the pulpit. Catholic bishops, in their pastoral letters ... at times criticize and even attack the government."

———————————

Are Christians free to evangelize? Billy Graham's visit to Poland in October 1978 seems to indicate they are. He was received by high government officials, was interviewed on national television, and seized the opportunity at the international press conference to proclaim the gospel to the many journalists present. Although his visit was sponsored by the Baptist Church and the Polish Ecumenical Council, the Roman Catholic church cooperated by placing their largest buildings at his disposal and by encouraging their people to attend. Many did so and responded positively to his message.

Yet evangelism is beset with peculiar difficulties. How are Roman Catholics to be reached who, though baptized and even practicing churchmen, nevertheless have no personal knowledge of Jesus Christ as Savior and Lord? This was the question that exercised the Methodist ministers whose conference I attended in May. They recommended the use of Christian homes for evangelistic Bible studies, since Vatican II encouraged Bible reading among the laity, and since Roman Catholics who might feel unable to attend a Protestant church have no comparable embarrassment about entering a Protestant home. The Methodist ministers acknowledged the need to develop programs to train their members in personal witness. They also emphasized that the reality of the living God must be visibly demonstrated both in the reverence of their public worship and in the love of their community life.

John R. W. Stott, "Cornerstone: Poland's Power of the Proletariat," *Christianity Today* 24, no. 17 (October 10, 1980): 50–51.

Part V

—

CHURCH CHALLENGES

Chapter 33

———

ANGLICAN EVANGELICALS
SPEAK OUT

A merican evangelicals whose only acquaintance with Anglicanism is with the Episcopal Church of the United States are often surprised to discover the strength of evangelical witness within the Church of England. Since the end of World War II the evangelical movement within England's national church has steadily grown and deepened. Starting as a despised minority, it became politely tolerated and is now a force that is respected by most, is looked to for leadership by some, and can be ignored by none.

The Church at large became aware of this development in 1967 when about a thousand people gathered at Keele University for the first National Evangelical American Congress. A decade later, just after Easter this year, nearly two thousand assembled at Nottingham University for the second, with the theme "Obeying Christ in a Changing World." The pre-congress study material had been published in three paperback symposiums entitled *The Lord Christ, The People of God,* and *The Changing World.* At the congress itself the authors responded to the responses they had received to these, and then the debate was taken a stage further in innumerable study groups. The participants (two-thirds of whom were lay men and women) threw themselves with evident relish into three and a half days of hard intellectual work. And each morning and evening in plenary session we celebrated the supreme Lordship of Jesus Christ with great joy.

Now the 20,000-word Nottingham Statement has been published by Falcon Press (50 p.). It claims to be neither a comprehensive nor an authoritative declaration of what Anglican evangelicals believe, for it contains both gaps and a few inner contradictions, and no part of the text received a final endorsement from more than one of nine subplenary sessions. Nevertheless, the Nottingham Statement does claim to be a faithful expression of the mind of the Nottingham Congress. It should stimulate and provide material for further debate.

In the statement, familiar evangelical beliefs are reasserted with conviction, but also often with a difference. For example, the Incarnation is called "the foundation truth on which Christianity rests" (para. B.1), and "the bishops of the Church of England as guardians of its doctrine" are solemnly called upon "to confirm the church's historic faith concerning the person of Jesus Christ the Lord" (B.2). At the same time, Jesus is declared to be "a real man in every way," and we confess that "we have not always taken full account of Jesus' humanness" (B.3). The "divine inspiration of Scripture, its entire trustworthiness, the sufficiency of its teaching for salvation, and its unique authority" are all reaffirmed (D.1), for "it is our abiding evangelical conviction that in order to obey Christ we must obey Scripture" (A.7). At the same time, we confess our failures in study and obedience, and we commit ourselves to a "creative listening" to the text that takes with proper seriousness the cultural horizons of both biblical author and Bible reader (D.2).

On the subject of mission, after an appreciative reference to the Archbishops' "Call to the Nation" in 1975, the hope is expressed that "some kind of 'Mission to the Nation' may follow it." Important convictions are then added that "regional enterprise is greatly preferable to a centrally imposed plan," and that "every coordinated evangelistic effort requires a common statement of faith and purpose, a diversity of approaches and methods, and a commitment to continuous outreach" (A.4).

The large central section of the statement is devoted to contemporary church issues that we evangelicals have sometimes ducked. The Church's identity is refreshingly redefined in terms of a threefold "commitment"—to "Christian truth" (Scripture as God's revelation and the creeds as the historic expression of Christian faith), to "a Christian lifestyle" (including the two sacraments of the Gospel), and to an "every-member ministry" (E.3). This latter point receives particularly strong emphasis. "Christianity is a one-caste religion. All Christians are equally called to minister to Christ in the world. ... Clerical professionalism has gravely inhibited the proper development of the diversity of ministries. We deplore the prevalent pattern of 'one-man ministries.' ... The New Testament pattern is always for a group of presbyters to form the leadership" (J.1 and 2). Moreover, "we repent of our failure to give women their rightful place as partners in ministry with men," a statement balanced by the qualification that many believe preserves a permanent biblical truth: "Leadership in the church should be plural and mixed, ultimate responsibility normally singular and male" (J.6).

Two sections bravely tackle questions of church unity as they relate both to the "Ten Propositions" now being debated by English churches and to the Roman Catholic Church. Our goal is reaffirmed on biblical grounds as a unity that becomes visible when Christians "not only share in a common baptism and a common confession of faith, welcome each other to the Lord's Table and work together in mission, but also merge their institutional structures to the point where there ceases to be any concept of 'each other' but only of a common life of all" (L.1). The present state of play in Anglican-Roman Catholic discussions is described: it is firmly but courteously stated that "agreement on fundamental doctrines must precede any formal act of reunion" (M.1); and some penetrating requests are made for clarification, e.g., whether the Roman Catholic Church now places itself under Scripture "as the final authority under Christ," whether it teaches that sinners are "justified by grace through faith, with their good works a fruit of justification and not a source of merit," how "the Eucharist is related to Christ's sacrifice," and what standing the Marian dogmas have (M.2).

On the thorny issue of establishment, the hope is expressed that the Church of England "will not seek to renounce, but to share with other Protestant churches the ancient constitutional ties that establish her as the church of this realm." "We value these," it is judiciously added, "not for privilege but for service, not for the church but for the nation," that is, in order that the church may accept its mission to the nation and its responsibility to be the nation's conscience (K.7).

The third section of the Nottingham Statement takes up questions of social ethics that were only broached ten years previously at Keele, and then with naïveté and tentativeness. Now, however, there are thoroughly thought through paragraphs on "power in our democracy" (which challenge "the accepted norm that ever-growing economic prosperity is the sole aim of a responsible society" and call for "real participation by the whole community in political power"—N.3 and 4), on "the power of the media" (both weighing their effects on society and welcoming the opportunities they afford for "human creativity in artistic terms"—P.1–3), on "the law and education" (Q.1–3), on "marriage and the family" (including also references to the single life, homosexuality, divorce and remarriage, and the differing roles of men and women—R.1–8), on "responsibility in mission" (in a multi-racial society, in urban areas, and in the world—S, T, and U), and on "global stewardship" (with reference to such matters as harvesting the world's resources, human rights, government aid, multi-national corporations, and simple lifestyles—V.1–10). It is extremely heartening to see evangelical Christians seeking to apply their biblical faith to such complex problems of today.

Looking back on the Nottingham experience, I was struck by the spirit of love, joy, and openness that characterized the debates. We by no means always agreed with one another, but we were given grace to listen to others with a new level of respect. Ten years ago at Keele we were not yet ready to face the charismatic controversy; at Nottingham it seemed already to belong to the past. The recent publication of the agreed evangelical statement *Gospel and Spirit* had defused it, and we expressed our "wish to live and work together from now on without any sense of the 'them and us' to which both sets have often been accustomed" (L.5). Several other areas of disagreement emerged. For example, the section on "power in our democracy" was thought by some to be faintly pink in color, and so includes an "alternative statement" (N.8) that was evidently written in a bluer ink. But the determination to face such differences in love and not conceal them is to be seen as a mark of growing evangelical maturity.

Besides, Nottingham (though important) was only an episode in our continuing domestic evangelical dialogue.

John R. W. Stott, "Cornerstone: Anglican Evangelicals Speak Out," *Christianity Today* 21, no. 19 (July 8, 1977): 30–31.

Chapter 34

EVANGELICALS AND
ROMAN CATHOLICS

"From the tyranny of the Bysshop of Rome and al hys detest-able enormities ... good lord, deliver us." Not a particularly Christian sentiment, one might think! But then it dates from long ago, as the quaint spelling indicates: the Litany of the English Prayer Book of 1552. The full petition contains references to both "tyranny" and "heresy," which reminds us that at the Reformation English nationalism went hand in hand with the recovery of biblical truth. Then for four long centuries there was virtually no rapproachement, only hostility and polemic.

What, then, should the attitude of evangelicals toward the church of Rome be *now,* since the astonishing *aggiornamento* that began with Vatican II, when the call was sounded to "let 'the word of the Lord run and be glorified' (2 Th. 3:1), and let the treasure of revelation entrusted to the Church increasingly fill the hearts of men" *(Dei Verbum* 26)? I have often asked myself this question and have always found it difficult to answer.

For what exactly is the church of Rome that one can relate to it? The old illusion of a monotholic structure has been shattered.

Today it appears almost as pluriform as Protestantism. What does it believe and teach? Has it really changed? Or is its old boast of changelessness and irreformability true?

Sometimes still our Protestant consciences are scandalized, as when in his "Credo of the People" Pope Paul described the redeemed as being "gathered round Jesus and Mary" in heaven. At other times a Catholic theologian will make a statement so Bible-based and Christ-centered that one wants to shout three cheers, give him a hug, and call him an evangelical.

But then another Catholic leader comes along with a counter-statement that takes us right back to the old theological liberalism we thought we were growing out of. Thus in his monumental *On Being a Christian* Hans Küng can assert that "the Scriptures are not themselves divine revelation; they are merely the human testimonies of divine revelation ..." (Haven't you heard that before somewhere?) Again, the Bible neither *is* God's word nor even *contains* it, he writes, but "the Bible *becomes* God's word ... for any one who submits trustfully ... to its testimony and so to the God revealed in it and to Jesus Christ." (Is Hans Küng also among the Barthians?)

In this confused condition of the Roman church, we must go on courteously pressing our evangelical questions. Reunion with Rome is inconceivable without the reformation of Rome. I recently signed an open letter (emanating from Latimer House, Oxford, and the Church of England Evangelical Council) that is addressed to the archbishops and bishops of the Anglican communion and that concerns relations between Anglican churches and the Roman and Orthodox churches. It expresses great joy over our common concern "for real and tested theological agreement as a pre-condition of closer churchly relationships." But it goes on to ask searching questions, e.g., whether the non-Reformed churches are yet ready "to test all their traditions ... by

Holy Scripture, as we shall seek to test ours, in order to amend what the Bible will not justify," and whether "justification" is indeed "God's free gift of acceptance, bestowed on sinners by grace alone, in and through Christ, and received by God-given faith alone." For if Vatican II was right that there is "a hierarchy of truths," then the doctrines of scriptural supremacy and free justification have preeminence among them.

This leads me to say that I fear that Archbishop Donald Coggan's call for Roman-Anglican intercommunion (which the Pope rebuffed) was premature. I know that there are some Roman Catholic communion services in which absolutely nothing is said or done that would offend evangelical consciences. I know too (and rejoice) that the so-called "Agreed Statement on the Eucharist" (though it has no authority in either church) unambiguously asserts that Christ's death on the cross was "the one, perfect, and sufficient sacrifice for the sins of the world," and that "there can be no repetition of or addition to what was then accomplished once for all by Christ." Again, I know that the word "transubstantiation" is not in the text of the agreement. Yet it is still there in a footnote as the traditional word Catholics use to indicate the "change in the inner reality of the elements" that is thought to take place. So, speaking personally, I do not think I could bring myself to participate in a Roman Catholic mass, even if it were authorized, until the doctrinal stance of the church has been officially reformed.

Instead, the right way forward seems to be that of personal friendship, joint Bible study, and candid dialogue with Roman Catholics. For this reason I was delighted to be a part of the Evangelical-Roman Catholic Dialogue on Mission, which took place in Venice in April. The eight-member Roman Catholic team had been appointed by the Vatican Secretariat for Christian Unity, while the eight evangelicals were an ad hoc international group, including Bishop Donald Cameron of Sydney, Australia, Professor Peter Beyerhaus of Tübingen, and Dr. David Hubbard, the president of Fuller seminary. We discussed the meaning of the words "mission," "salvation," and "conversion" and the possibilities of a common witness. Although we came together with some fears and suspicions of one another, soon the caricatures were discarded, and through patient listening we came to know, respect, and love one another in the Holy Spirit. We spent one evening sharing our personal experiences of Jesus Christ and our testimonies to him, and we rejoiced to recognize God's grace in one another.

For myself, I was constantly astonished to hear a Roman Catholic brother (or sister, for Joan Chatfield of the Maryknoll Sisters was a member of the Roman Catholic team) cite a biblical text in a discussion, quoting chapter and verse from memory. Nothing surprised me more, I think, than our degree of consensus on baptism. I have always supposed that Roman Catholics had a mechanical view of baptism and regarded all baptized people as *ipso facto* regenerate Christians. But no! They were in full agreement with this statement: "Baptism must never be isolated, either in theology or in practice, from the context of conversion. It belongs essentially to the whole process of repentance, faith, regeneration by the Holy Spirit, and membership of the covenant community, the church. None of us accepts a mechanical view of baptism."

We hope to meet again and to tackle in greater depth some of the main issues that still divide us. I find myself hoping and praying that evangelicals worldwide will take more initiatives to develop friendly conversations with Roman Catholics based on common Bible study. It would be tragic indeed if God's purpose of reformation were frustrated by our evangelical standoffishness. One of the Nottingham Congress's final "Declarations of Intent" concerned Roman Catholics and said: "We renew our commitment to seek with them the truth of God and the unity he wills, in obedience to our common Lord on the basis of Scripture."

John R. W. Stott, "Cornerstone: Evangelicals and Roman Catholics," *Christianity Today* 21, no. 21 (August 12, 1977): 30–31.

Chapter 35

———

ARE EVANGELICALS
FUNDAMENTALISTS?

D r. James Barr, Oriel Professor of the Interpretation of Holy Scripture in the University of Oxford, is one of our leading British theologians. He will probably be remembered for his contribution to the hermeneutical debate in *The Semantics of Biblical Language* (1961), in which he convincingly argues that the meaning of a word is to be determined less by its etymological history than by its contemporary use in context. He has written four major works since then.

Last year, however, he wrote a very different kind of book, *Fundamentalism*, which is not dispassionate but polemical, and which fiercely attacks fundamentalists or conservative evangelicals (whom he refuses to distinguish from one another). Our whole position is "incoherent," even "completely wrong" (p. 8), he asserts. Indeed, to him "fundamentalism is a pathological condition of Christianity" (p. 318), so that, far from it being "the true and ancient Christian faith," he is not even sure if it comes "within the range that is acceptable in the church" (pp. 343–44).

Two introductory comments need to be made. First, Barr refers several times to the research that lies behind his book, and claims that he has made a "very thorough review of fundamentalist literature" (p. 9). This is a false claim. He relies too heavily on the Scofield Reference Bible, which he calls "perhaps the most important single document in all fundamentalist literature" (p. 45), and popular presentations like the New Bible Commentary and New Bible Dictionary. He is unfair—even rude—to Norman Anderson and Michael Green, almost ignores F. F. Bruce and Howard Marshall, and does not begin to do justice to the reasoned argumentation of J. I. Packer in his *Fundamentalism and the Word of God* or J. W. Wenham in his *Christ and the Bible*.

I do not think he is any more surefooted when he turns to the American evangelical scene. He refers to Hodge and Warfield, the Princeton giants, and he quotes E. J. Carnell and G. E. Ladd appreciatively. But he has not read Carl F. H. Henry, for he refers to only one of his books and includes only two quotations from his pen, both of which he has taken from other authors.

My second general comment concerns his object in writing the book. It is not to change our minds, he says, but to understand and describe our "intellectual structure" (p. 9). This is strange. If we are so completely mistaken, should he not want to alter our opinions? The book is not a serious theological debate; he has little or no respect for the people he is criticizing. His tone ranges from the cynical and the patronizing to the contemptuous and even the sour. He attributes ignorance, prejudice, and hypocrisy to us. He also accuses us of making no "serious attempt to understand what non-conservative theologians think" (pp. 164 and 316). This may be true of some of us, but I fear that the boot is also on the other foot. *Fundamentalism* has increased my own determination that in all religious debate I will respect the other person, listen carefully to him, and struggle to understand him. There can be no understanding without sympathy and no dialogue without respect.

————————

In criticizing Barr's selectivity and tone, I am far from saying that we have nothing to learn from his attack. Here are three sensitive areas in which I think we should listen to him.

First, *tradition*. "The core of fundamentalism resides not in the Bible but in a particular kind of religion" (p. 11), he writes. That is, the religious experience and consequent tradition of evangelicals is normative for us, rather than Scripture. We "do not use the Bible to question and re-check this tradition"; instead, we "just accept that this tradition is the true interpretation of the Bible" (p. 37). This is often uncomfortably true. We do sometimes use our venerable evangelical traditions to shelter us from the radical challenges of the Word of God.

Secondly, *theology*. Fundamentalism, writes Barr, is "a theology-less movement" (p. 160). And the reason, he thinks, is that we are preoccupied with biblical studies and the defense of biblical authority. He gives no credit to the innovative work of Dutch theologians and some others, but as a generalization we cannot resist his stricture that we produce more biblical scholars than creative theological thinkers.

Thirdly, *interpretation*. Hermeneutics is Barr's own specialty, and here he scores some well-aimed points. "The inerrant text, given by divine inspiration, does not decide anything" (p. 302), he says. He is right. It needs to be understood and applied. But we evangelicals have always been much better at defending the authority of the Bible than at wrestling with its interpretation.

Dogmatic assertions about infallibility and inerrancy are no substitute for conscientious, painstaking studies.

Barr declines to accept a distinction between conservative evangelicals and fundamentalists, or even between "extremists" and "moderates." We are all lumped together in the same (to him) rather stinking manure heap. Is this fair? One of our characteristics is supposed to be "a strong hostility to ... modern critical study of the Bible" (p. 1). Yet he goes on to cite evangelicals who do attend to its historical and literary origins, while regarding them as inconsistent with their own principles. It is hardly just to condemn us for both doing and not doing the same thing, all in one breath.

My personal belief is that, in the original meaning of these terms, every true evangelical should be both a fundamentalist and a higher critic. In fact, I wrote that very thing in a small book as long ago as 1954. The original fundamentalist was insisting on such fundamental doctrines as the deity, virgin birth, substitutionary death and bodily resurrection of Jesus, in addition to the authority of the Bible, while the higher critic (as opposed to the lower or textual critic) was simply a literary critic who investigated the forms, sources, date, authorship, and historical context of the biblical books. But of course over the years both expressions have changed their image. The fundamentalist is now thought by many who use the term to be obscurantist, and the higher critic destructive, in their respective attitudes to Scripture.

Is there any difference, then, between an evangelical and a fundamentalist? I wonder if it is arbitrary to suggest the following distinction. The fundamentalist emphasizes so strongly the divine origin of Scripture that he tends to forget that it also had human authors who used sources, syntax, and words to convey their message, whereas the evangelical remembers the double authorship of Scripture. For this is Scripture's own account of itself, namely both that "God spoke to men" (Heb. 1:1) and that "men spoke from God" (2 Pet. 1:21). On the one hand, God spoke, deciding what he wished to say, although without crushing the personality of the human authors. On the other hand, men spoke, using their human faculties freely, though without distorting the message of the divine author.

This double authorship of Scripture naturally affects the way the evangelical reads his Bible. Because it is God's Word, he reads it like no other book, paying close attention to the context, structure, grammar, and vocabulary.

What if the two are in conflict? Barr is hostile to all harmonizers, to all (that is) who attempt to eliminate apparent discrepancies either between science and the Bible, or between different parts of the Bible, or between our theological understanding of the Bible and our historical critical methods in studying it. Here I find myself in almost total disagreement with him. Of course, if by harmonization is meant the twisting or manipulating of evidence, then it is dishonest. But it is not dishonest in the face of apparent discrepancies, to suspend judgment and continue looking for harmony rather than declare Scripture to be erroneous. On the contrary it is an expression of our Christian integrity, for it arises out of our basic conviction that there is only one living and true God, and that he is the God of Scripture and of nature, of theology and of history.

John R. W. Stott, "Cornerstone: Are Evangelicals Fundamentalists?," *Christianity Today* 22, no. 21 (September 8, 1978): 44–46.

Chapter 36

———

SEMINARIANS ARE
NOT TADPOLES

*Faith, life, and mission must be integrated
in the preparation of pastors-to-be.*

I have never been a seminary teacher—but please do not judge me unqualified to engage in the debate about seminary education. I was myself a seminary student once (though long ago); I have visited many theological colleges around the world, and seminarians have confided in me.

That something is wrong is generally conceded; the statistics of ministerial dropouts cannot be swept under the rug. The major cause is the gulf between the ideals of the seminary and the realities of the pastorate, which lead to disillusion, even to defection.

Some argue, "Jesus never founded a seminary," and call for their abolition; but this is a naive overreaction. Seminaries must maintain their goal of academic excellence. We need to learn from Prof. Richard Hofstadter who, in his *Anti-Intellectualism in American Life* (1962), traces the historical decline from the Puritan vision of the "learned minister" to the revivalist preacher who despises theology. Already by 1853, he argues, there was a widespread belief "that an intellectual clergyman is deficient in piety and that an eminently pious minister is deficient in intellect." Yet nobody who has felt the pain of Third World university students, as I have, who find themselves facing intellectual challenges their godly but uneducated bush pastor cannot even understand let alone help them meet, can doubt that the educational standards of the pastorate must keep rising with those of the population.

At the same time, theological students are not tadpoles—all head and nothing else. Their theologizing needs to encounter the spiritual, moral, and cultural ferment of the contemporary world: theology must be related to faith, life, and mission.

First, faith. All seminary professors hope that their students will be stronger believers when they leave college than when they entered. But how is their faith to ripen? The temptation is to try to coerce it.

Some seminaries thus require students to sign an elaborate doctrinal or denominational statement before they may enroll, and another before they may graduate. But how can we expect students to have a coherently articulated theology before they even begin serious theological study? And what kind of justice is it to make a degree dependent on toeing a party line instead of on successfully passing an examination? Other seminaries (particularly liberal ones) go to the opposite extreme. Far from trying to compel faith, they take a sick pleasure in trying to destroy it. They deliberately set out to undermine the beliefs a student brings to college.

These attempts to coerce faith or to demolish it make the same fundamental mistake: they confuse education with indoctrination. Indoctrination is incompatible with intellectual freedom, because by it the teacher tries to impose his or her mental authority upon the mind of the student. "The ideal educator," on the other hand, writes Arthur Koestler, "acts as a catalyst, not as a conditioning influence": he seeks to provide the stimulus and the context for free intellectual development.

Applying this principle to seminaries, wise students will choose one that is neither a hothouse nor a demolition yard, but a warm, supportive community of faith, committed yet open, reverent yet critical, in which they are encouraged to develop a Christian mind under the lordship of Christ, and so grow into Christian maturity. Only such a robust, first-hand faith can withstand the onslaughts of the unbelieving world.

Second, faith has to be related to life. A Christian mind is ineffective without a Christian character. The seminary needs to be a place that fosters personal growth and character formation, and expects theology to lead to doxology in both public worship and private prayer. It is a tragic example of declension from biblical standards that the principal gateway into the pastorate today is a theological examination, while a comparable examination of the candidate's character, behavior, moral standards, marriage, and home (as plainly required in 1 Timothy 3 and Titus 1) is seldom conducted.

How may seminarians be helped to grow up into Christ? Mainly, they need to find models in their teachers. Yet many complain that they feel alienated from their professors. Some seminaries try to solve this problem by appointing a chaplain, with special responsibility for the pastoral care of the students. This is good—but only if the faculty do not then regard their pastoral responsibility as having been delegated to him. To me the most impressive colleges are those in which professors and students meet one another regularly for fellowship, worship, discussion, and counseling.

A third dimension is needed for wholeness: mission. I have great sympathy for the advocates of TEE (theological education by extension) who emphasize that theological study is best done within one's own cultural setting, and not by being transported to some distant seminary. Although I do not myself believe that such on-the-job training is either required by the pedagogical example of Jesus or should even completely replace traditional seminary education, many seminaries need to do much more to break down the walls that divide them from the real world. Failure to do so encourages ivory tower theologizing, which proves inadequate after graduation and is a major reason for subsequent disillusionment.

Seminarians must, therefore, be personally and deeply involved in some form of mission, evangelistic or social or both. This should be on a regular basis, and in short midterm placements and vacations. Moreover, the theology taught in the seminary needs to be not only biblical, systematic, and historical, but also contextualized in the modern world. Some seminaries urgently need to develop a global perspective and a commitment to world mission. Others live in the past and concentrate on the defense and maintenance of ecclesiastical traditions. This may be right and necessary—but only if such traditions can stand the test of Christian scrutiny in the modern world.

Almost nothing is more important for seminarians than the development of skills in the hermeneutical task. How can they relate the ancient Book to the modern world? That is the paramount question. I would require all students to go to the movies and the theater as well as to the chapel and the classroom: screen and stage are mirrors of the world we live in. Classes need to discuss the contemporary culture exhibited there in order to develop a Christian response to it. Preaching is essentially the exposition of God's Word with such faithfulness and sensitivity that it makes a forceful impact on modern hearers. Yet pastors will never excel in this exacting discipline unless they have learned to soak themselves in both the sacred text and the secular scene, and to struggle with integrity to relate the one to the other.

Perhaps "integrity" is the key word. It is the quality of an integrated Christian, whose whole being has come under the liberating lordship of Jesus. An integrated Christian is growing in faith, life, and mission as a three-dimensional responsibility. It is to the development of such integrated Christian leaders that seminaries should devote themselves.

John R. W. Stott, "Cornerstone: Seminarians Are Not Tadpoles," *Christianity Today* 25, no. 3 (February 6, 1981): 54–55.

Chapter 37

———

PARALYZED SPEAKERS
AND HEARERS

The cure is recovery of Bible exposition.

Nothing troubles me more in church today than our Christian superficiality. So few of us are "mature in Christ." We deserve the rebukes Paul addressed to the Corinthians, for we are still babes when we should be adults, and need milk when we should be eating meat. While we rejoice at the astonishing statistics of church growth in some regions of the Third World, our euphoria should be tempered by the question of whether the growth is as deep as it is broad.

Observers differ in their diagnosis of the church's malady. For myself, I have no doubt that the major cause is what Amos called "a famine of hearing the words of the Lord" (8:11). E. L. Dargan, in his famous two-volume *History of Preaching,* sees the phenomenon partly as cause, partly as effect. On the one hand, a decline of spiritual life "is commonly accompanied by a lifeless, formal, unfruitful preaching," while on the other, "the great revivals of Christian history can most usually be traced to the work of the pulpit."

True, greater problems face modern preachers than their predecessors: much of contemporary culture is unfriendly to preaching. If the antiauthority mood makes many people less willing to listen to authoritative proclamation, the cybernetics revolution and the addiction to television make people less able to listen to anything. In addition, the atmosphere of doubt and the loss of confidence in the gospel have undermined the morale of many preachers. Thus there is paralysis at both ends—in the speaking and in the hearing.

The gravity of this situation becomes plain when we reflect on the biblical story, for the prosperity of God's people rose and fell according to their receptivity to his Word. Although his covenant with them was of his own initiative of grace, he yet hinged it on the condition "if you will obey my voice." Consequently, we hear him constantly appealing to them to listen, and complaining when they refused to do so: "I have persistently sent all my servants the prophets to them, day after day: yet they did not listen to me ... but stiffened their neck." These words are like a divine epitaph on the national grave. Similarly, in New Testament days Christ addressed his church through his apostles, instructing, admonishing, encouraging, and rebuking them. He still does. And the church's spiritual health depends on its response. A live church is always a listening church, but a deaf church is dead: that is the unalterable principle.

This is not to say that there are prophets and apostles in the church today with an authority equivalent to that of the biblical prophets and apostles, but that the preacher is called faithfully to expound their message. As he does so, God speaks, and the Holy Spirit brings the written Word to life. Hence the tremendous need for the church to recover the ministry of expository preaching. Christian preaching is not the proud ventilation of human opinions: it is the humble exposition of God's Word. Biblical expositors bring out of Scripture what is there; they refuse to thrust into the text what is not there. They pry open what appears closed, make plain what seems obscure, unravel what is knotted, and unfold what is tightly packed. In expository preaching the biblical text is neither a conventional introduction to a sermon on a largely different topic, nor a convenient peg on which to hang a ragbag of miscellaneous thoughts, but a master which dictates and controls what is said.

Exposition is not a synonym for exegesis, however. True biblical preaching goes beyond the elucidation of the text to its application. Indeed, the discipline of discovering a text's original meaning is of little profit if we do not go on to discern its contemporary message. We have to ask of every Scripture not only "What did it mean?" but "What does it say?" Perhaps it is the failure to ask both these questions, and to persevere with the asking until the answers come, which is the greatest tragedy of current preaching. We evangelicals enjoy studying the text with a view to opening it up, but we are often weak in applying it to the realities of modern life. Our liberal colleagues, however, tend to make the opposite mistake. Their great concern is to relate to the modern world, but their message is less than fully biblical. Thus almost nobody is building bridges between the biblical world and the modern world, across the wide chasm of 2,000 years of changing culture. Yet preaching is essentially a bridge-building exercise. It is the exacting task of relating God's Word to our world with an equal degree of faithfulness and relevance.

This earthing of the Word in the world is not optional. It is an obligation laid upon us by the kind of God we believe in, and by the way in which he has himself communicated with us, namely in Christ and in Scripture. In both he reached down to where the people were to whom he desired to disclose himself. He spoke in human language; he appeared in human flesh. Our bridges, too, must be firmly anchored on both sides of the cultural chasm, by refusing either to compromise the divine content of the message or to ignore the human context in which it has to be spoken. We have to plunge fearlessly into both worlds, ancient and modern, biblical and contemporary, and to listen attentively to both. Only then shall we understand what each is saying, and so discern the Spirit's message to the present generation.

If we are to build bridges for the Word of God to penetrate the real world, we have to take seriously both the biblical text and the contemporary scene, and study both. We cannot afford to remain on either side of the cultural divide. To withdraw from the world into the Bible (which is escapism), or from the Bible into the world (which is conformity), will be fatal to our preaching ministry. Either mistake makes bridge building impossible and noncommunication inevitable. On the one hand, we preachers need to be as familiar with the Bible "as the housewife with her needle, the merchant with his ledger, the mariner with his ship" (Spurgeon). On the other, we have to grapple with the much more difficult—and usually less congenial—task of studying the modern world. We have to look and listen and read and watch television. We have to go to the theater and the movies (though selectively), because nothing mirrors contemporary society more faithfully than the stage and the screen.

It has been a great help to me to have the stimulus of a reading group. Its members are intelligent young graduates (doctors, lawyers, teachers, architects, and others). We meet monthly when

I am in London, having previously agreed to read the same book, or see the same play or movie. Then we spend a whole evening together, share our reactions, and seek to develop a Christian response.

As the nineteenth-century German theologian Tholuck said, "A sermon ought to have heaven for its father and the earth for its mother." But if such sermons are to be born, heaven and earth have to meet in the preacher.

John R. W. Stott, "Cornerstone: Paralyzed Speakers and Hearers," *Christianity Today* 25, no. 5 (March 13, 1981): 44–45.

———

Chapter 38

SETTING THE SPIRIT FREE

WE CAN RECLAIM THE POWER OF
PENTECOST TO RENEW THE CHURCH

T he church is growing in many parts of the world; in some parts, very rapidly. But when the church grows rapidly, there is danger of a certain superficiality that deeply distresses sensitive Christians. In other places, the church is not growing. Its breath is stale, its growth is stunted, and its waters are stagnant.

Many people talk about the renewal of the church. Some speak of theological renewal, others of liturgical renewal, others of structural renewal, others of charismatic renewal, still others of pastoral renewal. We need the renewal of the church in all dimensions of its life.

Some people have such a narrow vision of the renewal of the church that they seek renewal of only a part, not the totality, of its life. All, however, agree that it is impossible for the church ever to be renewed without the work of the Holy Spirit. So the question is, What does a renewed church look like? What evidences does it give of the presence and the power of the Holy Spirit?

The answer to these questions is found in Acts 2, Luke's description of the Jerusalem church, indeed the first Christian church, when the people of God first became the Spirit-filled body of Christ. We learn from this description that a Spirit-filled Christian church has four major characteristics.

The First Mark: Study

The first characteristic is very surprising. If I had asked, "What do you think is the first mark of a Spirit-filled church?" I doubt very much if many would have thought of this: the first mark of a Spirit-filled church is its study. "They devoted themselves to the apostles' teaching," or "to the apostles' doctrine" (v. 42). They *devoted* themselves to it. They studied the apostles' doctrine. This was a learning and a studying church.

The Holy Spirit had opened a school in Jerusalem. He had appointed the apostles to be the teachers in the school, and there were 3,000 pupils in the kindergarten. The new converts were not enjoying some mystical experience that led them to despise their intellect. There was no anti-intellectualism. They did not despise the mind. They did not disdain theology, nor did they suppose that instruction was unnecessary. They did not say that because they had received the Holy Spirit, he was the only teacher they needed and they could dispense with human teachers.

Some people today say that, but these early, Spirit-filled Christians did not. They sat at the apostles' feet, they devoted themselves to the apostles' teaching, they were hungry for apostolic instruction. They were eager to learn all they could. They knew Jesus had authorized the apostles to be the infallible teachers of the church, so they submitted to the apostles' authority.

How can we devote ourselves to the apostles' teaching today? How can we submit to their authority? There is only one possible answer: the apostles' teaching has come down to us in its definitive form in the New Testament, which is precisely the teaching of the apostles.

When the canon came to be fixed in the second and third centuries, the test of canonicity was apostolicity. If it was not written by an apostle, does it come with the authority of the apostles? Does it contain the teaching of the apostles? Does it have the imprimatur of the apostles? Does it come from the circle of the apostles? If it was apostolic in one of these senses, then it was accepted as having a unique authority and therefore belonging to the canon of the New Testament Scriptures.

It is urgent for us in these days to recover an understanding of the unique authority of the apostles. They themselves were aware of it. They knew that Jesus had given them a unique authority, and the early church in the immediate post-apostolic period understood it very well, too. For example, Bishop Ignatius of Antioch, who flourished just after the last apostle had died, wrote: "I do not issue you commands like Peter or Paul, for *I* am not an apostle, but a condemned man." He was a bishop, but he was not an apostle and he did not have authority to issue commands as did the apostles.

This first mark, then, of a Spirit-filled church is humble submission to the teaching of the apostles. In other words, the Spirit-filled church is a biblical church, a New Testament church, an apostolic church, a church that is deeply desirous to conform its understanding and its living to this unique, infallible teaching of the apostles of Jesus Christ.

The Second Mark: Fellowship

The second mark of a Spirit-filled church is its fellowship: *koinonia* (v. 42). *Koinonia* is the fellowship of the Holy Spirit: there was no fellowship before Pentecost. There was friendship and camaraderie and so on, but there was no fellowship.

At the heart of the word *koinonia* is the adjective *koinos,* which means common. The *koinonia* expresses the commonness of the Christian church in two major respects. First, it expresses what we share *in* together, or what we possess in common. That, of course, is God himself and his saving grace. John wrote at the beginning of his first letter, "Our fellowship is with the Father and with his Son Jesus Christ." And Paul adds, "The fellowship of the Holy Spirit."

Fellowship, *koinonia,* is a trinitarian concept, because we have the same God as our Father, the same Jesus Christ as our Savior and Lord, and the same Holy Spirit as our indwelling Comforter. This is the element common to all Christians.

The *koinonia* bears witness not only to what we share *in* each other as our common possession, but what we share *out* as our common gift to others. What we *give* of ourselves and of our money and of our possessions is another indispensable mark of true *koinonia.* Where there is no generosity, there is no fellowship.

Luke tells of this generosity in Acts 2: "They were together, they had all things in common" (*koine,* v. 44). "They sold their possessions and gave according to every man's need."

These are very disturbing facts, the kind of facts that we, who live in the affluence of America and Europe, tend to skip over rather too quickly. What is the implication of this teaching? Must every Spirit-filled Christian follow the example literally?

I believe Jesus does still call some of his followers to total voluntary poverty. Mother Teresa is one example. Such Christians bear witness that a human being's life does not consist in the abundance of material possessions. I am also persuaded that Jesus does not call every disciple to total voluntary poverty. Christ and the apostles did not forbid owning private property.

In the early Jerusalem church, the selling of property and the giving were voluntary. The sin of Ananias and Sapphira was not that they kept back a part of the proceeds of the sale of their property, but that they kept back a part while pretending to bring the whole. Their sin was deceit and hypocrisy, not greed. Peter said to them, "Before you sold it, was it not your own?" (Acts 5:4), which is a very important piece of apostolic teaching. In other words, your property is your own; you are a steward of it. It is for you to decide in a conscientious way before God what you will do with your property and your possessions—how much you will keep and how much you will give away.

Although the selling and the giving were voluntary, we must not try to escape the challenge too easily, or get ourselves off the hook too quickly. Those early Christians really cared about the poor in their midst. They shared of their abundance, or affluence, according to need.

The Christian community is the one community in the world in which poverty should be abolished. Do we not believe that the church bears witness to the kingdom of God and that it is the kingdom of righteousness and the kingdom of justice? How can we permit gross economic inequality within the Christian community that is bearing witness to a kingdom in which such injustice is supposed to have been abolished?

There is also gross economic inequality between the affluent nations of the world and the poverty-stricken nations. There are 800 million destitute people in the world. Ten thousand people die of starvation every day: that is the official figure. These things should surely rest heavily on the conscience of the Christian. The Holy Spirit gives to those whom he fills a tender, social conscience. We should love the poor—especially in our midst, in the Christian family. We also have to help the millions of stricken brothers and sisters in the Third World.

The Third Mark: Worship

The third mark of a Spirit-filled church is worship. "They devoted themselves to the apostles' teaching and the fellowship and the breaking of the bread [which is almost certainly a reference to the Lord's Supper, probably with a fellowship meal thrown in as well] and the prayers" (v. 42). This is not a reference to private devotion, but to public prayer services or meetings. The Spirit-filled community is a worshiping community.

The Holy Spirit causes us to cry, "Abba, Father," and "Jesus is Lord." We worship in the Spirit and by the inspiration of the Spirit. Luke pictures a remarkable balance of the early Christian worship in two respects: first, it was both formal and informal. They worshiped both in the temple and in each other's homes, a very interesting combination. It is surprising that they continued to worship in the temple, but no doubt they wanted to reform it according to the gospel. I do not believe they attended the sacrifices in the temple, because they knew that these had been fulfilled in the sacrifice of Jesus. But they did attend the temple prayer services.

Young people who are understandably impatient with the inherited structures of the church can learn a valuable lesson here. The Holy Spirit is a patient spirit, but his way with the institution of the church is more the way of patient reform than of impatient rejection.

They supplemented the temple prayer services with more informal services in their homes. Why can't we do that? Why must we always polarize? Old fogies like me enjoy dignified services in the church; older members of the congregation sometimes feel a little embarrassed by the exuberance and spontaneity of informal home services when young people, who find it hard at times to take the dignity and the formality of the church, get out their guitars and testify and clap their hands. But adults need to experience spontaneity and exuberance, and young people need the experience of dignity. In other words, we need each other.

Every healthy local church will have not only the united service of dignity on the Lord's day, but it will divide the congregation into fellowship groups, which meet in each other's homes during the week. We need both; we must not choose between them.

A second example of balance is that the worship, in addition to being formal and informal, was both joyful and reverent. There is no doubt about the joy of those early Christians. They met to praise God with glad and sincere hearts. The word for gladness in the Greek means exultation: it expresses a high degree of joy. They had reason to be filled with joy. Had not God sent his Son into the world to take human nature to himself, to live upon this planet, to die, to rise again, to send the Holy Spirit? Had the Holy Spirit not come to take up his residence in their hearts? How could they not be joyful? One fruit of the Spirit is joy.

Sometimes when I attend a church service, I really think I've come to a funeral by mistake. Everybody is dressed in black. Nobody laughs and nobody smiles. The atmosphere is dismal. The hymns are played at a snail's pace, like a funeral dirge, and everything is lugubrious. If I could only overcome my Anglo-Saxon reserve, I would shout out in the middle of such a service, "*Cheer up!* Christianity is a joyful religion!"

A certain Salvation Army drummer was beating his drum so hard that the band leader had to tell him to pipe down a bit and not make so much noise. In his cockney accent the drummer replied: "God bless you, sir, since oi've been converted, oi'm so 'appy, oi could bust the bloomin' drum!" Every worship service ought to be a joyful celebration of the mighty acts of God in Jesus Christ.

But the joy of these early Christians was never irreverent. Fear came upon every soul—that fear which is reverence, or awe, in the presence of God. The living God had visited the city of Jerusalem; he was in their midst and they knew it.

Some people think that whenever the Holy Spirit is present in power there is noise; the more decibels the better. I enjoy noise, too; I don't mind when we clap and stamp and sing for joy. But sometimes when the Holy Spirit is present in power, there is silence; there is nothing to say. We can only bow down in speechless wonder and reverence before the greatness and the glory of almighty God. "The Lord is in his holy temple; let all the earth keep silence before him" (Hab. 2:20).

Joy and reverence need not be separated in Christian worship. Reverence and rejoicing do not exclude one another. We need to recover the balance of the early Christian worship, both formal and informal, both joyful and reverent.

The Fourth Mark: Evangelism

The fourth mark of the Spirit-filled church is its evangelism. "The Lord added to their number day by day those who were being saved" (Acts 2:47). If the marks of the Spirit's presence in the church were only study, fellowship, and worship, it would be a very self-centered community. The things that concerned the interior life of the church were studying, loving one another, caring for one another in the fellowship, worshiping God in the sanctuary. But what about the alienated world outside? The Holy Spirit is concerned about that, too.

There are several facts we must note about evangelism. The first is that the Lord Jesus himself did it. The *Lord* added to their number day by day those who were being saved. Nobody else can add to the church but Jesus. He is the head of the church; he is the Lord of the church. He reserves for himself the prerogative of adding people to the church.

Of course, he delegates to pastors the responsibility of admitting people by baptism into the visible church, but he adds people to the invisible church, the *real* church, the community of believers.

We live in such a self-confident age. Some people are preoccupied with the techniques of evangelism. Some books and articles suggest that world evangelization is going to be computerized quite soon. We need to use all the technology that God has put at our disposal, *so long as we remember that it is a servant only.*

The second fact about evangelism is that Jesus does two things together: he adds to the church those whom he is saving. He does not save them without adding them to the church and he does not add them to the church without saving them. Salvation and church membership go together. They did in those days and they still do today.

Third, Jesus did it every day. The evangelism of the Jerusalem church was not an occasional or sporadic thing. They did not organize a mission every five years, and in between let the missions sink back into bourgeois respectability. They evangelized continually. Jesus was adding to their number through the preaching of the apostles, through the witness of the Christians, through the love of their common life.

That is quite alien to many churches today. I know churches that have not had a convert for decades. They are not expecting converts and they are not getting converts. We need a rise in expectations that the Lord will add regularly to the church those who are being saved.

Looking back over these four marks of a Spirit-filled church, notice that they concern four major relationships. First, the early Christians were related to the apostles. They were eager to receive the apostles' instruction. A Spirit-filled church is an apostolic church, a New Testament church, a church anxious to learn from the apostles and to obey the apostles. Second, they were related to each other. They continued in the fellowship. They looked after the needy. The Spirit-filled church is a loving church, a caring church, a generous church.

Third, they were related to God. They worshiped God in the temple and in the home, and with joy and reverence. A Spirit-filled church is a worshiping church. Fourth, they were related to the world outside. They were engaged in continuous evangelism. A Spirit-filled church is a missionary church, because the Holy Spirit is a missionary Spirit.

What fascinates me is that these four marks of a Spirit-filled church, if I am not greatly mistaken, are exactly what young people in particular are looking for in the churches today. When I was in Argentina a few years ago, I met a group of Christian students. I learned they had been to every Protestant church in their city. None of the churches had satisfied them and therefore they had dropped out. They called themselves *"Christianos descalgados."* It is the term used if you go to the wall and lift a picture off the hook. They were "unhooked" Christians, or, if you like, unattached Christians.

I said, "Why? Why? What is it you were looking for in the churches that you could not find?" You can imagine my astonishment when they went straight down the line, without realizing what they were doing. First, they were looking for a teaching ministry in which the Bible was expounded with faithfulness and related to the contemporary world—a thoughtful, teaching ministry, equally faithful to Scripture and relevant to the modern world. Second, they were looking for fellowship: warm, loving, caring, supportive fellowship. Third, they were looking for worship, a sense of the living God and his greatness, not just a perfunctory ritual or liturgy. They sought a sense of the living God in the midst of his people, and a people who bowed down before him in wonder, love, and praise. Fourth, they said they were looking for compassionate outreach. They were sickened by the churches in their city because they were so self-centered. They saw the need for the churches to reach out into the community with compassion, both socially and evangelistically. Teaching, fellowship, worship, outreach: exactly the four marks of a Spirit-filled church, according to Scripture.

We do not need to wait for the Holy Spirit to come: he came on the day of Pentecost. He has never left the church. What we need to do is to surrender afresh to his sovereignty, to seek the liberating power of the Holy Spirit, to come to him in his fullness, both individually and as a community, that he may be given his rightful place. Then we shall find a church approaching this divine ideal in apostolic doctrine, loving fellowship, authentic worship, and compassionate outreach. May God make our church into that kind of a church.

John R. W. Stott, "Setting the Spirit Free: We Can Reclaim the Power of Pentecost to Renew the Church," *Christianity Today* 25, no. 11 (June 12, 1981): 17–21.

Part VI

—

SOCIAL CONCERNS

Chapter 39

REVERENCE FOR
HUMAN LIFE

C ontemporary society maintains a strangely ambivalent attitude toward the value of life. Life seems now cheap, now precious, on no clearly discernible principle.

For example, the British government saw nothing anomalous about including in its program of reform both the abolition of capital punishment and a wider freedom for abortion. And last year the Arts Council surrendered to public pressure and reprieved sixty catfish from a humane three-second electrocution, while in the same week the press gave considerably less publicity to the killing of two men and the injuring or maiming of twenty-seven others by a bomb planted in a Belfast public house.

Respect for life is naturally a subject of constant concern for every doctor—respect for the beginning of life (conception and birth), its continuance in growth to maturity, and its end in death. I am perhaps most hesitant to speak about the beginning of life since I read a comment quoted by Dr. Granville Williams in *The Sanctity of Life and the Criminal Law* (1958): "There seems to be something about the human reproductive system which throws the ecclesiastical mind off its balance." Certainly the whole subject is immensely complicated, with legal, medical, social, and economic implications as well as philosophical and moral ones.

My concern is to ask whether Christian faith can supply a guiding principle to help us find our way through the labyrinth of medico-moral problems. I believe it can. Let me, then, plot out the territory we are to traverse.

First, I hope to isolate the essential principle as being not so much the sanctity of life in general as reverence for *human* life in particular.

Second, I mean to defend this principle by setting it on its true (theological) basis.

Third, I will try to apply the principle of reverence for human life to medical practice and to some burning medical issues.

The Principle Isolated

My text, fundamental to my thesis, is Genesis 9:1–6:

> And God blessed Noah and his sons, and said to them, "Be fruitful and multiply, and fill the earth. The fear of you and the dread of you shall be upon every beast of the earth, and upon every bird of the air, upon everything that creeps on the ground and all the fish of the sea; into your hand they are delivered. Every moving thing that lives shall be food for you; and as I gave you the green plants, I give you everything. Only you shall not eat flesh with its life, that is, its blood. For your lifeblood I will surely require a reckoning; of every beast I will require it and of man; of every man's brother I will require the life of man. Whoever sheds the blood of man, by man shall his blood be shed; for God made man in his own image."

These purport to be the words of the Creator, from whom all life (human, animal, and vegetable) takes its origin. After the judgment of the Flood, God renews his blessing to man. He confirms both man's power of procreation (the command to be fruitful) and man's dominion over the whole animal creation. "Into your hand they are delivered" he says. This animal creation may serve man for food. However, though man might shed animal blood, he was not permitted to eat it, since blood is the symbol of life and life remains God's possession. And no animal or man might shed *human* blood with impunity: "Whoever sheds the blood of man, by man shall his blood be shed; for God made man in his own image."

It is important to recognize that capital punishment was divinely authorized not because human life (the murderer's) was cheap, but because human life (the victim's) was precious. Capital punishment in the Mosaic legislation was intended to bear witness to the value, the sanctity, of human life. The context puts this beyond question. Animal life might be taken (for food and clothing). But human life might not be taken, because man bears God's image. The only exception to this rule was the judicial execution of the murderer, whose life was forfeit precisely because he himself had violated the sanctity of human life.

The distinction between animal life and human life, between the permission to take the one and the prohibition against taking the other (except judicially), is the essential background to our discussion. It should protect us from either of two extreme positions. These extremes I will illustrate from two influential Germans who were contemporaries in the thirties and early forties.

Albert Schweitzer's philosophy was in some ways a mixture of Christianity and Buddhism. Its fundamental principle was "reverence for life," for *all* life. Schweitzer refused to distinguish between higher and lower forms, more or less valuable forms, because to do so (he said) would involve an entirely subjective judgment. How can we know, he asked, what significance any kind of life has? It was rumored that he would even decline to swat a fly in the operating theater at Lambaréné.

That Adolf Hitler went to the opposite extreme I hardly need say. Millions of Jews were liquidated in his gas chambers, and more than a quarter of a million non-Jews in his compulsory euthanasia centers. Many more millions were killed in the war into which he dragged the world.

Christians who take the biblical revelation seriously could not follow either of these men—although, to be sure, Schweitzer's philosophy is infinitely preferable to Hitler's.

We cannot follow Schweitzer and declare *all* life sacrosanct. Certainly we acknowledge God as the creator and sustainer of all life; we recognize, as Jesus taught, that ultimately it is he who feeds the birds of the air and clothes the flowers of the field; and we should set ourselves against all wanton destruction of animal and plant life. But at the same time we acknowledge that God gave man dominion over the animal creation, so that we have liberty to eat animal flesh, to harness animal labor to our service, to perform controlled experiments on animals for man's benefit, to exterminate harmful vermin, to put suffering animals painlessly to sleep.

At the other extreme, we cannot follow Hitler and declare *no* life sacrosanct. The compulsory euthanasia of the psychopath, the imbecile, or the senile on the ground that he is "useless" to society is abhorrent to us. Also abhorrent to many people is the contemporary pressure for unconditional abortion, and the tendency of many unmarried teen-age girls to regard abortion as, in one doctor's description, "physically and morally no more serious than having a tooth out."

But the fetus is not to be compared to a tooth. The fetus on the one hand and the psychopath on the other are at least to some degree human beings.

This, then, is the principle that our text isolates for us—not a reverence for life that regards all life as equally sacred, but reverence for human life. And reverence for human life is the result of reverence for man as a unique, indeed godlike, creature.

The Principle Defended

Respect for humanity, for human being and therefore human life, is (at least on paper) almost universal. For example, the Universal Declaration of Human Rights (1948) asserted in its preamble "the inherent dignity, and the equal and inalienable rights of all members of the human family." The same year the Declaration of Geneva, adopted by the World Medical Association, included the pledge, "I will maintain the utmost respect for human life, from time of conception"—which is a positive version of the Hippocratic Oath dating from the fifth century B.C. "not to give a deadly drug to anyone."

But what is the basis for this respect for human life? The humanist has no adequate answer. For if man is fundamentally an animal, why may we not treat him as we treat other animals? And if man is the present culmination of the evolutionary process why may we not adopt selective breeding, and the compulsory euthanasia of the physically and mentally defective, in order to give evolution a valuable shove and accelerate the development of the "super race" of which Nietzsche dreamed?

Yet almost everybody recoils from this. Is our reluctance to go this far an irrational prejudice of which we should seek to rid ourselves? Or is it a true instinct, a recognition of man's unique value? Do we shrink from treating man as an animal for the simple and sufficient reason that he is not an animal but a human personality, in consequence of which he is to be served and not manipulated, reverenced and not discarded?

Christians alone claim to have an adequate explanation for man's self-conscious uniqueness. It is a theological explanation that depends on two great doctrines.

First, *the doctrine of creation*.

Whatever mode God employed in creation (and the mode is eclipsed in importance by the fact), God made man in his own image or likeness. Although the Bible nowhere spells out exactly what this means, the implications are clear. For everywhere Scripture assumes man's qualitative difference from the animals, and rebukes or ridicules man when his behavior is more bestial than human in its irrationality or godlessness or selfishness.

The divine image in man is a complex of qualities that might be summarized as follows:

1. Man has an intelligence, a capacity to reason and even to evaluate and criticize himself.

2. Man has a conscience, a capacity to recognize moral values and make moral choices.

3. Man has a society, a capacity to love and to be loved in personal, social relationships.

4. Man has a dominion, a capacity to exercise lordship over creation, to subdue the earth, and to be creative.

5. Man has a soul, a capacity to worship, to pray, and to live in communion with God.

These capacities (mental, moral, social, creative, and spiritual) constitute the divine image, because of which man is unique.

Second, *the doctrine of redemption*.

The very word "redemption" presupposes that man has fallen from the condition in which he was made. He has become alienated from his original destiny. He needs to be remade in the divine image that has been distorted within him.

Christians believe that God so loved his creation, though spoiled by sin and hostile to him, that he sent his son Jesus Christ to effect the work of restoration. And the mission of Jesus shows plainly the value that God still puts on man, even on fallen man. "You are of more value than many sparrows," Jesus said. And "of how much more value is a man than a sheep?" He exhibited his care for man by his ministry of compassion, especially to the dropouts of human society. Above all, he gave his life for us; so completely did he identify himself with our sin and guilt that he bore in our place sin's grim penalty, death. And now, risen and exalted, he sends his Spirit actually to live within us and so to transform us into his own image.

So then, both creation (man's distinctive capacities) and redemption (Jesus Christ's birth, life, death, resurrection, and Spirit-gift) demonstrate, as nothing else does or could, the uniqueness of man in God's mind and purpose. These are, as it were, the gold standard against which the value of the human currency is to be assessed. They also supply the rationale of all service undertaken on man's behalf. If God made man in his own likeness, and humbled himself in Christ to serve and save him, it should be our honor to serve him too, and in particular to reverence his life. God says to us today, as Richard Baxter put it, "Did I die for them, and wilt not thou look after them? Were they worth my blood, and are they not worth thy labor?"

The Principle Applied

I am suggesting, however tentatively, that we have here the moral principle we need to guide us. Whether we are thinking of the embryo, the newborn baby, the youth, the middle-aged adult, or the elderly person, the essential question is: *Is this a human being?* If a patient is a human being made in the divine image, his life is to be reverenced, and the personal doctor-patient relation has to be preserved. For the patient is a human being, not an animal, and the medical attendant is a doctor, not a vet.

In trying to apply this principle, let us first consider *the fetus*, and the problem of abortion. Roman Catholics base their case against abortion on the premise that the fetus is a full human being, and that the decisive moment of humanization is conception. We must give them credit for being concerned about the right question (whether the human fetus is a human being or not) and, granted its affirmative answer to the question, its loyalty to logic and principle. But I cannot accept the premise on which the conclusion is based. Nor do I think we can draw a line at some arbitrary point called "quickening" or "viability" and declare the fetus to be human after that point but not human before it. It seems to me better and more biblical to think of the fetus throughout the gestation period as a *potential* human being, a human being in the making, but not yet an independent individual.

Then, if the choice has to be made, an abortion would seem morally permissible when the mother's life (perhaps interpreted to include her physical or mental health) is gravely at risk. For then the choice is between an actual human being and a potential human being.

That brings me to a second case, *babies born deformed*. This issue came to the forefront of public attention as a result of the Thalidomide tragedy of the early sixties. Madame van de Put killed her eight-day-old daughter because she had been born with no arms or shoulder structure, and with deformed feet. She was tried at Liège and acquitted of murder. One can feel nothing but the deepest sympathy for the mother. Yet I think it correct to say that *morally* this was a murder. Little Corinne van de Put, though terribly deformed, was a human being.

The Bible says much about the severely handicapped, and about the respect due to the blind, the deaf, the dumb, the mutilated, the leper. Even sin has not entirely destroyed God's image in man. If then the morally deformed are still said to be made in God's image (James 3:9), the physically deformed certainly are. We have no liberty to say that a damaged, deformed baby is not a human being.

The case of so-called monster babies is, I think, different. Since there are many forms, one cannot generalize. I take as my example the anencephalic, born with a brainstem (and therefore able to breathe) but without any cerebral cortex (and therefore, it seems, entirely without any capacity to think or choose or love or in fact grow into a human being). One can argue, of course, that every creature conceived and born of human parents is human. It is significant, however, that the Roman Catholic Church is prepared to entertain a doubt and will baptize "monster" babies only conditionally, saying, "If you are a man, I baptize you ..." I understand that it is a widely accepted (and I think justified) medical practice not indeed actively to destroy these babies but not to stimulate or resuscitate them and so to allow them to die.

This brings me to the hardest case of all, those sometimes termed *vegetables*. As a result of brain damage due to accident, disease, or senility, they fall into a deep coma, and their life appears more like that of a vegetable than of a human.

May we say that such a person is no longer a human being? that because he can no longer exercise his distinctively human capacities to think, choose, love, or pray, he has lost the divine image and may be treated as a vegetable? I think not. There is a difference between the congenital "monster" who has never had the capacity to become human and the human being who has become deprived of human powers. There is also our ignorance about the state of the soul of such a person whose brain has been damaged, and the relation between the two. It is also not without significance that the relatives continue to think of such a patient as a "he" and not an "it."

Nevertheless, if the brain has actually died, it would seem legitimate to allow the heart to die also, and not to keep activating it.

Further, if the brain (and/or body) has suffered such severe and irreparable damage that there is no hope of survival and in fact the process of dying has evidently begun, there comes a time in this case too when the patient's life should not be prolonged by so-called extraordinary means, but should be allowed to die in dignity and peace.

Norman St. John Stevas in his book *The Right to Life* (1963) quotes Lord Horder as having said that "the good doctor is aware of the distinction between prolonging life and prolonging the act of dying." Similarly, the useful report *Decisions about Life and Death* (1965) published for the Church of England Board of Social Responsibility refers to "a condition of artificially arrested death."

In this connection Karl Barth went so far as to ask whether "this kind of artificial prolongation of life does not amount to human arrogance." He goes on: "It is not now a question of arbitrary euthanasia [which he rejects]: it is a question of the respect which may be claimed by even the dying life as such." In quoting Barth, Dr. Paul Ramsey of Princeton adds his own comment: "To die is one way of being a human creature, and to be allowed to die a precious human right."

To recapitulate: the theological principle I have been trying to unfold and apply is that man is a unique creature, the object of God's loving care in both creation and redemption. The reason the Bible forbids the shedding of human blood (i.e., the taking of human life), except judicially, is that it is the life of a human being with a divine likeness. Therefore in complex medico-moral questions of life and death, the fundamental question we have to ask is whether the person concerned is a human being, and whether the treatment (or non-treatment) proposed is consistent with our answer to this question.

In conclusion, I suggest there are two simple lessons for medical practice.

First, a doctor should constantly remind himself that his patient is a person—not an animal to be treated as a vet might treat a dog, nor an interesting case to be added to his medical records, but a person, a human being, made in God's image. He is therefore, however annoying his temperament or repulsive his symptoms, to be cared for as someone of special value and worth.

Secondly, a doctor should respect and serve his patients accordingly. Vincent Edmunds and Jim Scorer in their book *Ethical Responsibility in Medicine* (1967) quote Joseph Lister, the pioneer of modern surgery: "There is only one rule of practice: put yourself in the patient's place." I hope I may echo this without impertinence, for a pastor is also called to care for people, though in a different way. I find I need to say to myself: "God made him in his own image. Jesus Christ died to save him. It is an honor for me to serve him."

I could not find a better illustration of all I have tried to say than that of Sir Frederick Treves's thoroughly Christian way of caring for the "elephant man" he found in a vacant greengrocer's stop opposite London Hospital in 1884. Treves describes him as "the most disgusting specimen of humanity" he had ever seen. He had an "enormous and misshapened head." A mass of bone projected from both his brow and his upper jaw, giving him a somewhat elephantine appearance, while spongy and evil-smelling skin, which looked like fungus or brown cauliflower, hung in bags from the back of his head, his back, his chest, and his right arm. His legs were deformed, his feet were bulbous, and he had hip disease. His face was expressionless, his speech spluttering and almost unintelligible. His left arm and hand were, by contrast, as shapely and delicate as a woman's.

To add to his suffering he was treated like an animal, hawked round the countryside from fair to fair and (though without police permission) exhibited to the curious for twopence a look. Treves writes: "He was shunned like a leper, housed like a wild beast, and got his only view of the world from a peephole in a showman's cart." He received less sympathy or kindness than a dog, and, terrified of staring eyes, he would creep into some dark corner to hide.

But Treves discovered he was a human being, John Merrick by name, age twenty-one, highly intelligent, with an acute sensibility and a romantic imagination. And when he was abandoned by the showman, Treves arranged for him to be cared for in a room at the back of the London Hospital, where three and a half years later he died in his sleep.

When first a woman visited Merrick, gave him a smile and a greeting, and shook him by the hand, he broke down into uncontrollable sobbing. But from that day his transformation began. He received many notable visitors, including Queen Alexandra, then Princess of Wales, and was enthralled by his visits to the pantomime and the countryside. Treves discovered him to be "a gentle, affectionate and lovable creature ... free from any trace of cynicism or resentment ... without an unkind word for anyone."

Gradually he changed "from a hunted thing into a man." But actually he had always been a man. It was Treves's remarkable reverence for human life that enabled John Merrick to lift up his poor misshapen head and gain some human self-respect, as a man made in the image of God.

John R. W. Stott, "A Guide for Doctors and Others: Reverence for Human Life," *Christianity Today* 16, no. 18 (June 9, 1972): 8–12.

Chapter 40

———

CHRISTIANS AND ANIMALS

What attitude should Christians adopt toward animals? This question has forced itself on the attention of many in Britain by the recent observance of Animal Welfare Year. It marked the centenary of the unamended *Cruelty to Animals Act* (1976), was supported by nearly seventy animal welfare societies, and aimed to promote more humane behavior toward laboratory animals, domestic pets, farm animals, and wildlife.

God has given to human beings a midway position between himself and the animals. In our physiology we are like them: we breathe like them ("living creatures" is a phrase applied to us both: Gen. 1:20, 24; 2:7), we eat and drink like them, and we reproduce like them (the command to "be fruitful" is addressed to us both: Gen. 1:22, 28). But in our higher faculties, and in the activities that these make possible (thinking, choosing, loving, creating, worshiping), we are unlike the animals and like God. In consequence, we combine the dependence on God that is common to all his creatures with a responsible dominion over the subhuman creation that is unique.

One extreme attitude to nature and to animals has been that of worship. Many ancient religions were pantheistic in tendency, identifying the gods with nature. The Egyptians worshiped the gods of sun, sky, air, earth, and water, and the Canaanites the "baals" or nature gods that were thought to have fertility powers. Both groups represented their deities in the form of either birds or beasts.

Still today popular Hinduism leans toward pantheism, and primitive animists live in dread of the spirits believed to inhabit mountains, forests, rivers, and animals. All such superstition is swept away by the uncompromising biblical assertion that the living God created the sun, the moon and stars, the earth, and the sea, and all creatures, and is supreme over them.

Yet we need to beware of more sophisticated ways of worshiping nature and its animals. The nineteenth-century Romantics were escapists in their back to nature call. Albert Schweitzer, for all his brilliance and dedication, held a quasi-Buddhist view of the inviolable sanctity of all life, so that he would never destroy living creatures, even disease-carrying flies. And pet-lovers sometimes become so sentimental in their attachment to a dog, a cat, or a parakeet that they give it a value belonging to people alone.

At the opposite extreme is the attitude of callous indifference to animals, and even of wanton destruction. True, man has been given dominion over earth and animals, but dominion is not another word for domination, still less for destruction. On the contrary, we are to be good stewards of the animal creation, and are responsible to God for our stewardship.

Can we, then, define more clearly the human attitude to animals taught by the Bible? I think we can. First, we should study them. God's works are "studied by all who have pleasure in them" (Ps. 111:2). All Christians should take an interest in natural history, especially town dwellers, who have to take greater initiatives to do so. As we study God's creatures, and so "think his thoughts after him," we marvel at them.

Scientists have developed hypodermic syringes from the fangs of snakes, aviation from bird flight, and radar from bats. There are moral lessons to learn as well. For animals shame us that they do by instinct what human beings should do by choice. Thus industry and forethought can be learned from ants (Prov. 6:6–11), repentance from migratory birds that fly away but always return (Jer. 8:4–7), obedience from the ox and donkey (Isa. 1:3), and faith from sparrows (Mt. 10:29–31, cf. 6:26).

Secondly, we may use them. God has given us permission to domesticate the animal creation, so that we may use their strength to carry our burdens (cf. Num. 7:1–11), their skins to clothe us (cf. Gen. 3:21), and their flesh to feed us (cf. Gen. 9:1–3; Mk. 7:19).

A few years ago I received a letter from a lady who attributed the world's ills to "the unhealthy and unnatural diet which man has chosen, namely the flesh of murdered animals," whereas (she argued) "the Bible repeats so many times *thou shalt not kill.*" She failed to see that this was a prohibition of murder, whereas the Bible also permits the killing of animals for food and clothing.

Thirdly, we are to be kind to them. Kindness to animals is enjoined in Scripture. For God himself created and sustains them, as he created and sustains us: "Men and animals are in your care" (Ps. 36:6, *Good News Bible*). So in the Old Testament animals were to be given their day's rest on the sabbath as well as humans (Ex. 20:10; 23:12), bird's-nesting was restricted (Deut. 22:6, 7), and oxen were not to be muzzled while threshing com (Deut. 25:4). In brief, "A good man takes care of his animals" (Prov. 12:10, *Good News Bible*).

How are we to apply these biblical principles to modern problems? Certainly if we have domestic pets, we must feed, house, and exercise them properly.

What about so-called factory farming? I think we should agree with the report of the Brambell Commission that any intensive farming should be outlawed (whatever its economic advantages) if it involves "a degree of confinement of an animal which necessarily frustrates most of its major activities which make up its natural behaviour," for "an animal should at least have sufficient freedom of movement to be able without difficulty to turn around, groom itself, lie down and stretch its limbs."

Probably the most controversial area of animal welfare has to do with vivisection, that is, experiments on living animals. Most of us would probably agree that such laboratory experiments are morally justifiable if they are absolutely necessary for medical research, and if they are conducted with the minimum of pain. What is now disturbing the British public is the fact that of the more than five million such experiments reported for 1975, over three and a half million were for non-medical purposes, namely for the development of commercial products ranging from food flavorings, detergents, and weedkillers to tobacco substitutes and cosmetics. It is encouraging that, in response to a memorandum on this topic submitted by a group chaired by Lord Houghton of Sowerby, the Home Secretary last year accepted the need to tighten up the administration of the law on animal cruelty. A Committee for the Reform of Animal Experimentation has also been formed.

A distinguished international group is proposing to submit to UNESCO in October this year a Universal Declaration of the Rights of Animals. The draft does not seem to me to recognize with sufficient clarity the uniqueness of what it calls "man as an animal species." Nevertheless, Christians should gladly affirm that "all animals have rights" under their Creator.

Finally, the Bible recognizes that all nature now "groans with pain" (Rom. 8:22). But we confidently look forward to the day when it will be liberated from its present bondage. Only then will all predation cease, and wolves and sheep, leopards and goats, cows and bears, calves and lion cubs will feed together, while even little children will care for them without any fear or danger (Isa. 11:6–9).

John R. W. Stott, "Cornerstone: Christians and Animals," *Christianity Today* 22, no. 9 (February 10, 1978): 38–39.

Chapter 41

———

WHAT IS HUMAN
LIFE ANYWAY?

*A Christian concept of euthanasia distinguishes
prolonging life from prolonged dying.*

I f only the word were still used in its true and original meaning, we would all believe in euthanasia. For it means "dying
well," and we who aspire to be good-living people should aspire
to be good-dying people too. Moreover, the "goodness" of the
dying process should include practical thoughtfulness in settling
our affairs and making our will, a calm trust in God who through
Christ has conquered death, and the reasonable expectation that
modern drugs can now relieve the symptoms and control the pain
which accompany much terminal illness.

Further, a Christian concept of euthanasia draws a legitimate
distinction between prolonging life and prolonging the process of
dying. The Hippocratic oath commits doctors to fight for human
life, but not to practice what has been aptly termed "meddlesome
medicine," namely the giving of useless and even distressing
treatment to a patient whose disease is irreversible. True terminal care should enable the dying to die with peace and dignity.

Indeed, as Professor Paul Ramsey of Princeton has written, "to be allowed to die is a precious human right." Similarly, in the use of drugs there is a distinction "between a determination to relieve suffering in order to minimize the trauma of death and a deliberate decision to precipitate death in order to end the trauma of suffering" (J. N. D. Anderson in *Issues of Life and Death*, 1976).

Nowadays, however, the term "euthanasia" is used (usually prefaced by the adjective "voluntary") as a euphemism for "mercy-killing." It describes the deliberate administration of a lethal dose to a patient who requests it and whose condition is burdensome but not fatal. In Britain the Voluntary Euthanasia Bill of 1969, which was rejected by Parliament, would have permitted such euthanasia in the case of a person suffering from "a serious physical illness or impairment reasonably thought ... to be incurable and expected to cause him severe distress or render him incapable of rational existence." But when does "rational existence" cease? In the contemporary debate, the advocates of "mercy-killing" concentrate less on the senile, whose dulled mental faculties tend to reduce their physical suffering, than on the young whose alert minds make their bodily incapacity all the more distressing.

Brian Clark's play *Whose Life Is It Anyway?*, which has been drawing enthusiastic crowds to the Savoy Theatre in London, presents a powerful argument for mercy-killing. Its main character is Ken Harrison (brilliantly played by Tom Conti), a professional sculptor who, paralyzed from the neck down as the result of an accident, will never be able to sculpt again. Throughout the play, able only to move his head and to speak, he lies in his hospital bed and occupies the center of the stage. One's deep sympathy is aroused for him by the heartless professionalism of the nursing Sister, the shallow evasiveness of the consultant ("I'm a Doctor not a Judge"), and the embarrassing insensitivity of the hospital chaplain who describes the patient as "God's chosen vessel into which people pour their compassion" (ribald guffaws from the audience).

The ground on which Ken Harrison bases his plea to be helped to end his life is straightforward: "I don't want to go on living, because I'm no longer human." "I'm dead already. ... Life is self-supporting; I'm not. I'm never able to direct anything. I'm in the power of other people." "It's a question of dignity. Now only my brain functions. I am in fact dead. It's an indignity; it's inhumane to preserve my life. Dignity starts with choice." His argument is paradoxical: since a life without choice is not a human life, the only way for him to become human again is to choose to die. The play therefore has a misleading title. The issue it raises is not "*whose* life is it anyway?" but "*what* is human life anyway?"

It is here, then, that our Christian critique of Ken Harrison's case would have to begin. If living means choosing, could he not equally have chosen to live rather than die? Besides, life is more than choice, more too than the artistic creativity in which he could no longer engage. Life is relationships. And Harrison's keen intelligence, sense of humor, and warmth of personality make rich relationships possible for him. But he shuns these, and this to me is the most significant flaw in the play. Although consultant, psychiatrist, resident intern, Sister, nurse, social worker, cleaner, attorney, and judge all come in and out of the ward in the course of their duties, Ken Harrison receives no visitors. He has broken his engagement, and asked his fiancée and his parents not to visit him. No friends come to see him either. But this creates an artificial situation. By cutting himself off from those who love him most he has deliberately dehumanized his own life. Further, no reference is made either to the possibility of a relationship with God, or to the afterlife.

Joni Eareckson offers us a striking contrast, the more telling because it comes from real life, and not from the stage. For she too is a quadriplegic, who as an athletic girl of seventeen broke her neck in a diving accident in Chesapeake Bay. In *Joni* (Zondervan, 1976), her bestselling autobiography, she is splendidly honest about her struggles with despair. "Why can't they just let me die?" she asked. When she realized that she would never walk again, or use her arms, or be able to marry her boyfriend, she was bewildered and angry, she felt betrayed by God, and she tried to escape into a world of fantasy. Attempting to recall her to reality, her friend Diana said to her: "The past is dead, Joni, you're alive." "Am I?" Joni responded; "This isn't living."

How, then, did Joni come to reevaluate the fundamental meaning of human life? It is partly that she acquired extraordinary skill in drawing and painting with her mouth. More than that, she was surrounded by the supportive love of her parents, sisters, and friends. But most important of all, she gained a spiritual perspective. She came to see that her paralysis was only temporary, that one day she will receive a new and glorious body, and that meanwhile her chair is a "tool" to fashion her like Christ. For by it, as she once told 2,000 young people in Kansas City, "God transformed an immature and headstrong teenager into a self-reliant young woman who is learning to rejoice in suffering." Her second book *A Step Further* (Zondervan, 1978) expresses a yet stronger resolve to "let God be God" and a yet clearer conviction that "suffering gets us ready for heaven." (See review, p. 36.) I guess she might even agree, despite all her frustration and grief, that she is more genuinely human now, not less. Her example is an inspiration to many.

John R. W. Stott, "Cornerstone: What Is Human Life Anyway?," *Christianity Today* 23, no. 13 (April 6, 1979): 32–33.

Chapter 42

PEACEMAKING IS
A MANAGEMENT
RESPONSIBILITY

For Christians, mutual service replaces mutual
suspicion and cooperation replaces competition.

D uring the winter of 1978–79 there was industrial civil war
in Britain. We had strikes of bakers, of garbage and other
road haulage, railway workers, ambulance drivers, journalists and
teachers, and of hospital social workers. During the first three
months of 1979 more than five million working days were lost
through industrial disturbances, which are more than half the
total for the whole of 1978. Something went sour in our society.

Social turmoil is of special concern to Christians because we
are in the business of right relations. Reconciliation is at the top
of our agenda because it is at the heart of our gospel. Jesus is
the world's supreme peacemaker, and he tells his followers to be
peacemakers too. But how?

A vital biblical principle is spelled out in 1 Kings 12. Despite
his wisdom, Solomon had been a tyrant. His ambitious building

program had been completed only by the use of forced labor. Industrial relations were at an all-time low. So when he died, the people described his oppressive regime as a "heavy yoke" and begged his son Rehoboam to lighten it. Moreover, the elder statesmen advised him to heed their appeal: "If you will be a servant to this people today and serve them ... they will be your servants" (v. 7).

Nevertheless, this principle remains the essential basis of every constitutional government and democratic institution. It is the principle of mutual service arising from mutual respect. It is service based on justice rather than mere expediency, for it recognizes people as human beings with human rights, made in God's image, and deserving our respect as we deserve theirs. This is the fundamental truth behind the Old Testament instruction to care for the handicapped and destitute, and to administer justice impartially in the law courts, as well as behind the New Testament teaching about the regard masters and servants should show each other, since they have the same Lord and Judge.

Turning from biblical principle to contemporary society, the contrast is glaring. For what we have is an adversary situation born of suspicion, instead of a service situation born of trust. Moreover, it is deeply embedded in our stratified British society. As David Steel, the leader of the Liberal Party, said before the recent General Election: "The major single defect in British society ... remains its class-ridden nature. Class division ... bedevils ... industrial relations ..." In consequence, many people feel underprivileged and alienated; what motivates them when they agitate for higher pay is not greed so much as grievance.

Such a situation of strife is incompatible with the spirit of Jesus Christ, and in his name his people should set themselves against it. But how can mutual suspicion be replaced by mutual service, and competition by cooperation?

First, we should *abolish discrimination*. This applies to everything which perpetuates a "them-us" confrontation. What, for example, is the justification for making wage earners clock in, while the salaried staff do not? Or for restricting the former to a rather sleazy "works canteen" (workers cafeteria) while the latter have a posh "staff restaurant"?

Behind these symbols of discrimination there lies the reality of social injustice, namely the unjustified disparity between the high paid and the low paid. I do not think that total egalitarianism is the Christian way, for God himself has not made us equal in natural endowments. What Christians should oppose, however, is the inequality of privilege. Is it really beyond the wit of man to devise a graduated pay scale, which covers the whole range of workers, managers, and directors, which rewards training, skill, responsibility, achievement, and long service, plus conditions of dirt and danger (as well as responding to the laws of supply and demand), and which is seen to be just because all disparity is rationally justified?

Secondly, we should *increase participation*, both in decision making and profit sharing. In many companies the workers lack self-respect because they lack responsibility. They feel oppressed because they are powerless. Other people—remote, faceless people—make all the decisions for them. Their only role is to obey. But decision making is part of our humanness. To be a human being is to make responsible choices. To deny to adults a share in making decisions about matters that affect them is to treat them like children, even like machines.

In the last century Christians opposed slavery because by it humans were dehumanized by being *owned* by others. In this century we should oppose all labor arrangements in which humans are dehumanized by being *used* by others—even if they have signed away their responsibility in a voluntary contract. Thank

God that on both sides of the Atlantic various experiments in industrial democracy are being made, whose purpose is to create a positive partnership between management and workers in the development of company strategy and in the making and implementing of decisions.

Profit sharing also rests on biblical principle: "The laborer is worthy of his hire." If a company prospers, the workers as well as the shareholders should benefit, whether in bonuses, in stock, or in pension.

Thirdly, we should *emphasize cooperation*. Labor unions were developed in the nineteenth century, as an indispensable protection of workers against exploitative bosses. Are they not an anachronism in the twentieth century? The tragedy is that confrontation is now built into the very structures of industry. Why should we assume that this structural confrontation is inevitable and everlasting? Why should we not dream of better structures that express cooperation instead? When management and labor are locked in confrontation, the public suffers; but when they cooperate in the service of the public, their relations to each other improve.

Good labor relations in contemporary society constitute a powerful challenge to Christians, whom God calls into business or industry, to help organize their company on the principle of mutual respect and service, to eliminate all unjustified discrimination, to facilitate full participation in power and profit, to develop cooperation in the service of the public, and so to demonstrate the possibility of industrial relations that are harmonious.

We Christians should not acquiesce in bad industrial relations as if they were inevitable. Even the unregenerate have an inborn sense of justice and compassion. Better relations are possible. We need both to exemplify them in the Christian fellowship and to work for them in the world, remembering the words of the Lord

Jesus, "Blessed are the peacemakers, for they shall be called the children of God."

John R. W. Stott, "Cornerstone: Peacemaking Is a Management Responsibility," *Christianity Today* 23, no. 22 (September 22, 1979): 36–37.

Chapter 43

———

PRESERVING THE RICHNESS
OF RACIAL DIVERSITY

"I have a dream that one day ... little black boys and black girls will be able to join hands with little white boys and white girls as sisters and brothers. ... With this faith we will be able to transform the jangling discords of our nation into a beautiful symphony of brotherhood." So said Martin Luther King in his famous "dream" speech in Washington, D.C., not long before his assassination. His dream lives on. It needs to be dreamed not only in the United States, and in Southern Africa, but in Britain as well.

Britain has now suffered 20 years of racial tension, beginning in 1958 when racial violence erupted in Notting Hill (London) and in Nottingham. There followed a decade in which four *Commonwealth Immigration Acts* were passed. These made Christians ashamed not because they limited immigration (which every country must do) but because the legislation was weighted against colored immigrants. Meanwhile, Mr. Enoch Powell, M.P., was fomenting racial tension by emotive speeches about "watching the nation heaping up its own funeral pyre" and about Britons "becoming strangers in their own country." Then some measure of justice was secured for racial minorities by two *Race Relations Acts* (1968 and 1976), since the first created a board to hear complaints and promote reconciliation, while the second created a "Commission for Racial Equality" that put teeth into the enforcement of the law.

But in 1967 the National Front, a coalition of the extreme right, came into being. Its policy is to stop immigration, promote repatriation, and fight communism. Its leaders had all been involved previously in Nazi activities and were ardent admirers of Hitler. Colin Jordan said in 1959, "I loathe the Blacks—we're fighting a war to clear them out of Britain," while John Tyndall's fourth "Principle of British Nationalism" (1966) was to "oppose racial integration and stand for racial separateness." Fortunately, such extreme statements are those of a small racist minority. Nevertheless, the well-researched book *Racial Disadvantage in Britain*, by David J. Smith (Penguin, 1977), documents the conclusion that, especially in employment and housing, "there is still very substantial racial discrimination" against nonwhite people.

A growing number of British Christians are deeply troubled by this stain on our society, and the Evangelical Race Relations Group is seeking to spread facts, allay fears, and arouse concern. Above all we need to think biblically about the issue. Let me draw out some basic principles from Paul's great Areopagus speech (Acts 17).

First, Paul affirmed the unity of the human race, or the God of creation. For God had "made from one every nation of men" (v. 26), and all human beings are therefore his "offspring" (28, 29). We evangelicals rightly reject the concept of "the universal fatherhood of God and the universal brotherhood of men" if it is used to deny the special fatherhood and fellowship God gives to his redeemed people. But we should acknowledge the truth about creation it expresses. All men and women, having been created in God's image, are equal before him in worth, and therefore have an equal right to respect. Moreover, this human unity is not destroyed by interbreeding. Martin Webster of the National Front stated his view in 1975 that "racialism is the only scientific and logical basis for nationalism," and that "the identity of the British nation" would be "destroyed by racial interbreeding." But this is a historical and biological myth. The British nation was actually created by interbreeding. There is no such thing as "pure British blood."

Second, Paul affirmed the diversity of ethnic cultures, or the God of history. For the "periods and the boundaries" of the nations are in God's hand (26). The apostle was probably alluding to the primeval command to multiply and fill the earth. It was certainly this human dispersal that inevitably resulted in the development of distinctive cultures. Now culture is the complement of nature. What is "natural" is God-given and inherited; what is "cultural" is manmade and learned. Culture is an amalgam of the beliefs, values, customs, and institutions every society develops and transmits to the following generation. Scripture celebrates the colorful mosaic of human cultures, and even declares that their "glory" will be brought into the New Jerusalem (Rev. 21:24). This being so, we should seek to ensure that human society remains multicultural, and does not become monocultural. For cultural diversity is a source of human enrichment.

Third, Paul affirmed the finality of Jesus Christ, or the God of revelation. For "now he commands all men everywhere to repent," having raised Jesus from the dead and appointed him the universal Judge (30, 31). The apostle refuses to acquiesce in the multi-religious condition of Athens. He does not hail the city as a living museum of religions. No, its idolatry was abhorrent to him. We learn, therefore, that to welcome the diversity of cultures does not imply an acquiescence in the diversity of religions. On the contrary, Christians who appreciate cultural achievement must at the same time resist the idolatry which lies at the heart of many cultures. We cannot tolerate any rivals to Jesus Christ. They "provoke" us, as they did Paul (16). We must therefore proclaim to all mankind that the God they may "worship as unknown" (23) has actually made himself known, uniquely and decisively, in Jesus Christ.

Fourth, Paul affirmed the glory of the Christian community, or the God of redemption. For God acted through Jesus Christ to abolish the barriers which divide human beings from one another and to create a single new humanity. His fullest exposition of this theme is in Ephesians. Luke only hints at it in Acts 17 by mentioning two converts by name, "Dionysius the Areopagite and a woman named Damaris" (34). Here was the nucleus of the new society of Jesus, in which men and women of all social, racial, and cultural origins are reconciled to each other through him.

Whatever policies a country may develop for racial integration, they must reflect and not compromise these four theological truths. Because of the unity of the human race we must demand equal rights for racial minorities. Because of the diversity of ethnic cultures, we must renounce cultural imperialism and seek to preserve the riches of every culture. Because of the finality of Jesus Christ, we must insist that religious freedom includes the right of Christians to propagate their faith, and we must not deny this right to others. Because of the glory of the new community in Christ, we must rid it of all lingering racism and strive to make it a model of multiracial harmony.

Jesus calls all his followers to be peacemakers. We must pray, witness, and work, to the end that the multiracial dream may come true.

John R. W. Stott, "Cornerstone: Preserving the Richness of Racial Diversity," *Christianity Today* 23, no. 25 (November 2, 1979): 42–43.

Chapter 44

———

CALLING FOR
PEACEMAKERS IN A
NUCLEAR AGE, PART I

Christ's ministry is not symbolized by the whip but by the cross.

The contemporary build-up of the superpowers' nuclear arsenals is a horrendous reality. Each Poseidon submarine has 10 missiles, each of which has 14 MIRV warheads, each of which is equivalent to the Hiroshima bomb. So one submarine carries enough power to destroy 140 Hiroshimas. America's 11,000 nuclear warheads could annihilate the complete world population 12 times over, SALT II sets a ceiling on the number and type of missiles, but not on warheads, so that within a few years the two superpowers are likely to have between 20 and 30 thousand of them. What lunacy is this?

Five nations are now known to have both nuclear weapons and delivery systems, while five more have the capability to develop them. SIPRI (the Stockholm International Peace Research Institute) forecasts that by 1985 the nuclear club may have grown to 35 member nations.

Nobody can predict with any accuracy how much devastation a nuclear war would cause. It would depend on a number of factors. But the U.S. Congress document *The Effects of Nuclear War* (1979) says that "the minimum consequences would be enormous." It provides four case studies ranging from a single megaton weapon attack on a city the size of Detroit or Leningrad to "a very large attack against a range of military and economic targets" in which the USSR struck first and the U.S. retaliated. The former would mean up to two million dead, and the latter up to 77 percent of the American population (about 160 million) and up to 40 percent of the Russian. Moreover, many more millions would die later of their injuries, or starve or freeze to death the following winter, while in the long term cancer would claim yet more victims.

It is against this background of horror that we need to hear again the words of Jesus: *Blessed are the peacemakers, for they shall be called God's children.* Peacemaking is a divine activity, and we can claim to be authentic children of God only if we seek to do what our heavenly Father is doing. Thus, the basis for peacemaking is theological: it derives from our doctrine of God.

To be sure, the God of the Bible is a God of both salvation and judgment. But not equally so, as if these were parallel expressions of his nature. For Scripture calls judgment his "strange work"; his characteristic work, in which he delights, is salvation or peacemaking. Similarly, Jesus reacted to willful perversity with anger, uttered scathing denunciations upon hypocrites, drove the money-changers out of the temple. He also endured the humiliation and barbarities of crucifixion without resistance. Thus we see in the ministry of the same Jesus both violence and nonviolence. Yet his resort to violence of word and deed was occasional, alien, uncharacteristic; his characteristic was nonviolence; the symbol of his ministry is not the whip but the cross.

It is on the ground of this theology—of this revelation of God in Christ and in Scripture—that we Christians must all be opposed to war and dedicated to peace. Of course, throughout the centuries different Christians have formulated their conclusions differently. Some have been total pacifists, arguing that the example and teaching of Jesus commit his disciples to renounce the use of force in any form and to follow instead the way of the Cross, that is, of nonviolent love. Others have seen that according to Paul, officers of the state are "ministers of God" appointed to reward good conduct and punish bad, have argued that Christian citizens may share in the state's God-given role, and have sought to extend it into the international arena in terms of the "just war." Although this notion has been expressed in various forms, it may be said to have at least four essential aspects.

First, the cause must be righteous. That is, the war must be defensive not aggressive, its goal must be to secure justice and peace, and it may be justified only as a last resort after all attempts at reconciliation have failed.

Second, the means must be controlled. The two key words have been used regarding the limitation of violence. One is "proportionate." That is, the degree of injury inflicted must be less than that incurred. The other word is "discriminately." Police action is essentially discriminate, namely the arresting, bringing to trial, and punishment of specific criminals. Similarly, a war could not be in any sense "just" unless directed only against enemy combatants, leaving civilians immune. This principle is enough to condemn the saturation bombing of German cities in World War II (as Bishop George Bell of Chichester had the courage to argue in the House of Lords), and the fact that Hitler started it is no excuse. I believe the same principle is sufficient to condemn the use of strategic nuclear weapons. Because they are indiscriminate in their effects, destroying combatants and noncombatants alike, it seems clear to me that they are ethically indefensible, and that every Christian, whatever he may think of the possibility of a "just" use of conventional weapons, must be a nuclear pacifist. As the Roman Catholic bishops expressed it at Vatican II: "Any act of war aimed indiscriminately at the destruction of entire cities or of extensive areas along with their population is a crime against God and man himself. It merits unequivocal and unhesitating condemnation" (*Gaudium et Spes,* par. 80).

Third, the motive must be pure, for in no circumstances whatever does Christianity tolerate hatred, cruelty, envy, or greed. And fourth, the outcome must be predictable: there must be a reasonable prospect of victory, and of gaining the just ends for which the war is fought.

My point, however, is not so much to weigh the respective arguments which some adduce for total pacifism and others for the "just war" position, but rather to emphasize that the advocates of *both* positions are opposed to war. Both should be able to affirm the statement made by the Anglican bishops at successive Lambeth conferences (1930, 1948, 1968) that "war as a method of settling international disputes is incompatible with the teaching and example of the Lord Jesus Christ."

So then, although "just war" proponents may seek to justify engagement in war in certain restricted circumstances, they should never seek to glorify it. They may acquiesce in it with the greatest reluctance and the most painful qualms of conscience, but only if they perceive it as the least of all the alternative evils. And we should steadfastly refuse to glamorize war; war remains inhuman, unchristian, bestial. It is peacemaking we are to glorify. In brief, the only possible way Christians can try to justify war is to present it as the only possible way to make peace.

In my next "Cornerstone" article I hope to make some practical suggestions about Christian peacemaking.

John R. W. Stott, "Cornerstone: Calling for Peacemakers in a Nuclear Age, Part I," *Christianity Today* 24, no. 3 (February 8, 1980): 44–45.

Chapter 45

CALLING FOR PEACEMAKERS IN A NUCLEAR AGE, PART II

There are practical initiatives by which Christians can cool the international climate.

I n the February 8 issue I wrote about the appalling size of the superpowers' arsenals, the economic madness of current worldwide "defense" spending, the predictable effects of nuclear war, and the theological grounds for peacemaking. Jesus' seventh beatitude retains its full validity: *Blessed are the peacemakers, for they shall be called God's children.*

But what can it mean to be a Christian peacemaker amid the frightening realities of the nuclear age? What practical peacemaking initiatives are possible?

First, Christian peacemakers must recover their morale. There is a tendency among today's church members either to grow so accustomed to the balance of terror that we lose our sense of outrage, or to become so pessimistic that we acquiesce to it with a feeling of helplessness. But to give up either feeling or hoping is to have parted company with Jesus Christ. We need to join others in seeking to reverse the arms race.

Second, Christian peacemakers must be more diligent in prayer. I beg you not to dismiss this statement as a piece of pietistic irrelevance. For Christian believers it is nothing of the sort. Jesus our Lord specifically commanded us to pray for our enemies; do we? Paul laid down, as the first duty of every gathered congregation, the responsibility to pray for their national leaders, so that "we may lead a quiet and peaceable life" (1 Tim. 2:1–2). He thus attributed peace to prayer. Today virtually every church has a period of intercession in its public worship. Is it perfunctory or real? Supposing the whole church family during this period were to unite in fervent, concentrated prayer for rulers, for enemies, for peace, freedom, and justice in the world? What might God not do in response?

Third, Christian peacemakers must supply an example of a community of peace. It is impossible for Christians to maintain a credible witness for peace in the world unless the church is itself seen to be a community of peace. If charity begins at home, so does reconciliation. We need to obey the teaching of Jesus *first* to be reconciled to our brother and *then* to come and offer our worship (Matt. 5:23–24). We need to forgive our enemies, mend our broken relationships, ensure that our homes are havens of love, joy, and peace, and banish from our church all malice, anger, and bitterness.

God's purpose is to create a new, reconciled society. He wants his new community to challenge the value system of the secular community, and to offer a viable alternative. Not that this is easy. God's own peacemaking involved the blood of the cross.

———————

Fourth, Christian peacemakers must contribute to confidence building. There has been a lot of study of the postures of aggression which human beings adopt when they feel threatened. But not enough study has been done on the behavior of states under threat. Have you ever asked yourself how much Soviet behavior may be aggressive not so much because they are ambitious for power as because they feel threatened? How far could their aggressive stance be a sign not of imperialism but of insecurity?

On this matter opinions differ sharply. Some believe the Soviet Union is committed to world conquest by force. They point to Korea (1950), Hungary (1956), the Cuban missile crisis (1962), Czechoslovakia (1968), and to Afghanistan, Angola, Ethiopia, and other countries today. They are convinced Russia is utterly unscrupulous in its imperialistic designs.

Others believe that, although world conquest is indeed the Marxist goal, the Soviet Union is committed to the battle of ideas and to political infiltration, and that the nation's main concern is the security of its far-flung borders. The Soviet Union has good reason to be jumpy, they add, since already twice this century its territory has been invaded by Germans.

Whichever explanation is right, we must agree that each superpower perceives the other as a threat, and that Christians should support any means to reduce this confrontation of suspicion and fear.

The Helsinki Final Act (1975) spoke of "confidence building measures" (CBMs) whose purpose was to remove the fear of sudden attack and develop reciprocal trust. The kind of CBMs in view were the establishment of demilitarized buffer zones, advance notification of military maneuvers, the exchange of information and observers, and verification measures to enforce arms control agreements. It seems to me, however, that there is also scope for the development of Christian CBMs. I understand that the Mennonite Central Committee arranges student exchanges between the U.S. and both Poland and East Germany. Ought not Christian travel agencies to organize more tour groups to visit the Soviet Union? It is reliably reported that between 15 percent and 20 percent of Russians still are church members. Yet the links between American and Russian Christians are minimal. A strengthening of this fellowship could be influential.

Fifth, Christian peacemakers must promote more public debate. In England in the fifties and sixties the campaign for nuclear disarmament was headline news. In the seventies the debate died down, but in the eighties it must be revived. Fresh questions need to be asked. Is the nuclear arsenal a deterrent any longer? Does it not now offer more peril than safety? Could it ever be justifiable to buy national defense at the cost of millions of civilian lives? Does not the Bible roundly condemn "the shedding of innocent blood"? Is not national morality in the end more important than national security?

But Christians need at the same time to be realistic. The call for immediate, total, unilateral nuclear disarmament seems to me unrealistic. What Christians could do, however, is to call for a unilateral gesture of disarmament, as an example of the "audacious gestures of peace" which Pope John Paul II has canvassed. I believe we should press our governments to make an unequivocal public pledge that they will never be the first to use a strategic nuclear weapon. We could also call on them to declare at least a temporary moratorium on the development and testing of new nuclear weapons systems.

Of course, we shall not succeed in building a utopia of peace and plenty on earth. Jesus said, "There will be wars and rumors of wars." Not till he returns will all swords be beaten into ploughshares and spears into pruning hooks. But this fact cannot be made an excuse for building sword and spear factories. Does

Christ's prediction of famine inhibit us from feeding the hungry and seeking a more equitable distribution of food? No more can his prediction of wars inhibit us from seeking peace. God himself is a peacemaker. If we want to qualify as his authentic children, we must be peacemakers too.

John R. W. Stott, "Cornerstone: Calling for Peacemakers in a Nuclear Age, Part II," *Christianity Today* 24, no. 5 (March 7, 1980): 44–45.

Chapter 46

———

ECONOMIC EQUALITY AMONG NATIONS

A CHRISTIAN CONCERN?

*We are tempted to use the enormous complexity of
international economics as an excuse to do nothing.*

T he 1980s have ushered in the Third Development Decade,
but without much optimism. Although during the first two
development decades some progress was made in the economic
growth of Third World countries, as well as in public health, life
expectancy, and literacy, the gap in average per capita income
between the rich and poor nations still widened considerably.

According to the World Bank's 1979 Report on World
Poverty "about 800 million people still live in absolute poverty,
with incomes too low to ensure adequate nutrition, and without adequate access to essential public services." The Brandt
Commission Report on International Development Issues, published this past February, adds that 17 million children under five
die every year, and that in 34 countries more than 80 percent of
the people are illiterate. These facts, comments West German

ex-chancellor Willy Brandt, constitute "the greatest challenge to mankind for the remainder of the century."

The call for a "New International Economic Order" was thus issued; it was first formulated in 1973 at the meeting of non-aligned countries in Algiers. It demands radical restructuring of world economy in the interests of developing countries, and expresses their determination to gain *economic* independence along with the *political* independence they have recently gained. The UN General Assembly endorsed this in 1974 and published a "Charter of Economic Rights and Duties of States." The NIEO is a plea for more direct aid and credit facilities, the right to regulate multinationals, the removal of trade barriers, and more adequate representation in international decision-making structures like the International Monetary Fund. Little progress has been made to implement these proposals. The United Nations Conference on Trade and Development in Nairobi in 1976 and in Manila in 1979 are regarded by most as disappointing and by some as failures.

How should Christians react to the growing demand from the Third World for economic justice? There are two major biblical principles that should help us to think and feel "Christianly" about it.

The first is *the principle of unity*. It was Adlai Stevenson in 1965 who likened the earth to a little spaceship in which we travel together, "dependent on its vulnerable supplies of air and soil." Barbara Ward elaborated the theme in her book *Spaceship Earth* (1966) and developed it further in *Only One Earth* (1972). She bemoaned the lack of "any sense of planetary community," and added that human survival depends on our achieving "an ultimate loyalty to our single, beautiful and vulnerable Planet Earth."

This is clearly a biblical vision. "The earth is the Lord's and the fulness thereof, the world and those who dwell therein" (Ps. 24:1).

That is, God has created a single people (the human race) and placed us in a single habitat (the planet earth). "Be fruitful and multiply, and fill the earth and subdue it" was his original command (Gen. 1:28). The whole earth was to be developed by the whole people for the common good; all were to share in its God-given resources. This divine purpose has been frustrated by the rise of competitive nations, who have carved up the earth's surface, and who now jealously guard their part of its fossil fuels and mineral deposits. But we cannot evade our responsibility to the poor on the ground that they belong to other nations and therefore do not concern us. The major point of the parable of the good Samaritan is that true neighbor love ignores racial and national barriers. We Christians should be pioneering the way, by repenting of all selfish nationalism and by developing instead a global perspective. For "the chief new insight of our century," writes Barbara Ward in her latest book, *Progress for a Small Planet* (1979), is "the inescapable physical interdependence" of all human beings. We are one people inhabiting one planet. We *are* our brother's keeper.

The second biblical truth concerns *the principle of equality*, which Paul develops in 2 Corinthians 8:8–15. He grounds his appeal for the poor Judaean churches on the theology of the Incarnation—that is, on the gracious renunciation of Christ who though rich became poor so that through his poverty we might become rich (v. 9). It was a renunciation with a view to an equalization. It should be the same with the Corinthians: "Your abundance at the present time should supply their want ... that there may be equality" (v. 14).

An important qualification is necessary, however. The equality the Bible commends is not a total egalitarianism. It is not a situation in which all of us become identical, receiving identical incomes, living in identical homes, equipped with identical furniture, and wearing identical clothing. Equality is not identity. We know this from the doctrine of creation. For the God who has made us equal in dignity (all sharing his life and bearing his image) has made us unequal in ability (intellectually, physically, and psychologically). The new creation has even increased this disparity, bestowing on us who are "one in Christ Jesus" different spiritual gifts or capacities for service.

How, then, can we put together this biblical unity and diversity, equality and inequality? Perhaps in this way: since all have equal worth, though unequal capacity, we must secure equal opportunity for each to develop his or her particular potential for the glory of God and the good of others. Inequality of privilege must be abolished in favor of equality of opportunity. At present, millions of people made in God's image are unable to develop their human potential because of illiteracy, hunger, poverty, or disease. It is, therefore, a fundamentally Christian quest to seek for all people equality of opportunity in education (universal education is arguably the principal means to social justice), in trade (equal access to the world's markets), and in power sharing (representation on the influential world bodies that determine international economic relations).

We are all tempted to use the enormous complexity of international economics as an excuse to do nothing. Yet this was the sin of Dives. There is no suggestion that Dives was responsible for the poverty of Lazarus either by robbing or by exploiting him. The reason for Dives's guilt is that he ignored the beggar at his gate and did precisely nothing to relieve his destitution. He acquiesced in a situation of gross economic inequality, which had rendered Lazarus less than fully human and which he could have relieved. The pariah dogs that licked Lazarus's sores showed more compassion than Dives did. Dives went to hell because of his indifference.

I hope in my next article to make some suggestions as to what we who live in comparative affluence could and should do to help the world's 800 million destitute people.

John R. W. Stott, "Cornerstone: Economic Equality among Nations: A Christian Concern?," *Christianity Today* 24, no. 9 (May 2, 1980): 36–37.

Chapter 47

———

THE JUST DEMANDS OF
ECONOMIC INEQUALITY

*We become personally culpable when
we acquiesce to the status quo.*

I n my article in the last issue I argued that equality is not a synonym for identity; that by creation, equality of human worth
and inequality of human ability are combined; and that what
we should be seeking is equal opportunity for all human beings
(through education, medical care, housing, nutrition, and trade)
to develop their full, God-given potential. This is the minimum
that love and justice should demand.

Such an acceptance of responsibility is not the same as an
admission of guilt. To apportion blame for the present situation
of worldwide economic inequality seems to me neither possible
nor profitable. It is certainly not God's fault, since he has provided
ample resources for everybody. Nor is it the fault of the poor, for
almost invariably they were born in it. But neither is the situation
necessarily our fault, although our colonial forefathers doubtless
had a share in creating it and our governments in perpetuating
it by not tackling the problem more energetically. We ourselves

become personally culpable, however, only if we acquiesce in it by doing nothing. Yet what, in practice, can we do?

To begin with, God may well be calling more Christian people than hear and respond to his call to give their lives in the service of the poor and powerless, in practical philanthropy or Third World development, in politics, or in economics. I would love to see in every country a team of well-qualified Christian economists band together both to work out new international economic policies and to labor for political solutions. Yet this is bound to be the calling of only a minority. What can the rest of us do?

First and foremost, there is the challenge to *our heart*. When Jesus saw the multitudes, hungry and leaderless, he was moved with compassion, and then fed them or taught them or both. It was compassion that aroused and directed his action, and it is compassion that we need most. We have to feel what Jesus felt—the pangs of the hungry, the alienation of the powerless, and the indignities of the wretched of the earth. For ultimately, the unacceptable inequalities between North and South are neither political nor economic, but rather moral. Until we feel moral indignation about worldwide social injustice and strong compassion for worldwide human suffering, I seriously doubt if we shall be moved to take action.

The challenge to *our head* comes next. We need to inform ourselves of the facts. The Third World lies at our gate today much as Lazarus lay at the rich man's. Dives may not have known he was there, but a plea of ignorance would not have exonerated him. Nor can we plead ignorance. Nearly all of us drink tea and coffee, probably sweeten it with sugar, eat bananas, and wear textile clothing. We cannot enjoy these things responsibly if we remain indifferent to the wages and living conditions of those who produce them, and to the trade agreements by which they become available to us. So we should take steps to find out. Does the daily paper we read have adequate Third World coverage? Do we subscribe to a magazine devoted to Third World needs? Is there a "Work Development Movement" in our country for us to join (as there is in Britain), which exists to supply the public with factual information? More personally still, could we make friends with a Third World citizen or travel to some region of the Third World in order to educate ourselves at first hand? Or could we offer ourselves for short-term service in a developing country? And does our church have a "world development group" in addition to a "world mission group," whose responsibility is to inform itself and to keep the congregation informed?

Our mouth also needs to be involved. We have a duty to spread the information we have obtained in order to arouse the concern of our relatives, friends, and colleagues as well. It is only when we are sure of our facts (for we all have a tendency to pontificate from a position of ignorance) that we shall be equipped to join in any form of political agitation. Most communities have pressure groups, which are seeking to influence public opinion and increase public concern about development issues. They could benefit from a Christian contribution to their thought and action; it is anomalous that sometimes humanists show more compassion for the deprived than Christians. Again, most congressmen have times when they are available to the public (British members of Parliament borrow an expression from the medical profession and call them "surgery hours"), Christians should take advantage of such opportunities to ask informed questions about trade tariffs and quotas, to press for the government to increase its ODA (Official Development Assistance), and to inquire why, in Tanzanian President Julius Nyerere's words, so many developing countries are forced to "sell cheap and buy dear."

Finally, there is *our pocket*. Emotional arousal, self-education, and political agitation are all necessary. But there is an element of hypocrisy about all of them if they are not accompanied by personal commitment. In comparison to the 800 million destitute people of the world, we who subscribe to CHRISTIANITY TODAY are rich. We could not afford it otherwise! Now, we should be thankful to God our Creator and Father for the good things he has given us to enjoy; a negative asceticism—self-denial as an end in itself—is a contradiction of the biblical doctrine of creation, for it overlooks the generosity of God "who richly furnishes us with everything to enjoy" (1 Tim. 6:17). At the same time, we have to remember the numerous biblical warnings against the dangers of wealth (that it easily engenders pride, materialism, and a false sense of security), against the evils of covetousness, and against the injustice of condoning the inequalities of privilege. So, recalling the principles of unity and equality which I elaborated in my previous article, most of us (for I include myself) ought to give more generously to aid and development, as well as to world evangelization. In order to do so, we ought further to develop a simple lifestyle. The two most discussed sentences in the Lausanne Covenant (1974) read: "All of us are shocked by the poverty of millions and disturbed by the injustices which cause it. Those of us who live in affluent circumstances accept our duty to develop a simple lifestyle in order to contribute generously to both relief and evangelism."

I am writing this a few days before the International Consultation on Simple Lifestyle to be held in London, and naturally I am in no position to anticipate its findings. But I am confident that it will remind us of the biblical call to renounce covetousness and to cultivate contentment. I hope it will summon us deliberately to develop a standard of living lower than we could afford, out of solidarity with the world's poor. It is true that such a purposeful renunciation of luxurious living would not solve the world's economic problems or transform the poverty of the destitute into plenty. But it would be a sign and symbol of our Christian obedience, of our love for the needy, and of our resolve to imitate that grace of our Lord Jesus Christ who, though rich, became poor in order that through his poverty we might become rich.

John R. W. Stott, "Cornerstone: The Just Demands of Economic Inequality," *Christianity Today* 24, no. 10 (May 23, 1980): 30–31.

Chapter 48

DOES LIFE BEGIN
BEFORE BIRTH?

We cannot fix criteria of humanness and then conclude
that, lacking these, the fetus is not human.

I n both the United States and the United Kingdom the recent
liberalization of abortion laws has become for Christians a
major moral issue. In England and Wales, since David Steel's 1967
Abortion Act, although illegal abortions have not decreased, the
annual average of legal abortions has increased from 10 to more
than 100,000. For every five babies born alive, one is now aborted.
A human fetus is being destroyed every five minutes.

What is the issue? Proabortionists begin with the rights of the
mother (especially her right to choose) and see abortion as little
more than a retroactive contraceptive. Antiabortionists begin
with the rights of the unborn child (especially his or her right to
live) and see abortion as little less than prenatal infanticide. The
former appeal particularly to compassion, and cite situations
in which the mother and/or her family would suffer intolerable
strain if the unwanted pregnancy were allowed to come to term.
The latter appeal particularly to justice, and stress the need to

defend the rights of an unborn child who cannot defend himself. But we must not set compassion and justice in opposition to one another. Compassion needs moral guidelines; without the ingredient of justice it is bound to go astray.

The moral question concerns the nature and status of the human fetus. If "it" were only a lump of jelly or blob of tissue, then of course it could be removed without qualms. But "it" is actually a "he" or "she," an unborn child. What is the evidence for this assertion?

We begin (as we always must) with the Bible. The author of Psalm 139 looks back to the antenatal stage of his existence. Three words sum up what he affirms. First, *creation.* He seems to liken God both to a potter who "formed" his inmost being and to a weaver who "knit him together" in his mother's womb (v. 13). Although the Bible makes no claim to be a textbook of embryology, here is a plain affirmation that the growth of the fetus is neither haphazard nor automatic but a divine work of creative skill.

The second word is *continuity.* The psalmist surveys his life in four stages: past (v. 1), present (vv. 2–6), future (vv. 7–12), and before birth (vv. 13–16), and in all four refers to himself as "I." He who is writing as a full-grown man has the same personal identity as the fetus in his mother's womb. He affirms a direct continuity between his antenatal and postnatal being.

The third word is *communion,* or relationship. Psalm 139 is arguably the most radical statement in the Old Testament of God's personal relationship to the individual. Personal pronouns and possessives occur in the first person (I, me, my) 46 times and in the second person (you, yours) 32 times. Further, the basis on which God knows us intimately (vv. 1–7) and attaches himself to us so that we cannot escape from him (vv. 7–12) is he formed us in the womb and established his relationship with us then (vv. 13–16).

These three words supply us with the essential biblical perspective in which to think. The fetus is not a growth in the mother's body (which can be removed as readily as her tonsils or appendix), nor even a potential human being, but a human life who, though not yet mature, has the potentiality to grow into the fulness of the humanity he already possesses. We cannot fix criteria of humanness (like self-consciousness, reason, independence, speech, moral choice, or responsive love) and then conclude that, lacking these, the fetus is not human. The newborn child and the senile old person lack these also. Nor can we draw a line at any point and say that after it the child is human and before it, not. There is no "decisive moment of humanization," subsequent to conception, whether implantation, or "animation" (when some early fathers, building on Aristotle, supposed that the fetus receives a rational soul, a boy at about one month and a girl at about two), or "quickening" (a purely subjective notion, when the mother first feels the fetus move), or viability (which is getting earlier and earlier), or birth (when the child takes his first independent breath). All these are stages in the continuous process by which an individual human life is developing into mature human personhood. From fusion onwards the fetus is an "unborn child."

The rest of Scripture endorses this perspective. An expectant mother is a "woman with child." When the pregnant Elizabeth (carrying John the Baptist) was visited by the pregnant Mary (carrying Jesus) and heard her greeting, "the babe leaped in her womb for joy" (Luke 1:41, 44). The same truth is confessed in the creed, since he who "was conceived by the Holy Spirit, born of the Virgin Mary, suffered under Pontius Pilate" was throughout—from conception to death—one and the same "Jesus Christ, God's only Son, our Lord."

This biblical evaluation of the humanness of the fetus is confirmed by modern medical science. In the 1960s the genetic code was unraveled. We now know that from the moment the ovum is fertilized by the penetration of the sperm, the zygote has a unique genotype distinct from both parents. The 23 pairs of chromosomes are complete. The sex, size, and shape, the color of skin, hair, and eyes, the intelligence and temperament of the child are already determined. At 3 to 3½ weeks the tiny heart begins to beat. At 4 weeks, although the embryo is only a quarter of an inch long, the head and body are distinguishable, as are also rudimentary eyes, ears, and mouth. At 6 to 7 weeks brain function can be detected, at 8 every limb has begun to appear, including fingers and toes, and at 9 to 10 weeks the child can use his hands to grasp and his mouth to suck his thumb. By 13 weeks, when the pregnancy is only one-third through—and when abortions usually begin—the embryo is completely organized, and a miniature baby lies in his mother's womb. He can alter his position, respond to pain, noise, and light, and have an attack of hiccups. Even his fingerprint is already unique. From then on he merely develops in size and strength.

If, then, the life of the fetus is a human life, with the full potentiality of growing into an adult human person, we have to think of mother and unborn child as two human beings at different stages of maturity. Doctors have to consider that they have two patients, not one, and seek the well-being of both. Lawyers and politicians have to think similarly, in accordance with the United Nations Declaration of the Rights of the Child (1959), that children need "special safeguards and care, including appropriate legal protection, *before as well as after birth.*" Christians will want to demand "extra" safeguards and care before birth because at this stage the child is helpless to protect himself, and the God of the Bible defends the powerless.

So "we have to assert as normative the general inviolability of the fetus" (Archbishop Michael Ramsey in 1967). Most Protestant theologians go on to say that, in certain extreme cases of urgent necessity, when the continuance of the pregnancy threatens to kill the mother, or drive her to suicide, or render her a complete "physical or mental wreck" (the McNaughten judgment in 1938) and so significantly shorten her life, it would be morally justifiable to sacrifice her unborn child in order to spare her. But in such circumstances death in some form is already present; "the doctor has not introduced death into the case" (Oliver O'Donovan in *The Christian and the Unborn Child,* 1973). The Christian conscience rebels against the notion that an unborn child may be destroyed because his birth would be a "burden" to the mother or her family. This argument could equally justify the destruction of a newborn child, the comatose victim of a car crash, or an imbecile. Yet such merciless "mercy killing" is totally unacceptable in a civilized community, as Dr. Francis Schaeffer and Dr. Everett Koop have powerfully argued in *Whatever Happened to the Human Race?*

If we Christians campaign for a stricter abortion policy, as we should, we must both back it up with an educational program to reduce unwanted pregnancies and also accept full responsibility for its social effects and ensure that mothers receive the personal, social, medical, and financial support they need. Louise Summerhill, the founder of *Birthright,* rightly said, "We help rather than abort. We believe in making a better world for babies to come into, rather than killing them."

John R. W. Stott, "Cornerstone: Does Life Begin before Birth?," *Christianity Today* 24, no. 15 (September 5, 1980): 50–51.

Chapter 49

WHO, THEN, ARE THE POOR?

One could answer this question rationally, with the cool detachment of statistics. There are 4.3 billion inhabitants of planet Earth, and one-fifth are destitute. Every day, 10,000 succumb to starvation, and die. Meanwhile, more than another one-fifth live in affluence, consume four-fifths of the world's income, and contribute to Third World development the derisory annual sum of $45 billion, while spending 21 times that amount on armaments.

Or one could approach the question emotionally, with the hot-blooded indignation aroused by the sights, sounds, and smells of poverty. Arriving in Calcutta a few weeks ago, I found the city enveloped in a malodorous pall of smoke from a myriad fires fueled with cow dung. An emaciated woman clutching an emaciated baby stretched out an emaciated hand for *baksheesh*. A quarter of a million people sleep on the city's sidewalks, and human beings are reduced to foraging like dogs in its garbage dumps.

There is a third way of approaching the question of the poor—one that should stimulate our reason and emotions simultaneously—and that is through Scripture. Consider Psalm 113:5–8:

"Who is like the LORD our God, who is seated on high, who looks far down upon the heavens and the earth? He raises the poor from the dust, and lifts the needy from the ash heap, to make them sit with princes ..."

What is distinctively characteristic of Yahweh, the psalmist writes, is not just that he reigns on high, or that he condescends to our depths, but that he actually "raises the poor from the dust." That is the kind of God he is. Hannah quoted this after the birth of Samuel; Mary alluded to it when she learned she was to be the mother of the Messiah. Jesus kept repeating that "he who exalts himself will be humbled, while he who humbles himself will be exalted."

Who, then, are "the poor" whom God "raises from the dust"?

First, and economically speaking, there are *the indigent poor,* deprived of the basic necessities of life. God commanded his people in the law not to harden their hearts or shut their hands against the poor, but to maintain those who could not maintain themselves, taking them home and feeding them without charge. If an Israelite loaned money, he was not to exact interest. If he took a pledge, he was not to go into the poor person's house to fetch it, but to wait outside until it was brought. If he took as pledge the person's cloak, he was to restore it before nightfall, because a cloak by day was a blanket by night. Employers were to pay wages to their workers on the same day. Farmers were not to reap a field "to its very border," or gather the gleanings of the harvest, or strip a vine or olive tree bare; the leftovers were for the poor, the alien, the widow, the orphan.

The wisdom literature underlined this: "Blessed is he who considers the poor." Why? Because "he who mocks the poor insults his Maker," whereas "he who is kind to the poor lends to the Lord." No wonder our Lord fed the hungry, made friends with the poor, and promised that if we do likewise we shall find ourselves ministering to him "in this distressing disguise" (as Mother Teresa puts it).

———————————

Second, and sociopolitically speaking, there are *the powerless poor,* the victims of human oppression. The Old Testament recognizes that poverty is sometimes due to laziness, gluttony, or extravagance, but usually attributes it to the sins of others. Moreover, injustice tends to deteriorate because the poor are powerless to change it. Yet if the poor have no human helper, God "stands at the right hand of the needy" and "maintains the cause of the afflicted." So the law contains strong prohibitions against perverting the justice due to the poor, the wisdom literature requires kings and judges to "give justice to the weak and fatherless" and "maintains the rights of the poor and needy," and the prophets fulminate against national leaders who "trample the head of the poor into the dust." Thus, the concern of the biblical writers goes beyond philanthropy to social justice.

Third, and spiritually speaking, there are *the humble poor.* Oppressed by men, they look to God for help, and put their trust in him. So "the poor" came to be a synonym for "the pious," and their condition a symbol of and stimulus to the dependence of faith. This is specially clear in the Psalter; for example, "this poor man cried, and the LORD heard him, and saved him out of all his troubles" (Ps. 34:6).

In these ways God "raises the poor from the dust," for he lifts them out of the dust of penury, oppression, and helplessness. God concerns himself both with the *materially* poor and powerless, and with the *morally* humble and meek. Yet his attitude to these groups differs, for the former is an outward and sociological condition which he opposes, while the latter is an inward and spiritual condition which he approves.

The only community in which these concepts are combined is a church that is witnessing to the kingdom of God. The Old Testament expectation was of an ideal king who would "judge the poor with righteousness," "decide with equity for the meek of the earth," and grant these blessings to the "humble and lowly." The fulfillment in Jesus corresponds to this, for he spoke of the righteousness of his kingdom and at the same time said that the good news would be preached, and the kingdom given, to "the poor." These can be neither the sociologically poor (or salvation would be limited to the proletariat), nor the spiritually poor (or the facts of Jesus' ministry to the poor and hungry would be overlooked), but to those who are both. To them the kingdom of God is proclaimed as a free gift of salvation and as a promise of justice.

The Christian church should exemplify these truths. On the one hand, it consists entirely of the spiritually poor, who acknowledge that they have no merit to plead, and so receive the kingdom as a gift. On the other hand, the church should not tolerate material poverty in its own fellowship. If there is one community in the world in which justice is secured for the poor and need is eliminated, this should be the church.

The church, if it exemplifies both ideals of the kingdom, will bear witness to the paradox of poverty. If we want the new community of Jesus to offer a radical alternative to the world around us, then we must set ourselves simultaneously to eradicate the evil of material poverty (because we hate injustice) and to cultivate the good of spiritual poverty (because we love humility).

If we ask how we well-to-do Christians should express solidarity with the poor, it seems that the first option, to "become poor," is the vocation of some but not all. The selling and giving of the early Jerusalem Christians was clearly voluntary. The opposite extreme, to "stay rich and ignore the poor," is not an admissible option.

The rich cannot ignore the poor of this world, but must do something for them. A rich Christian is not a contradiction in terms; but a Christian who lives richly, spending his wealth upon self and family, is a contradiction. The third option, to which all of us are called, is to live a life of generosity and of simple contentment. "We brought nothing into the world, and we cannot take anything out of the world; but if we have food and clothing, with these we shall be content" (1 Tim. 6:7–8).

John R. W. Stott, "Cornerstone: Who, Then, Are the Poor?," *Christianity Today* 25, no. 9 (May 8, 1981): 54–55.

Conclusion

———

JESUS IS LORD! HAS
WIDE RAMIFICATIONS

As I lay down my Cornerstone pen after four years to depart soon for a sabbatical leave, I ask myself if any discernible theme has united my monthly contributions to CHRISTIANITY TODAY. I have not developed a single motif in any deliberate way, for I have written *ad hoc* articles as they have arisen out of my studies and travels. Yet I think the fundamental truth underlying each is that *Jesus Christ is Lord*. Of the widespread ramifications of the lordship of Jesus, I seem to have concentrated on three.

The first is theological, and concerns the deity of his person. Since the publication of *The Myth of God Incarnate* (1977), I have written three pieces about the Christological debate, and about the gravity of allowing flagrant Unitarian heresy to be unanswered, unchecked, and undisciplined in the church. The central issue is neither one of semantics (the meaning of words like "myth," "incarnation," "nature," and "person") nor of credal formulation (whether the Chalcedonian definition is adequate for our day), but rather of salvation (whether Jesus can in any sense mediate between God and mankind if he is not himself both God and man) and of discipleship (for we cannot worship him, believe in him, or obey him if he is not God).

Yet on these points, disputed as they are today with a great display of learning, the New Testament leaves us no room for doubt. The early Christians not only called Jesus "Lord," in spite of their knowledge that *kyrios* was the Septuagint rendering of the sacred divine name "Yahweh," but actually applied to Jesus a variety of texts and concepts which in the Old Testament related to Yahweh. So they worshiped him.

Indeed, "Christolatry" (the worship of Christ) may be said to have preceded "Christology" (the developed doctrine of Christ). Moreover, the New Testament letters contain no hint that the divine honors given to Jesus were the subject of controversy in the church, as was the case, for example, with the doctrine of justification. There can be only one explanation of this. Already by the middle of the first century, the deity of Jesus was part of the faith of the universal church. It cannot and must not be compromised today.

To confess that "Jesus is Lord" has ethical as well as theological implications. The counterpart of his lordship is our discipleship, and authentic discipleship involves bringing all our thinking and living under his authority. We evangelicals have always held this in theory, but tended to restrict Christ's dominion to personal ethics.

———————

In recent years, however, we have begun to take more seriously the great challenge of social ethics. We are latecomers in this field and have a lot of catching up to do. So I have struggled to write on euthanasia and abortion, work and unemployment, industrial and race relations, the nuclear horror and the new international economic order. I have been criticized: "Stott is abandoning evangelism for social action," my detractors have said. This is not true. What I have been trying to do is to become a more integrated Christian, whose principle of integration is the lordship of Jesus.

What does it mean to "have the mind of Christ" and "be renewed in the spirit of our minds" (1 Cor. 2:16; Eph. 4:23), so that we think Christianly about even so-called secular topics? How can we "take his yoke upon us and learn from him" as our Teacher and Lord, and seek to "take every thought captive to obey Christ" (Matt. 11:29; 2 Cor. 10:5)? I sometimes wonder if our minds are the last stronghold to capitulate to Jesus the Lord. Of course, major questions remain to be answered in the contemporary hermeneutical discussion. Yet we can safely say that no hermeneutical method or conclusion can be Christian which fails to honor Christ by enthroning him as Lord.

Further, world mission or worldwide evangelization is best understood under the rubric of Jesus Christ's lordship. I have written about this on several occasions. The universal commission to go and make disciples of all the nations was the direct consequence of the universal authority which the risen Lord claimed to have been given (Matt. 28:18–19). As Bishop Lesslie Newbigin has aptly expressed it in his book *The Finality of Christ* (1969): "The universality of Christ's lordship over all nations and over all creation is not, in the New Testament, a ground for leaving all the nations as they are. It is on the other hand exactly the ground for the Church's mission to preach repentance to every man and to all nations."

"We preach ... Jesus Christ as Lord," writes Paul (2 Cor. 4:5). If we are to follow his example, we shall have to reject all false positions that in one way or another contradict the New Testament's witness to his supremacy. For example, the pluralism which seeks to preserve all religions, each in its own integrity, and the syncretism which prefers to blend them both deny the uniqueness and the finality of Jesus. Universalism is a more subtle enemy of evangelism. It claims to exalt Christ's lordship by declaring that all people will acknowledge it in the end; but in principle it makes the proclamation of the gospel unnecessary, and fails to recognize that evangelism presents people with a choice, so that some confess "Jesus is Lord," while others cry "Jesus be cursed" (1 Cor. 12:3; Rom. 10:9–10).

There are evangelical as well as liberal hindrances to evangelism, however, of which we need to repent. There is the spiritual lethargy manifested in a narrow parochialism and inhibiting us from developing a global concern. Then there is arrogant imperialism that attempts to impose our culture on others, fails to respect theirs, and makes our message unacceptable.

Another grave obstacle is our chronic evangelical divisiveness, whereby we are competing with one another instead of cooperating, and so confuse our hearers who want to choose Christ but find themselves presented instead with a choice between his followers.

Finally, there is our tendency to overemphasize verbal proclamation at the expense of the visual. It is another case of "this ought you to have done, and not left the other undone." Jesus plainly told us to let our light so shine before men that they may see our good works and glorify our heavenly Father (Matt. 5:6). Thus words and works, hearing and seeing, truth and love belong inseparably to each other.

No incentive to evangelism is greater than a vision of the exalted Lord Jesus and a zeal, even a "jealousy," for his glory. God has superexalted him and given him the preeminent name in order that every knee should bow to him and every tongue confess him Lord. Then we must share the Father's desire for the universal acknowledgement of the Son. It was "for the sake of the Name" that the first Christian missionaries went out (Rom. 1:5; 3 John 7); the same concern for the honor of his name should motivate us today.

Jesus is Lord!

John R. W. Stott, "Cornerstone: Jesus Is Lord! Has Wide Ramifications," *Christianity Today* 25, no. 11 (June 12, 1981): 55.

EVANGELISM PLUS

John Stott reflects on where we've been and where we're going.

INTERVIEW BY TIM STAFFORD

I n 2004, *New York Times* columnist David Brooks wrote that if evangelicals chose a pope, they would likely select John Stott. Stott, 85, has been at the heart of evangelical renewal in the U.K. His books and biblical sermons have transfixed millions throughout the world. He has been involved in many important world councils and dialogues, not least as chair of the committees that drafted the Lausanne Covenant (1974) and the Manila Manifesto (1989)—two defining statements for evangelicals. For more than 35 years, he has devoted three months of every year to traveling the globe, with a particular emphasis on churches in the majority world. He is ideally suited to comment on evangelicals' past, present, and future. *CT* senior writer Tim Stafford interviewed him at his home in London.

As you see it, what is evangelicalism, and why does it matter?

An evangelical is a plain, ordinary Christian. We stand in the mainstream of historic, orthodox, biblical Christianity. So we can recite the Apostles' Creed and the Nicene Creed without cross-ing our fingers. We believe in God the Father and in Jesus Christ and in the Holy Spirit.

Having said that, there are two particular things we like to emphasize: the concern for authority on the one hand and sal-vation on the other.

For evangelical people, our authority is the God who has spoken supremely in Jesus Christ. And that is equally true of redemption or salvation. God has acted in and through Jesus Christ for the salvation of sinners.

I think it's necessary for evangelicals to add that what God has said in Christ and in the biblical witness to Christ, and what God has *done* in and through Christ, are both, to use the Greek word, *hapax*—meaning once and for all. There is a finality about God's word in Christ, and there is a finality about God's work in Christ. To imagine that we could add a word to his word, or add a work to his work, is extremely derogatory to the unique glory of our Lord Jesus Christ.

You didn't mention the Bible, which would surprise some people.

I did, actually, but you didn't notice it. I said Christ and the bib-lical witness to Christ. But the really distinctive emphasis is on Christ. I want to shift conviction from a book, if you like, to a person. As Jesus himself said, the Scriptures bear witness to *me*. Their main function is to witness to Christ.

Part of your implication is that evangelicals are not to be a negatively inspired people. Our real focus ought to be the glory of Christ.

I believe that very strongly. We believe in the authority of the Bible because Christ has endorsed its authority. He stands between the two testaments. As we look back to the Old Testament, he has endorsed it. As we look forward to the New Testament, we accept it because of the apostolic witness to Christ. He deliberately chose and appointed and prepared the apostles, in order that they might have their unique apostolic witness to him. I like to see Christ in the middle, endorsing the old, preparing for the new. Although the question of the New Testament canon is complicated, in general we are able to say that canonicity is apostolicity.

How has the position of evangelicals changed during your years of ministry?

I look back—it's been 61 years since I was ordained—and when I was ordained in the Church of England, evangelicals in the Church of England were a despised and rejected minority. The bishops lost no opportunity to ridicule us. Over the intervening 60 years, I've seen the evangelical movement in England grow in size, in maturity, certainly in scholarship, and therefore I think in influence and impact. We went from a ghetto to being on the ascendancy, which is a very dangerous place to be.

Can you comment on the dangers?

Pride is the ever-present danger that faces all of us. In many ways, it is good for us to be despised and rejected. I think of Jesus' words, "Woe unto you when all men speak well of you."

Going back to the *hapax*, it's a very humbling concept. The essence of evangelicalism is very humbling. You have William Temple saying, "The only thing of my very own which I contribute to redemption is the sin from which I need to be redeemed."

We have also seen an immense growth of the church worldwide, largely along evangelical lines. What do you see as its significance?

This enormous growth is a fulfillment of God's promise to

Abraham in Genesis 12:1–4. God promised Abraham not only to bless him, not only to bless his family or his posterity, but through his posterity to bless all the families of the earth. Whenever we look at a multiethnic congregation, we are seeing a fulfillment of that amazing promise of God. A promise made by God to Abraham 4,000 years ago is being fulfilled right before our very eyes today.

You know this growing church probably as well as any Westerner does. I wonder how you evaluate it.

The answer is "growth without depth." None of us wants to dispute the extraordinary growth of the church. But it has been largely numerical and statistical growth. And there has not been sufficient growth in discipleship that is comparable to the growth in numbers.

How can the Western church, which surely has problems of its own, fruitfully interact with the non-Western? Right now many churches are sending mission teams all over the world.

I certainly want to be positive about short-term mission trips, and I think on the whole they are a good thing. They do give Westerners an awfully good opportunity to taste Southern Christianity and to be challenged by it, especially by its exuberant vitality. But I think the leaders of such mission trips would be wise to warn their members that this is only a very limited experience of cross-cultural mission.

True mission that is based on the example of Jesus involves entering another world, the world of another culture. Incarnational cross-cultural mission is and can be very costly. I want to say, please realize that if God calls you to be a cross-cultural missionary, it will take you 10 years to learn the language and to learn the culture in such a way that you are accepted more or less as a national.

So there's really no replacing the long-term missionary.

I think not, except of course for indigenous Christians.

What about what some call the greatest mission field, which is our own secularizing or secularized culture? What do we need to do to reach this increasingly pagan society?

I think we need to say to one another that it's not so secular as it looks. I believe that these so-called secular people are engaged in a quest for at least three things. The first is transcendence. It's interesting in a so-called secular culture how many people are looking for something beyond. I find that a great challenge to the quality of our Christian worship. Does it offer people what they are instinctively looking for, which is transcendence, the reality of God?

The second is significance. Almost everybody is looking for his or her own personal identity. Who am I, where do I come from, where am I going to, what is it all about? That is a challenge to the quality of our Christian teaching. We need to teach people who they are. They don't know who they are. We do. They are human beings made in the image of God, although that image has been defaced.

And third is their quest for community. Everywhere, people are looking for community, for relationships of love. This is a challenge to our fellowship. I'm very fond of 1 John 4:12: "No one has ever seen God; if we love one another, God abides in us, and his love is perfected in us." The invisibility of God is a great problem to people. The question is how has God solved the problem of his own invisibility? First, Christ has made the invisible God visible. That's John's Gospel 1:18: "No one has ever seen God; the only God, who is at the Father's side, he has made him known."

People say that's wonderful, but it was 2,000 years ago. So in 1 John 4:12, he begins with exactly the same formula, nobody has ever seen God. But here John goes on, "If we love one another, God abides in us." The same invisible God who once made himself visible in Jesus now makes himself visible in the Christian community, *if we love one another*. And all the verbal proclamation of the gospel is of little value unless it is made by a community of love.

These three things about our humanity are on our side in our evangelism, because people are looking for the very things we have to offer them.

And therefore you're not despairing of the West.

I'm not despairing. But I believe that evangelism is specially through the local church, through the community, rather than through the individual. That the church should be an alternative society, a visible sign of the kingdom. And the tragedy is that our local churches often don't seem to manifest community.

Do you want to talk about preaching?

I never tire of doing that. I'm an impenitent believer in the importance of preaching. Of course, that's biblical preaching.

Biblical preaching has fallen on hard times in many places. What do you say to a pastor who is desperately trying to hold his congregation's attention and really doesn't have the confidence that enables one to just preach from a biblical text?

It's the same issue across the globe. Churches live, grow, and flourish by the Word of God. And they languish and even perish without it.

So the Langham Partnership International has three basic convictions. Conviction one is that God wants his church to grow. One of the verses that expresses this best is Colossians 1:28–29, in which Paul says we proclaim Christ, warning everybody and teaching everybody in all wisdom, in order that we may present everybody mature in Christ. There's a plain call to maturity, to grow up out of babyhood.

Second, they grow by the Word of God. I suppose you could concede that there are other ways by which the church grows, but if you take the New Testament as a whole, it's the Word of God that matures the people of God.

Which brings me to the third conviction, that the Word of God comes to the people of God mainly, though not exclusively, through preaching. I often envisage on a Sunday morning the amazing spectacle of the people of God converging on their places of worship all over the world. They're going to medieval cathedrals, to house churches, to the open air. They know that in the course of the worship service there will be a sermon, and it should be a biblical sermon, so that through the Word of God they may grow.

When I enter the pulpit with the Bible in my hands and in my heart, my blood begins to flow and my eyes to sparkle for the sheer glory of having God's Word to expound. We need to emphasize the glory, the privilege, of sharing God's truth with people.

Where do we evangelicals need to go? We've been through quite a trip in the last 50 years.

My immediate answer is that we need to go beyond evangelism. Evangelism is supposed to be evangelicals' specialty. Now, I am totally committed to world evangelization. But we must look beyond evangelism to the transforming power of the gospel, both in individuals and in society.

With regard to individuals, I'm noting in different expressions of the evangelical faith an absence of that quest for holiness that marked our forebears, who founded the Keswick movement, for example, and the quest for what they sometimes called scriptural holiness or practical holiness. Somehow *holiness* has a rather sanctimonious feel to it. People don't like to be described as holy. But the holiness of the New Testament is Christlikeness. I wish that the whole evangelical movement could consciously set before us the desire to grow in Christlikeness such as is described in Galatians 5:22–23.

Regarding social transformation, I've reflected a great deal on the salt and light metaphors, the models that Jesus himself chose in Matthew 5 in the Sermon on the Mount. "You are the salt of the earth; you are the light of the world." It seems to me that those models must be said to contain at least three things.

First, that Christians are radically different from non-Christians, or if they are not, they ought to be. Jesus sets over against each other two communities. On the one hand there is the world, and on the other hand there is you, who are the dark world's light. Jesus implied that we are as different as light from darkness and salt from decay.

Second, Christians must permeate non-Christian society. Salt does no good if it stays in the saltshaker. Light does no good if you hide it under a bed or bucket. It has to permeate the darkness. So both metaphors call us not just to be different, but to permeate society.

The third, the more controversial implication, is that the salt and light metaphors indicate that Christians can change non-Christian society. The models must mean that, because both salt and light are effective commodities. They change the environments in which they are placed. Salt hinders bacterial decay. Light dispels darkness. This is not to resurrect the social gospel. We cannot perfect society. But we can improve it.

My hope is that in the future, evangelical leaders will ensure that their social agenda includes such vital but controversial topics as halting climate change, eradicating poverty, abolishing armories of mass destruction, responding adequately to the AIDS pandemic, and asserting the human rights of women and children in all cultures. I hope our agenda does not remain too narrow.

Tim Stafford, "Evangelism Plus: John Stott Reflects on Where We've Been and Where We're Going," *Christianity Today* 50, no. 10 (October 2006): 94–99.

Epilogue

"A PLAIN, ORDINARY CHRISTIAN"

*John Stott made extraordinary contributions
to the global evangelical movement.*

TIM STAFFORD

"An evangelical is a plain, ordinary Christian," John Stott told *Christianity Today* in an October 2006 interview. From his conversion at Rugby secondary school in 1938 to his death on July 27, Stott exemplified how extraordinary plain, ordinary Christianity can be. He was not known as an original thinker, nor did he seek to be. He always turned to the Bible for understanding, and his unforgettable gift was to penetrate and explain the Scriptures. As former *CT* editor Kenneth Kantzer wrote in these pages in 1981, "When I hear him expound a text, invariably I exclaim to myself, 'That's exactly what it means! Why didn't I see it before?' "

Until his conversion and subsequent call to Christian ministry, Stott seemed headed for the diplomatic corps. A skilled linguist, he excelled in the study of French at Cambridge University before going on to excel equally in theology. No one doubted Stott's

diplomatic potential. In his ministry, he retained the best qualities of that calling, to faithfully and skillfully represent someone else.

Beginning Years

Like any good diplomat, Stott knew exactly who he was and where
he came from. Born into an emotionally close and cultured doctor's
family, he spent virtually his entire life in the same London neighborhood. As a child he attended All Souls Church, sometimes sitting
in the balcony and dropping wads of paper on ladies' hats below.
At his ordination in the Church of England in 1945, Stott became
curate there and then, in 1950, rector of the badly war-damaged
church. He would remain on staff for the rest of his days.

Stott was thoroughly English in stereotypical ways: incisive,
cool, time-conscious, orderly, and balanced. Though he had a great
gift for friendship, he was not given to small talk or self-revelation.
(He did have a wry sense of humor and was a talented amateur
musician.) A lifelong bachelor, he showed a formidable capacity
for work. When he was immersed in a writing project, he could
happily keep his own company for weeks on end at his retreat
in Wales, grinding out page after page of well-regulated prose.

At the same time, he relished the world around him in all its
variety. Perhaps nothing showed this so obviously as his lifelong
love for birdwatching, which biographer Timothy Dudley-Smith
says bordered on an obsession. In his later decades, Stott spent a
great proportion of his time traveling, much of it in third-world
(he called them "majority-world") countries. Time for birds was
nearly always included. He traveled without an entourage, sometimes preaching in a cathedral one day and under a tree the next,
meeting the mighty and the lowly and staying in their homes. As a
London pastor, too, he formed strong attachments to a wide variety of humanity. When he encountered opposition or criticism,

he would seek out an exchange of views. He did not enjoy conflict, but he was committed to dialogue.

Right from the beginning, Stott was passionate about evangelism. The man who led him to Christ, E. J. H. Nash, or "Bash," worked for Scripture Union in the elite English public schools. Stott had been raised to attend church and read the Bible daily, but as a young student he had no understanding of personal salvation. Bash shared with him the scene from Revelation 3, of Jesus standing at the door and asking to come in. It seized Stott's understanding, and shortly thereafter he became a Christian. Bash soon put Stott to work, talking to other boys about what he had discovered. By the time Stott reached university, he was running evangelistic Scripture Union holiday camps.

Best known today as a Bible expositor and teacher, Stott initially made a reputation as an evangelist. At All Souls, he led many to Christ while teaching the congregation how to evangelize friends and neighbors. All Souls was an inner-city church with a striking mix of the well-off and the indigent, and Stott was determined to neglect neither side. He firmly believed that the local church should be a locus for evangelism. One of his first books, published in 1952, was *Parochial Evangelism by the Laity*.

J. I. Packer remembers that Stott "in his younger days ... was a brilliant and hard-worked student evangelist." He was the chosen speaker for a considerable number of InterVarsity Christian Fellowship's week-long campaigns at British universities, particularly Cambridge and Oxford. These later extended to North America and throughout the Commonwealth. From these evangelistic talks came one of his best-selling books, *Basic Christianity* (1958), which has been translated into 25 languages and has sold well over a million copies.

Billy Graham first visited England in 1946, and Stott met him while sharing open-air preaching at Speakers' Corner in Hyde

Park. In 1954, he welcomed Graham for his 12-week Harringay crusade, and the two became warm friends, bonding through an active, shared commitment to evangelism.

Evangelical Resurgence

Fundamentally, though, Stott was a church minister, one who became the leading figure in a resurgence of British evangelicalism, particularly within the Church of England.

Conservative evangelicals were a despised minority when Stott was ordained, without a single bishop in the Church of England. In response, Stott showed his ingenuity as a social entrepreneur, fostering organizations meant to encourage younger evangelical clergy, and spearheading a durable set of evangelical conferences.

Most of all, he modeled confidence and intellectual strength. "I remember reading his books as a young student," says Old Testament scholar Chris Wright, whom Stott later chose to lead Langham Partnership International, his majority-world ministry of biblical scholarship and preaching. "They were so clearly argued you felt that you had a case."

Stott believed the mind was a gift from God. In an evangelical world tempted to rely on proof texts and emotive stories, Stott drilled down deep into Scripture to display its power. Many people, hearing Stott preach for the first time, said they had never heard the Bible expounded with such clarity and depth. His passion was to learn what God said and to let it shape all of life.

His practice of evangelism demonstrated that "plain, ordinary Christianity" could appeal to all classes of people. What evangelicals most treasured—the person and work of Jesus Christ, and the Scriptures that testified to them—he showed to be potent resources for winning the world. Largely through Stott's leadership, British evangelicalism was transformed from a defensive backwater into an engaged and significant movement.

Lausanne Leader

Stott was every inch an evangelical, but always a reforming evangelical. He recognized that evangelicalism sometimes sank down into mere piety, whereas the Bible spoke of a robust transformation of the world brought about by God's people engaged in mission. As a London pastor, Stott increasingly prodded evangelicalism to reclaim its heritage of engagement with the social issues of the day.

As he once remarked, "In the early 1960s, I began to travel in the Third World, and I saw poverty in Latin America, Africa and Asia as I had not seen it before. It became clear to me that it was utterly impossible to take that old view." The "old view" was that preaching was a Christian's preeminent task, and that deeds of compassion were strictly secondary. As Stott probed the Scriptures, he saw that Jesus' Great Commission encompassed a practical concern for life and health.

One of Stott's most significant books, *Issues Facing Christians Today* (1984), addressed crucial concerns of contemporary society, such as abortion, industrial relations, and human rights. In 1982, he helped to launch the London Institute for Contemporary Christianity, which offered classes and lectures on a wide variety of pressing topics.

His greatest impact in the area of social concern came somewhat inadvertently. In 1974, the Billy Graham Evangelistic Association convened an International Congress on World Evangelization at Lausanne, Switzerland. Among the thousands of delegates and speakers, about half came from majority-world countries. The gathering's wide representation resembled meetings of the World Council of Churches, but the excited atmosphere of unified mission was unprecedented. Many participants grasped for the first time the global dimensions of the evangelical church. Almost 30 years later, historian Philip Jenkins would write *The Next Christendom: The Coming of Global Christianity* (2002). But according to David Jones, former president of John Stott Ministries, at Lausanne, "Jenkins's book was there in the faces and minds of people."

Delegates had to overcome great differences in perspective between the West and the majority world, and the relationship between evangelism and social concern was an emotional hot button. According to some, Christians were called to preach the gospel, full stop. Others thought such a stance amounted to callous indifference toward countries battered by poverty and injustice.

Stott gave the opening address. He began with characteristic humility, calling for "a note of evangelical repentance." Then, with a lucid exposition of Scripture, he addressed this potential impasse.

> Here then are two instructions, "love your neighbor" and "go and make disciples." What is the relation between the two? Some of us behave as if we thought them identical, so that if we have shared the Gospel with somebody, we consider we have completed our responsibility to love him. But no. The Great Commission neither explains, nor exhausts, nor supersedes the Great Commandment. What it does is to add to the command of neighbor-love and neighbor-service a new and urgent Christian dimension. If we truly love our neighbor we shall without doubt tell him the Good News of Jesus. But equally if we truly love our neighbor we shall not stop there.

Stott's speech made it possible for delegates to rethink their positions, and to conceive of preaching and social action working in tandem. He managed the same trick in chairing the committee that drafted the Lausanne Covenant. Stott's diplomatic skill was never more evident, as he chaired potentially fractious meetings, getting people to listen to each other's views. He worked tirelessly behind the scenes to draft and redraft the covenant, finding wording that would capture various points of view without doing violence to any. The resulting document expressed a common mission that most delegates could enthusiastically endorse, while providing a basic statement of purpose for future evangelical groups. Lausanne was a defining moment in global evangelicalism. Billy Graham was the indispensable convener, but John Stott was the indispensable uniter.

Living Legacy

What has John Stott left behind? His legacy lives on in his church, for generations a vital, grounded, evangelical community in the heart of London. To this day, All Souls serves as a beacon for visitors from all over the world. Langham Partnership, preeminent among the organizations he launched, increasingly reflects a global partnership of evangelicals concerned for scholarship, literature, and preaching in the majority world.

His books, too, continue to speak eloquently: clear, precise, stimulating, and balanced. His commentaries cover much of the New Testament, bridging the gap between scholarly works and thoughtful works for lay people. Many people consider *The Cross of Christ* (1986) Stott's magnum opus, but his entire corpus is a summing up of evangelical Christianity: dominated by the Bible, but full of a sense of Cross-centered mission.

For all his skill and intellect, his writing, his entrepreneurial energy, and his brilliant preaching, Stott's ultimate legacy may be the vast number of people he mentored and befriended all over the world.

Far earlier than most, Stott recognized the vitality and strength of the church in the majority world. He began to spend an increasing share of his time there as he retired from the day-to-day responsibilities of leading All Souls.

Most of his work in the majority world was, from a Westerner's perspective, invisible. He met thousands of church leaders, often young men and women struggling to find their place. He procured theological study books for those without access to good libraries. He arranged scholarships in England and the United States for qualified doctoral candidates. He demonstrated biblical preaching, and he modeled modesty and a simple lifestyle. He made hundreds if not thousands of friends, becoming a bridge between cultures.

"Naturally, by temperament, he was an introvert," remembers Chris Wright. "He was very happy to be in his own company. Yet he gave himself to so many people, remembering names, knowing their families, knowing their children, writing letters, praying for them. He was constantly praying for people."

"There have been mixed feelings about the West among our leaders," says Ajith Fernando, a Methodist church leader and head of Youth for Christ in Sri Lanka. "Sometimes I feel an anger close to racism has arisen in the minds of Christian leaders out of the sense that Western leaders do not understand the concerns of people in the rest of the world. There is a suspicion that what they want is to fulfill their agenda in our countries—another form of colonialism? With people like John Stott around, it was impossible for me to nurture such feelings. ... Here was humility personified. We are grateful that he gave so much time coming to the poorer nations not with some huge program which would impress the whole world, but simply to teach us the Bible."

Latin American theologian C. René Padilla remembers vividly an early encounter with Stott. Arriving in Argentina on a rainy night, they walked to their lodgings and deposited two pairs of mud-covered shoes. "In the morning, as I woke up, I heard the sound of a brush—John was busy, brushing my shoes. 'John!' I exclaimed, full of surprise, 'What are you doing?' 'My dear René,' he responded, 'Jesus taught us to wash each other's feet. You do not need me to wash your feet, but I can brush your shoes.'"

Theologian David Wells, who came to Christ at a 1959 John Stott mission in South Africa, later shared a household with him for five years in the early 1960s. "His leadership was effective," Wells says, "because of his personal integrity and his Christian life. ... He was known all over the world, but when you met him he was a most devout, humble Christian man. His private life was no different from his public life. It was the same person. That's another way to say that he had integrity. There was no posing."

One would like to say that such is the nature of plain, ordinary Christians. Not all live up to it. John Stott did.

Tim Stafford, "A Plain, Ordinary Christian," *Christianity Today* 55, no. 9 (September 2011): 45–48.

SUBJECT INDEX

SCRIPTURE INDEX

Old Testament

New Testament